BECOMING
the WOMAN
I WANT TO BE

Bethany House Books
by Donna Partow

Becoming a Vessel God Can Use
Becoming a Vessel God Can Use Prayer Journal
Becoming the Woman I Want to Be
Living in Absolute Freedom
Standing Firm
This Isn't the Life I Signed Up For
This Isn't the Life I Signed Up For AudioBook
This Isn't the Life I Signed Up For Growth Guide
Walking in Total God-Confidence
A Woman's Guide to Personality Types

EXTRACTING THE PRECIOUS
2 Corinthians
Isaiah
Galatians
Nehemiah

DONNA PARTOW

BECOMING
the WOMAN
I WANT TO BE

A 90-DAY JOURNEY TO RENEWING
SPIRIT, SOUL, & BODY

BETHANYHOUSE

MINNEAPOLIS, MINNESOTA

Published by Bethany House Publishers
11400 Hampshire Avenue South
Bloomington, Minnesota 55438

Bethany House Publishers is a division of
Baker Publishing Group, Grand Rapids, Michigan.

Printed in the United States of America

Library of Congress Cataloging-in-Publication Data

Partow, Donna.
    Becoming the woman I want to be: 90 days to renew your spirit, soul, and body / by Donna Partow.
        p. cm.
        ISBN 0-7642-2294-5 (pbk.)
    1. Christian women—Prayer-books and devotionals—English. I. Title.

BV4844.P325   2004
248.8'43—dc22   2003022235

DONNA PARTOW is a Christian communicator with a compelling testimony of God's transforming power. Her uncommon transparency and passion for Christ have been used by God at women's conferences and retreats around the country. She is the bestselling author of numerous books and has been a popular guest on more than two hundred radio and TV programs, including *Focus on the Family*.

If your church sponsors an annual women's retreat, perhaps they would be interested in learning more about the author's special weekend programs. For more information, contact: *www.donnapartow.com*.

CONTENTS

The Pathway to
Becoming the Woman I Want to Be

Two years ago I was visiting my sister in New Jersey when I suddenly got the urge to take the infamous "good hard look at my life." I grabbed a notebook and pen and then headed outdoors to sit on a picnic bench. As I sat there prayerfully pondering how I had lived up until that point, and considering what I wanted my future to look like, I realized there were only a very few things that actually mattered. My family. My key relationships—with God, myself, and the world around me. My values. My character. It was, for me, a remarkably clearheaded moment. I had started the process by evaluating what I had accomplished with my life and initially planned to continue by listing what I hoped to accomplish with however many days I have remaining. But something clicked.

Life isn't so much about what you *do*. It's more about who you *are*. Of course, who you *are* has a profound impact on what you *do* and how you do it. But I fear many of us get it backward. We define who we are by what we do.

So the question became: what kind of person do I want to be? I sketched out, in words, a picture of the woman I want to be in terms of my relationships, values, and character. If it's okay with you, I'd like to open up that notebook— and open my soul to you. Each statement reflects not who I am right now but who I hope to become. Some statements you will relate to as universal human goals; others are more personal. Here's what I wrote, word for word:[1]

- ☩ I am, first and foremost, a child of God who seeks to walk daily in truth— to live what I believe.
- ☩ I live my life in a spirit of prayer, practicing the presence of God at all times and in all my affairs.

---

[1] Okay, you caught me—one item was too personal to print :)

✿ I strive for health and wholeness in my spirit, soul, and body. I seek healing whenever needed.

✿ I seek to raise godly children who fulfill their full potential in all areas of their lives.

✿ I strive to minister in power under God's anointing that lives will be dramatically changed through my writing and speaking. I am constantly learning and growing so I have worthwhile things to share with others.

✿ I desire and work toward peace within and around me. I cultivate harmony in all my relationships by being gracious, no matter how difficult the circumstances.

✿ I live every day, every moment, enthusiastically. I receive each opportunity and encounter as a gift to be celebrated.

✿ I am thankful to God and all who deserve my thanks.

✿ I put a smile on my face and inspire a smile in everyone I meet.

✿ I work hard at everything I do. I always do my best.

✿ My mission is to help as many people as I can in as many ways as I can.

✿ I endeavor to show myself, and the world, my "inner princess" by walking with my head held high and caring for my outward appearance.

I liked what I saw and began to get excited. Yes! That's the woman I want to be! Imagine the impact such a life could make, even if I never accomplished anything according to the world's standards. Just conducting myself on the planet in such a way would automatically touch the lives of virtually everyone I came in contact with. I wouldn't have to dream up "stuff" I could do for God (which used to be my personal specialty). I wouldn't even have to volunteer for any church committees to serve him effectively. Instead, ministry would flow naturally out of my heart directly into the hearts of others.

Then the thought occurred to me: what has held me back from becoming the woman I want to be? Some deep emotional trauma? Permanent personality flaws? Lack of cooperation from the people around me? A shortage of faith? No willpower?

For the next several months I searched for the answer. And I think I just might have found it! The pathway to becoming the woman I want to be is found in actively pursuing maximum health in my spirit, soul[2], and body. I realized that each area profoundly affects the others. It's hard to be a woman of prayer (thus cultivating a healthy spirit) when you can't get out of bed a little earlier than the rest of your family because you're too exhausted (because you have an unhealthy

---

[2]The soul encompasses your mind, your will, and your emotions.

10

body). And it's hard to have a positive impact on the people around you when you're negative, discouraged, and depressed (a reflection of an unhealthy soul).

Gradually it became apparent that I could not have optimal health in one area without attending to all three areas. They were too intricately bound. If you're anything like me, you've struggled to keep all of this in balance. Perhaps you've had a time of spiritual renewal when you were active in a Bible study or attended a retreat that rekindled the flame of your first love for God. For weeks, or even months, your spirit was vibrant and healthy. But you neglected your body and eventually physical exhaustion wiped out your spiritual zeal.

Or perhaps you joined a gym and began getting in shape—but you skipped your quiet time so you could exercise first thing in the morning. Next thing you knew, you were more concerned about how your clothes fit than you were about the fact that you were routinely throwing fits.

Perhaps you began seeing a counselor to deal with emotional issues in your life and gained tremendous insight into why you do the things you do. You determined to make changes but simply couldn't muster enough energy or willpower to implement them. Perhaps you didn't realize all that coffee and those doughnuts were weakening your ability to function effectively. Your soul's well-being was ultimately compromised by your unhealthy body.

If we are going to become all that God desires us to be, it will require a synergistic approach. We cannot focus on one area to the exclusion of the other two. Our goal needs to be optimal health in spirit, soul, and body.

In the past you may have pursued a variety of strategies—or "Things"—toward becoming the woman you want to be. Perhaps it went something like this:

- ✛ You heard a sermon on the importance of memorizing Scripture so you purchased a Scripture memory program at the Christian bookstore. Thing 1.
- ✛ Next you heard a preacher on the radio who admonished everyone to read the Bible daily. He even offered a little chart you could use to track your progress, so you called the radio ministry and ordered your Bible reading chart. You posted it on your refrigerator. Thing 2.
- ✛ Then all the ladies at your church were abuzz about the importance of praying God's Word. So you purchased a book that provided Scripture-based guided prayers. Thing 3.
- ✛ Then you attended a women's conference where the speaker emphasized the importance of prayer journaling. So you went to her book table and purchased a prayer journal. Thing 4.
- ✛ You were juggling these four activities, when one of your co-workers

mentioned that your real problem was "sweating the small stuff." The way to overcome that habit, she explained, was to recite positive affirmations. During your lunch hour, you stopped in at Barnes & Noble to pick up a book filled with affirmations to recite. Thing 5.

✣ Although you rarely watch television (Of course not! You are a devoted Christian and you have more important things to do with your time—like juggling Things 1 through 5), one day you happened on *Oprah* or *Good Morning America*. The day's renewal featured a dynamic author/expert who promised you could change your life or make it over if only you had a new life strategy. "Yes," you exclaimed aloud. "Enough sitting around pondering. I need to get up and take action." Fortunately, just before the renewal ended, they explained how you could register for a seminar near you. Thing 6.

✣ While at the seminar (reference the aforementioned Thing 6), the speaker emphasized the importance of getting an attitude adjustment. What you really needed, she explained, was an audio series filled with uplifting messages. So you clambered to the product table, along with a zillion of your closest friends, and procured some uplifting CDs or audiotapes. Thing 7.

✣ One day you discovered a site on the Internet that espoused the importance of maintaining a daily food diary. Indeed, it claimed that research indicates those who maintain a food journal are 90 percent more successful in their dieting efforts than those who do not. So you signed up for the renewal (just $19.95 per month) and added the interactive daily food diary to the favorite pages section on your computer. Then all you had to do was log on each day, go to the Web site, fill in the form, and voila! You jumped ahead of 90 percent of the dieting population. (They didn't mention that this process takes about twenty minutes since the site is so slow because it's bogged down with advertisements for every diet pill, potion, and renewal ever conceived by the mind of man. But that's no problem. You won't mind the inconvenience. You know you can keep up with it anyway.) Thing 8.

✣ You ran into an old girlfriend you hadn't seen in several months and she looked fabulous! "What on earth are you doing?" you ask. "Well, I'm following this new fitness renewal that's sweeping the nation. I might even win a million dollars if I can transform myself in the next twelve weeks. It's awesome. The book explains, step by step, everything you have to do. You should get it!" Back to the bookstore. Thing 9.

✣ Well, right about now, you're feeling completely defeated. You've tried Things 1 through 9 and haven't managed to transform your spirit, soul, or body. You're weary and discouraged. Fortunately, a friend invites you out to lunch, and when you mention feeling down, she gives you the name and number for a great counselor. You call to make an appointment the next day. Thing 10.

Can I make a small confession? I have actually done all of the above! Yes indeed, I know all about Thing 1 through Thing 10. Especially Thing 10. If you pursued even half of those Things trying to find the pathway to becoming the woman you want to be, no doubt you found it impossible to juggle it all. What I've tried to do—for your benefit as well as mine—is bring everything together in one place.

Let me explain how the renewal works by describing the daily routine and the rationale behind each component.

Spirit

Cultivating a healthy spirit requires devoting time each day to the spiritual disciplines of Scripture memory, Bible reading, praying Scripture-based prayer, and prayer journaling. All four are included right here on these pages. Each day features:

Scripture to memorize

The first item on your daily journey is your Scripture to memorize. Every five days you will be assigned a new memory verse to ponder. At the end of ninety days, you will have mastered eighteen passages, all of which are directly related to our theme of renewing your spirit, soul, and body. Some passages are favorites you may already know; others may be unfamiliar to you. Please give careful attention to both varieties. (At the back of the book these eighteen passages are printed on cards to cut out and carry in your purse or post on the refrigerator to help you memorize them on the go.)

Passage to read

Each day you will have a Bible passage to read. To be completely honest, when I've read books in the past that instructed me to go look up such and such Scripture, I found myself getting frustrated—or I simply guessed what I thought the passage was about (based on the reference or the contextual clues provided by the author). I'm one of those people who can't always sit down at a desk—

with three versions of the Bible, *Strong's Exhaustive Concordance,* and *Vine's Expository Dictionary* on hand—while I'm working through a book like this. I'm guessing that at least some of you know what I'm talking about. That's why I have printed out the entire text of each Scripture passage on these pages for your convenience.

Guided prayer

I have put a great deal of thought, effort, and prayer into the process of writing out a guided, Scripture-based prayer each day, derived from the daily passage. Please, don't rush past these. Instead, slowly pray through each one. I would strongly encourage you to pray them aloud. That way, the words become more than just marks on a page. They become the prayer of your own heart.

When you not only base your prayer requests on Scripture but actually turn Scripture into a prayer, you don't have to worry whether or not you are praying according to God's will—you are.

A prayer from your heart

Next, space has been provided for you to write out your own prayer. Please, please, please do not skip this exercise, as I truly believe prayer journaling is a powerful tool for spiritual growth. This is also a good way for you to practice turning Scripture into prayer, a skill that will yield spiritual benefits throughout your lifetime.

Soul

Yesterday I was asked to sum up my salvation experience within the allotted one inch of space on a preprinted form. I wrote: "Saved by the blood of Jesus in July 1980. Been justified. Being sanctified. Will some day be glorified." Rather pithy, wouldn't you say? I share that not only because I thought it was, in fact, rather pithy but also because it demonstrates an important point. We have been declared justified in God's sight. Our sin is no longer held against us, and we have been granted entrance into heaven. That work has already been accomplished. It is an established fact. A done deal. It is on that basis alone that we will one day stand before the throne of God and be transformed into his likeness (glorification). But in between what happened on the day of your salvation and what will happen to you one glorious day, the process of working out that salvation takes place.

For many years I was puzzled by the verse "Work out your own salvation with fear and trembling" (Philippians 2:12 NKJV). I knew we couldn't earn our salvation, so what were we supposed to work on? Here's what I believe it means: take what God has already accomplished in your spirit and let it transform your soul—your mind, your will, and your emotions. Yes, God has made it possible for you to enjoy heaven in heaven, but you can enjoy a little of heaven down here on earth.

The chapter goes on to make several important points, the first of which is best clarified by the Amplified Bible:

"[**Not in your own strength**] for it is God Who is all the while effectually at work in you [energizing and creating in you the power and desire], both to will and to work for His good pleasure and satisfaction and delight" (v. 13, emphasis added).

If God's only concern were your eternal salvation, you would have been directly transported to heaven on the day you accepted Christ. But the fact is, God chose to leave you here for a specific purpose. He has Kingdom work for you to complete before you leave earth. God himself gives you the energy and the power and the desire to complete the good works he prepared in advance for you . . . but you've got a part to play, too. You can't just lie on your bed and pray for God to do the rest.

Although praying is the ideal starting point, it won't get you over the finish line. You have to get up and put forth some serious effort. You have to apply that energy and power and desire, using it to move forward and take the necessary steps as an act of your will. God gives us freedom. He will never violate your will or force you to live a certain way. But he will give you the energy, power, and desire—in other words, everything you could possibly need—to fulfill your life purpose. But only you can get on that path, put one foot in front of the other, and walk worthy of your high calling.

In case you are still unclear about what that path might look like, the Bible spells it out plainly in the next two verses:

"Do everything without complaining or arguing, so that you may become blameless and pure, children of God without fault in a crooked and depraved generation, in which you shine like stars in the universe" (Philippians 2:14–15).

Did God provide a checklist of things to "accomplish"? No! God gives instructions concerning the type of character we are to demonstrate—the kind of woman he wants you to be. And as you live that way, you will indeed shine like a star in the universe. That's your assignment right there. The rest is just details.

Since God specifically mentions "do everything without complaining or arguing" as the key to shining like stars in the universe, our soul focus (did you catch the little pun?) during the next ninety days will be developing an attitude of thankfulness, although we will explore other soul issues, as well.

Affirmation to recite

The way to transform your mind is not by trying to rid yourself of the garbage you've been fed over the years and the negative thinking patterns that have held you captive in the past. (If that approach worked, I would be Mother Teresa by now. Trust me, it doesn't work!) Instead, deliberately turn your attention to the positive—and I want you to be very aggressive about it. I'm not talking about becoming a Pollyanna or wasting your time on wishful thinking. No, I'm talking about renewing your mind with the truth of God's Word. The other day I heard someone say that what most of us need is brainwashing, using God's Word as the soap. Here's how Webster's Dictionary defines brainwash: "to teach a set of ideas so thoroughly as to change a person's beliefs and attitudes completely."[3] Sounds pretty good, doesn't it? Maybe it's time for you to get serious about washing your brain.

To assist you in this process, I have written a daily affirmation (positive statement of biblical truth). However, it won't be enough simply to read the daily affirmation. Frankly, that will do you no good. You will need to recite the affirmations aloud, over and over and over, until they begin to transform you from the inside out. As you fill your mind with the truth about who God is and all the good things he has done in the past and desires to do in the future, the negative will eventually get washed away.

All of the affirmations are rooted in Scripture and most are simply rephrased Bible passages. Here again, as you observe for ninety days how I have done this, you will be able to transform Bible verses into affirmations on your own. I cannot overemphasize how important these affirmations are! I believe they are an extremely powerful component of this ninety-day renewal.

Action to take

As you think new thoughts, your attitude will begin to change. Gradually, with a new attitude, the words you speak and the way you respond will change.

---

[3] *Webster's New World Dictionary.*

Your behavior—the actions you take—will change. This is what the Scripture means when it says "be transformed by the renewing of your mind" (Romans 12:2). Then something wonderful will begin to happen: you'll notice that people respond to you differently. Your circumstances begin to change. It becomes a positive cycle of blessing.

Each day I will give you some action to take to implement what you're learning in a practical way. This is your opportunity to apply the force of your will toward a positive end.

Attitude adjustment

The final component of the soul portion of your ninety-day renewal addresses your emotions. Let's go back to the dictionary for a moment. Emotion is defined as a "strong feeling." My edition points out: "Emotion is used of any of the ways in which one reacts to something without careful thinking."[4] So your emotions are a reflection of who you are when you're not thinking—it's the gut-level you. It's what the Bible means when it says, "For out of the overflow of the heart the mouth speaks" (Matthew 12:34). Yet, as we shall discuss throughout our journey together, your thinking directly affects your emotions. Indeed, the best way to get a handle on your emotions is to change the way you think and what you think about. Each day I will offer some suggestions directed toward changing your thinking or giving you something encouraging to think about.

The last component to address on your journey to becoming the woman you want to be is your body. Let's face it: how you feel physically has a profound impact on your spirit and soul. Each day is divided into two distinct areas: diet and exercise.

Diet

I am not a doctor or dietician. I'm not a nutritionist. I'm just a fellow human being who has figured out that what I eat directly impacts my emotions and energy level. It therefore directly impacts my ability to live the kind of life God desires for me.

---

[4] *Webster's New World Dictionary.*

It's not my intention to overhaul your entire eating routine or put you on a strict regimen. Instead, I will suggest relatively minor additions and gradual changes. Again, rather than focusing on the negative—what you shouldn't eat and what you have to give up—I've focused on the positive. As you incorporate enough positive dietary choices, I believe the negative will automatically dissipate.[5]

For example, starting in the second week, I am asking you to consume sixty-four ounces of water per day.[6] That's a fairly large quantity of fluids. I think you may find it difficult to consume your usual four cans of soda or five glasses of iced tea *in addition* to all that water. The more water you drink, the less food you'll eat. From Day 1, you'll be encouraged to eat as many vegetables as you can from the approved list. By increasing your vegetable intake, you will cut down on the volume of starchy, sugar-laden carbohydrates you can consume. Pretty tricky, eh?

Since the ninety-day renewal incorporates a series of one- and two-day fasts, let me say a few words on the subject before we begin. If you have any medical concerns about fasting, talk with your doctor first. Obviously, those who have blood-sugar-related diseases need to seek special guidance before undertaking a fast. First, the benefits:

- Fasting enables us to focus on the needs of our spirit rather than the demands of our body.

- Fasting provides a wonderful opportunity for us to practice saying "No"—something many Americans have forgotten how to do, to our own detriment.

- Fasting allows the body to rest from the task of digestion, enabling it to devote more resources to cleansing and healing.[7]

- "Thousands of people throughout the world fast regularly not to cure any particular disease, but because they consider fasting to be an effective way to cleanse the body from accumulated wastes, build up physical stamina and resistance against disease, and revitalize and rejuvenate the functions of all their vital organs."—Paavo O. Airola, N.D., Ph.D.[8]

- Fasting can increase life span and make people more resistant to the diseases

---

[5] Always check with your doctor before making dietary changes.
[6] Each day you are assigned a special morning "tonic" to cleanse your system. You can deduct the water thus consumed from your total sixty-four ounces.
[7] David and Anne Frahm, *Healthy Habits* (Colorado Springs, CO: Pinon Press, 1993), 171.
[8] Ibid., 173.

of aging including diabetes and Alzheimers.[9]

Some fasting guidelines:

- First and foremost: Do *not* consume caffeine while fasting! If possible, eliminate caffeine a few days before your fast.
- Be aware that you may experience headaches, jitters, shivering, nausea, diarrhea, and other side effects as your body "detoxifies" itself. This is especially true if you have been eating an unhealthy diet for many years. Don't give up your fast! This is *good news*. It means your body is getting rid of the junk.
- You might want to eat a salad or steamed vegetables and then take a warm bath before going to bed on the eve of your fast. This jump-starts your body's cleansing processes.
- Eat healthy foods for several days prior to your fast.
- Don't gorge yourself on junk food the night before.
- You might consider purchasing one of the forty-eight-hour diet juices for some (but not all) of your fasts. I've found that these lessen the possible side effects of fasting, especially headaches.
- If you have a juicer, you can consume a small amount of fresh vegetable juices during your fast.
- Drink at least one half gallon of water—preferably one gallon—per day.
- You may add a little fresh lemon or a small amount of cranberry juice concentrate (available at health food stores) to your water.
- The day after your fast, try to eat healthy and light. For breakfast, you might start with fresh fruits, then a salad for lunch. Resist the temptation to eat starchy or sugar-laden foods, as these will undo the health benefits of your fast.
- If a complete fast is not possible, you may consider a partial fast. For example, fast from solids, restricting yourself to liquids such as protein shakes, fruit juice, soup, etc. (I often do this type of fast.) Or you might fast from a food group or favorite food.
- If your doctor advises against any form of fasting from food, consider alternative fasts, such as "fasting" from TV, the Internet, telephone, music, reading (other than your Bible), etc.
- Prepare your family's meals in advance; slow-cooker meals are wonderful because you can throw the food in and forget it. Your family can serve themselves without too much involvement on Mom's part. Pray for your family

---

[9]According to the online edition of the Proceedings of the National Academy of Sciences, Tue Apr 29.

while they enjoy their meals. When I am fasting, I often use mealtimes to read aloud to my children.

- ✠ Keep your schedule light if at all possible. Run errands in advance, put your household in good order by getting ahead of schedule on chores, etc.
- ✠ Enlist your family's support. Explain to them why you are fasting. Ask them to pray for you and not tempt you with food offerings.
- ✠ You can be certain the Enemy of your soul will do everything in his power to dissuade you from fasting. He knows you are about to tap into some powerful spiritual resources. Be determined, in advance, to resist every temptation he will send your way.

Exercise

Even though I am a certified personal trainer, I believe my most important credential is this: I'm a middle-aged woman who's finding it increasingly difficult to stay in shape. I realize how vitally important exercise is to my overall sense of well-being, so I've done a great deal of research into what works and what doesn't in the area of physical fitness. If you have the time, money, and inclination to join a gym or register for a formal workout class, I think that's absolutely awesome. You can bypass my daily exercise admonition, which will be included for the benefit of everyone else.

I prefer to keep it simple. I've found three things that work best for me, so that's what I'm recommending to you. My top three fitness strategies are: Walking. Bouncing. And strength training. If you can find a fitness partner—a friend to join you in these activities—so much the better. I've always exercised more consistently when I've had a friend to keep me motivated. I currently have two fitness partners: my twelve-year-old daughter Leah and her little sister, Tara, age six.

For walking, all you need is a great pair of shoes. (Don't try to save money here. Invest in a quality shoe designed specifically for walking, not running, cross-training, or anything else.) I realize some readers may have physical limitations that prevent them from implementing the fitness component of this renewal. Please do not be discouraged if you are unable to walk very far—or perhaps not at all. Pray, asking God to show you the best way to care for your body. He created you and he has the answers! Meanwhile, focus on those aspects of the ninety-day renewal that are within your reach.

For bouncing (jumping), a mini-trampoline (also called a rebounder) is ideal. It's cheap, quick, fun, and, best of all, is easy on your joints. "Rebounding cleanses and decongests [the body's lymphatic system], increases immunity, offers an aerobic workout, increases circulation and muscle strength, reduces cellulite and body fat, lowers cholesterol, [while improving] coordination and balance. . . . And all of this can be accomplished in the privacy of your own home, in a very small area, with one piece of equipment."[10] If you can't jump, you can derive many of the same health benefits simply by sitting on it while someone else bounces it for you.[11] You can bounce either barefoot or with sneakers. There's no need to leap into the air; just jump lightly, especially in the beginning. If at any point you become "winded," simply rock up and down on the soles of your feet. Mini-tramps are extremely popular right now and are widely available at fitness stores or over the Internet. Be sure to follow the instructions that come with your mini-tramp.

For strength training, I recommend a super-short workout video/DVD such as the eight-minute workouts by Jorge Cruise (*www.jorgecruise.com*) or Jaime Brenkus (available at *www.amazon.com*). There's no need to undertake an hour-long video, unless you want to transform yourself into a fitness model. In that case, rumor has it that *The Firm* workout videos are among the best on the market (*www.firmdirect.com*). For the average woman, long workouts are overkill. Besides, if you're like most women, you'll quickly burn out. Short workouts with consistency will prove far more effective than an intense fitness craze that doesn't last. Along with the video, you will want to obtain dumbbells. I suggest beginning with three different weights. For the novice: 2, 3 and 5 lbs.; for the intermediate: 5, 8 and 10 lbs.; and for the advanced: 10, 12 and 15 lbs. To determine which weights to begin with, go to a fitness store and guesstimate which weight you can curl twelve times. When you find the weight you can "just barely" curl twelve times, that's your middle weight dumbbell. Purchase one just a little lighter and one just a bit heavier.[12]

As always, before undertaking any form of physical fitness renewal, be sure to check with your doctor.

I've launched an on-line support group to help you be motivated. Visit *www.donnapartow.com* for more details.

Let's Begin

Now you have a clear overview of what the next ninety days will feature. I hope you're excited about the prospect for positive change in your life. If you stick with the renewal, I'm convinced you'll agree your efforts will be well rewarded in the end. It's my prayer that this book will help you become the woman you want to be.

---

[10]*www.purejoylivingfoods.com/products/needackRebounder.shtml*
[11]Ann Louise Gittleman, *The Fat Flush Plan* (NY: McGraw-Hill, 2002), 93.
[12]Jorge Cruise, *8 Minutes In the Morning* (NY: HarperCollins, 2003), 37–38.

What You Will Need for the Exercise Program:
☐ A good pair of sneakers
☐ Mini-trampoline or rebounder
☐ Eight-minute workout video of your choice, along with recommended dumbbells (optional)
☐ Upbeat praise music (to listen to while you bounce)
☐ 64-oz. refillable water bottle
☐ A partner or group of partners

What You Will Need for the Diet:

WEEK(S)	FOOD
1-3, 8-13	☐ 2 lemons per week
1-13	☐ Multivitamins
1-13	☐ Ester-C
2-13	☐ One 64 oz.-container (if you are in one place all day) or two 32-oz. containers suitable for taking water with you (if you are on the go). Each morning fill the bottle(s) and finish it (them) before the day is through. This approach assumes your tap water is suitable. If your tap water is unsuitable, you'll need to purchase bottled water.
2-13	☐ Bottled water if necessary (Be sure you purchase enough to consume sixty-four ounces per day.)
2-13	☐ Vegetables from the approved list (see below)—as many as you think you and your family can possibly consume in a week.
2-13	☐ Eggs (usually two per day)
4-13	☐ Essential Fatty Acids (capsules or liquid) (also called EPAs)*
4-8	☐ Unsweetened cranberry juice*
4-8	☐ Psyllium husk*
5-7	☐ Protein shake mix (Make sure you buy a low-carb brand. Vanilla or strawberry flavor works best.)
5-7	☐ Frozen raspberries or strawberries
6-13	☐ Healthy proteins (i.e., fish, poultry, lean beef, tofu, all-natural peanut butter)
9-13	☐ Bragg's Apple Cider Vinegar*
9-13	☐ Locan honey
11-13	☐ Apples and/or grapefruit

A note about Ester-C and Bragg's Apple Cider Vinegar: While you'll find several types of vitamin C and various brands of apple cider vinegar, I recommend these because I think they're the best on the market.

*Items marked with an asterisk will probably require a trip to a health food store. If it's a long trip, you may want to acquire all of the items up front.

Approved Vegetables[13]

Buy as many of the following vegetables each week as you think you and your family can realistically consume in that week. Be careful not to overestimate on fresh produce or you'll risk spoilage—and wasted money. Do not shy away from frozen vegetables, as they are often just as nutritious as fresh produce. Of course, if you prefer organically grown and/or fresh produce, that is fine.

Asparagus	Eggplants	Peppers
Broccoli	Greens	Radishes
Brussels sprouts	Green beans	Spinach
Cabbage	Lettuce	Tomatoes
Cauliflower	Onions	Water chestnuts
Celery	Parsley	Zucchini
Cucumbers		

Vegetables to eat in moderation include:

Beets	Potatoes
Corn	Yams
Peas	

---

[13]My thanks to Carrie Carter, M.D., author of *Thrive!* (Bethany House Publishers, 2003) for her assistance in preparing the list of recommended vegetables.

Week 1

Scripture to memorize:

> *May God himself, the God of peace, sanctify you through*
> *and through. May your whole spirit, soul and body*
> *be kept blameless at the coming of our Lord Jesus Christ.*
> *The one who calls you is faithful and he will do it.*

1 THESSALONIANS 5:23–24

Passage to read:

Out of the depths I cry to you, O Lord;
> *O Lord, hear my voice.*
Let your ears be attentive
> *to my cry for mercy.*
If you, O Lord, kept a record of sins,
> *O Lord, who could stand?*
But with you there is forgiveness;
> *therefore you are feared.*
I wait for the Lord, my soul waits,
> *and in his word I put my hope.*
My soul waits for the Lord
> *more than watchmen wait for the morning,*
> *more than watchmen wait for the morning.*

PSALM 130:1–6

Guided prayer:

Dear Lord, hear my voice. You know the weaknesses of my spirit, soul, and body. Today, once again, I realize my need for your mercy. Forgive me for neglecting myself. So often I have failed to cultivate my spirit by not spending time with you in prayer or in the study of your Word. I have allowed my mind to be filled with clutter. I have not trained my will to choose rightly but have *instead lived by my impulses. Too often, my emotions have raged out of control, causing me to say and do things I later regretted. My body bears witness that I have not always cared for it as I should. I have treated it like a trash can, rather than the temple of your Holy Spirit.*

Lord, I know that if you were to keep a record of all my sins, I could not stand before you. But with you, there is forgiveness. I thank you that, even as I confess these sins, you have removed them as far as the east is from the west. Praise you, Lord! I ask you now to sanctify my spirit, soul, and body, and I thank you that your Word says you will be faithful to fulfill all your good promises to me. Amen.

A prayer from your heart:

_____

_____

_____

_____

Affirmation to recite:

I forget those things that are behind me, including all of my personal short-comings in the area of spiritual disciplines, diet, and exercise. I am pressing toward what lies ahead: a bright future filled with health in my spirit, soul, and body.

BASED ON PHILIPPIANS 3:13

Action to take:

On the following lines, write out a list of twenty-five things you want to have, do, or be.

For example, you might want to *be* an awesome mother, *have* a mountain bike, and memorize the book of James (*do*). You don't need to have any certain number of items in each category. And don't overanalyze your answers at this point. This is a gut level exercise, so move through it quickly, writing down whatever pops into your head.

Twenty-Five Things I Want to Have, Do, or Be

1. _____
2. _____
3. _____
4. _____
5. _____
6. _____
7. _____
8. _____
9. _____
10. _____
11. _____
12. _____
13. _____

14. _____
15. _____
16. _____
17. _____
18. _____
19. _____
20. _____
21. _____
22. _____
23. _____
24. _____
25. _____

Attitude adjustment:

He has half the deed done who has made a beginning.

HORACE

Congratulations! Today you've made a start toward improving your spirit, soul, and body. You've moved one step closer toward becoming a Brand-New You! The you God intended you to be on the day he created you. Don't be discouraged by all the areas in your life you think need improvement. Instead, focus on the progress you've made just by picking up this book and reading this far. (You *did* read The Pathway to *Becoming the Woman I Want to Be,* right? If not, go back and read it before accepting my hearty congratulations!) Rejoice that you've made a new beginning! The things you once only dreamed of doing, being, and having should now seem more possible than they ever have before . . . because I promise you they are!

Body

Diet:

☐ First thing this morning, drink an eight-ounce cup of hot lemon juice. (Bring water almost to a boil. Place a quarter of a lemon in the water and allow to steep for a few minutes. Squeeze the lemon. Drink up. I'll say more about the benefits of lemon water later. Meanwhile, if a quarter of a lemon upsets your stomach, back down to an eighth, etc.)

☐ Take a good multivitamin and Ester-C.

☐ Eat as many raw or steamed veggies (from the approved list, page 23) as you can.

Exercise:

☐ Bounce on your mini-trampoline for two to three minutes.

☐ Walk briskly for fifteen minutes.

DAY TWO	TODAY'S DATE

Spirit

Scripture to memorize:

May God himself, the God of peace, sanctify you through
and through. May your whole spirit, soul and body
be kept blameless at the coming of our Lord Jesus Christ.
The one who calls you is faithful and he will do it.

1 THESSALONIANS 5:23–24

Passage to read:

The Lord your God is testing you to find out whether you love him with all
your heart and with all your soul. It is the Lord your God you must follow, and

him you must revere. Keep his commands and obey him; serve him and hold fast to him.

DEUTERONOMY 13:3–4

Guided prayer;

Dear Lord, your Word reveals that you do, indeed, test your people. I know you have tested me in the past . . . and I have not always passed those tests. I thank you that today is brand-new, another day in which I can choose to follow you wholeheartedly. Lord, I know your heart is filled with love toward me and that every test that comes my way flows from your heart of love. You desire to see—and to show me—whether I will love you with all my heart and with all my soul.

I desire to keep your commands and obey you, to serve you and hold fast to you. Strengthen me, by the power of your Holy Spirit, to live a life that honors you. Open my spiritual eyes to see the tests that come my way today. I know I will be tested to see how serious I am about my commitment to becoming healthy in spirit, soul, and body. I know my own desires will tempt me to take the "easy" way out. I may not want to follow the diet or exercise renewal. I might prefer watching television rather than reading something uplifting. At those moments, I pray I will remember what I have purposed in my heart and draw my strength from you. Amen.

A prayer from your heart:

_____

_____

_____

_____

Affirmation to recite:

I have the power to change my life, because the spirit of the Lord rests upon me. I can learn a new way of living because I have a spirit of wisdom and understanding.

BASED ON ISAIAH 11:2

Action to take:

Go back through the Twenty-Five Things list you created yesterday. For each item, indicate if it falls under the category of something you want to have (put an H next to that item), something you want to do (D), or who you hope to become (B). It might be interesting to note how many items you had of each:

H = _____   D = _____   B = _____

What do the numbers listed above tell you about yourself? (There's no right answer!)

_____

_____

Next, list the top five items in each category in the space below:

Have	**Do**	**Be/Become**
1. _____	_____	_____
2. _____	_____	_____
3. _____	_____	_____
4. _____	_____	_____
5. _____	_____	_____

Attitude adjustment:

From now on you'll be traveling the road between who you think you are and who you can be. The key is to allow yourself to make that journey.

WORDS OF WISDOM FROM THE FATHER IN THE MOVIE *THE PRINCESS DIARIES*

You picked up this book because you want to make positive changes in your life. On the second day of your journey, you've gained a clearer picture of who you want to become, what you want to do, and what you hope to have in your lifetime. Please do not be discouraged if it seems like the journey ahead of you is long. Just take it one day at a time. It's my prayer that by the end of these ninety days you'll be greatly encouraged to see how much closer you are to that final destination of becoming the woman you want to be. As you become all God intended for you, the doors will open up for you to experience the very best this life has to offer. More to the point, you'll have a greater appreciation for what you already have. But remember: you'll never become who you want to be by remaining who you are.

Diet:
- [ ] Drink eight ounces of hot lemon water upon rising.
- [ ] Take a multivitamin and Ester-C.
- [ ] Eat as many raw or steamed veggies as you can.

Exercise:
- [ ] Walk briskly for fifteen minutes.

DAY THREE	TODAY'S DATE

Scripture to memorize:

May God himself, the God of peace, sanctify you through
and through. May your whole spirit, soul and body
be kept blameless at the coming of our Lord Jesus Christ.
The one who calls you is faithful and he will do it.

1 THESSALONIANS 5:23–24

Passage to read:

Hear, O Israel: The Lord our God, the Lord is one. Love the Lord your God with all your heart and with all your soul and with all your strength. These commandments that I give you today are to be upon your hearts. Impress them on your children. Talk about them when you sit at home and when you walk along the road, when you lie down and when you get up. Tie them as symbols on your hands and bind them on your foreheads. Write them on the doorframes of your houses and on your gates.

DEUTERONOMY 6:4–9

Guided prayer:

Dear Lord, I acknowledge you today as my God. I desire to love you with all my heart, with all my soul, and with all my strength. Jesus said if I love you, I will obey you. Yet how can I obey what I do not know? How can I believe what I do not understand? Lord, this moment, I ask you to press your commandments upon my heart. I want to cooperate with you by meditating upon your Word and letting it fill my mind. Today, as I go about my daily tasks— walking, driving, housecleaning, cooking, exercising, interacting with friends and family—may I be mindful of your Word. I renew my commitment to memorizing Scripture. Holy Spirit, I invite you to remind me, throughout the day, of that commitment and bring to my remembrance those passages I have committed to

31

memory (and those I am studying even now). I ask you to provide at least one opportunity for me to share a portion of Scripture with someone today. Amen.

A prayer from your heart:

_____

_____

_____

_____

Affirmation to recite:

I am cooperating with God as he transforms me day by day. I am pressing on toward the prize God has in store for me.

BASED ON PHILIPPIANS 3:14

Action to take:

Rewrite (or type) the Top Five list you created yesterday and post it somewhere you will see it often. The refrigerator door and bathroom mirror work well for me. Try to read the list every day for the next week or so to remind yourself of the woman you want to be.

Attitude adjustment:

If one advances confidently in the direction of his dreams, and endeavors to live the life which he has imagined, he will meet with success unexpected in common hours.

HENRY DAVID THOREAU

No doubt you've figured it out by now: dreams don't unfold overnight. I once heard it said, "The average overnight success took twenty years to succeed." During all that time, they kept the dream alive by working daily toward its fulfillment. Dreaming, envisioning the woman you want to be, is just the first step on a journey you'll be traveling the rest of your life. You won't become the woman you want to be tomorrow just because you set some goals today. But you can move closer to becoming that woman if you advance confidently in the direction of your dreams.

If you're going to dream, you might just as well dream big. Small dreams never got anyone out of bed in the morning. Give yourself permission to believe great things can happen. As the woman you want to be begins to emerge, new opportunities will emerge as well. New experiences. New friends. New insights. Get ready and be on the watch for them!

Diet:
- [ ] Drink eight ounces of hot lemon water upon rising.
- [ ] Take a multivitamin and Ester-C.
- [ ] Eat as many raw or steamed veggies as you can.

Exercise:
- [ ] Bounce for two to three minutes.
- [ ] Walk briskly for fifteen minutes.

DAY FOUR	TODAY'S DATE

Scripture to memorize:
May God himself, the God of peace, sanctify you through
and through. May your whole spirit, soul and body
be kept blameless at the coming of our Lord Jesus Christ.
The one who calls you is faithful and he will do it.

1 THESSALONIANS 5:23–24

Passage to read:

One of them, an expert in the law, tested him with this question: "Teacher, which is the greatest commandment in the Law?"

Jesus replied: "'Love the Lord your God with all your heart and with all your soul and with all your mind.' This is the first and greatest commandment. And the second is like it: 'Love your neighbor as yourself.' All the Law and the Prophets hang on these two commandments."

MATTHEW 22:35–40

Guided prayer:

Dear Lord, thank you for telling us plainly what your priorities are. Sometimes we make the Christian life so complicated. Yet Jesus said it's really very simple. You desire for us to love you and love each other. Lord, I desire to love you with all my soul. That's why I am choosing, even now, to fill my mind with thoughts of your character. To discipline my will to choose the path of obedience. To fill my heart with your promises so that my emotions will stay in check, resting securely in your love. Lord, I acknowledge that I have looked to others to fill that place in my heart that you alone can fill. And because of that emptiness inside—that desperate need to feel loved—I have been unable to love others in the way you have commanded. I ask you to flood my heart with an awareness of your love for me today. Heal those insecure places in my heart that cause me to be self-protective, self-seeking, and self-consumed. Fill me to overflowing so that loving others is as natural to me as breathing. Amen.

A prayer from your heart:

_____

_____

_____

_____

Affirmation to recite:

I rest securely in God's loving care. I know he has an awesome plan for my future. Plans to prosper me and not to harm me.

BASED ON JEREMIAH 29:11

Action to take:

Share a copy of your Top Five list with a trusted friend. Ask her to mark her calendar eighty-six days from now to check on your progress toward your goals.

Attitude adjustment:

Love God and do whatever you want.

ST. AUGUSTINE

Many Christians think that following God involves adhering to a set of rules and regulations. I remember one Christian author posing the question (in fact, I think it was a chapter title in one of his books), "Can a Christian drive a BMW?" I'm pretty sure his answer was "No." The Pharisees had more rules than you could shake a stick at! And they followed the letter of the law with tremendous determination and religious zeal.

Was Jesus pleased with them? No. He told them, in essence, "You're making this way more complicated than it needs to be." I like the way Augustine put it: "Love God and do whatever you want." If you love God, you'll walk in close communion with him. If you walk in close communion with him, you'll become more and more like him. Since God loves people, you'll love people too. If you love people, you'll be a loving person who does the right thing *from the heart* rather than *from a rulebook*. Love God. Love people. Don't worry about the rest.

Body

Diet:
- ☐ Drink eight ounces of hot lemon water upon rising.
- ☐ Take a multivitamin and Ester-C.
- ☐ Eat as many raw or steamed veggies as you can.

Exercise:
- ☐ Walk briskly for fifteen minutes.

DAY FIVE	TODAY'S DATE

Spirit

Scripture to memorize:

> May God himself, the God of peace, sanctify you through
> and through. May your whole spirit, soul and body be kept
> blameless at the coming of our Lord Jesus Christ.
> The one who calls you is faithful and he will do it.

1 THESSALONIANS 5:23–24

Passage to read:

The Lord is my shepherd, I shall not be in want.
He makes me lie down in green pastures,
he leads me beside quiet waters,
he restores my soul.
He guides me in paths of righteousness
for his name's sake.
Even though I walk
through the valley of the shadow of death,
I will fear no evil,

for you are with me;
your rod and your staff,
they comfort me.
You prepare a table before me
in the presence of my enemies.
You anoint my head with oil;
my cup overflows.
Surely goodness and love will follow me
all the days of my life,
and I will dwell in the house of the Lord
forever.

PSALM 23

Guided prayer:

Dear Lord, I thank you for being my shepherd, the one who looks after me and guides my steps. Thank you for providing everything I need—help me to see and truly believe that my needs are met. I recognize and confess my tendency to confuse my wants and needs. I realize how often that confusion robs me of the peace you desire for me to experience. This day I desire to find rest even in the midst of my busy life. Help me to enjoy the green pastures and quiet waters along the way. To relish those early morning moments alone with you. To sit and enjoy the sun rising or setting. To listen to the sound of running water or chirping birds. Teach me how to cultivate peace and quiet within my own soul. Restore my soul, Lord.

Renew my mind, will, and emotions today. Let me walk in paths of righteousness, consciously determining to do what is right, rather than what is convenient or commonplace. Lord, I also acknowledge that hard times will come my way—that is an inevitable fact of life. Help me not to overreact or panic or give way to fear. Rather, let me rest securely within even when there is hardship without. I acknowledge, too, that I will have enemies. Not everyone will like me. But even in the midst of my enemies, you prepare a table before me, providing all that I need to enjoy my life. You anoint my head with the oil of your Holy Spirit, so my mind is cleansed and renewed. I thank you that goodness and love follow me wherever I go. Amen.

A prayer from your heart:

_____

_____

_____

_____

Affirmation to recite:
Goodness and love follow me wherever I go. I am richly blessed!

BASED ON PSALM 23

Action to take:
Create your own prayer oasis, a special place you can go each day to focus on your relationship with God and becoming the woman you want to be. One of my friends, who lives here in Arizona where the sun shines most of the year, has a prayer garden. She enjoys sitting outside at her picnic table, with a cup of tea and her Bible, early in the morning. Another friend spends time on her front porch swing, which affords a beautiful view of a neighboring farm.

I have a beautiful prayer room filled with dried flowers, cheerful pictures, candles, and many of my most treasured possessions. I love to sit in my rocking chair with my prayer basket by my side. For my last birthday, a friend bought me a tabletop waterfall. It has made a wonderful addition to the room.

You may not be able to go outdoors or set aside an entire room, but if you look carefully enough, you will surely find a little corner somewhere in your home. Transform it. Make it your favorite place and you'll be more likely to spend time there.

I would encourage you to create a prayer basket (so, if weather permits, you can always go outside, perhaps to a park). Your prayer basket should include: your Bible, this book, pens, highlighters, Post-it notes, note cards, tissues, hand cream, and lip balm. (I don't know if you're like me, but the minute I sit down to have my morning devotions, I suddenly remember a million things I have to do or people I want to call. I jot it down on a Post-it note and move on. Or, as I'm praying for someone, I might decide to write him a quick note. The other big three for me are: stuffy nose, dry hands, and chapped lips. So I'm prepared and don't have to walk away from my prayer chair. Your prayer basket will evolve as you discover the items that routinely "drive you from your chair" and prepare accordingly.

Before you go to bed tonight, set your alarm for thirty minutes earlier than you usually wake up and report directly to your prayer room.

Attitude adjustment:

Discipline is the human effort to create the space in which God can be generous and give you what you need.

Henri Nouwen

God will not love you any more if you assert your will, make the decision, and put forth the effort to create a prayer oasis. God will not love you more if you wake up thirty minutes earlier each day to devote to prayer and reflection. These actions do not benefit God. (Although I'm sure it does his heart good to see his child trying. Don't you love to see your children putting forth an honest effort?) These actions benefit *you* and those around you. When you set aside time for spiritual disciplines, you put yourself in a place where it's easier to recognize and receive the blessings God desires to shower upon you. Get ready to receive!

Diet:
- ☐ Drink eight ounces of hot lemon water upon rising.
- ☐ Take a multivitamin and Ester-C.
- ☐ Eat as many raw or steamed veggies as you can.

Exercise:
- ☐ Bounce for two to three minutes.
- ☐ Walk briskly for fifteen minutes.

DAY SIX	TODAY'S DATE

Scripture to memorize:

My soul finds rest in God alone;
my salvation comes from him.
He alone is my rock and my salvation;
he is my fortress, I will never be shaken.

PSALM 62:1–2

Passage to read:

Oh, how I love your law!
I meditate on it all day long.
Your commands make me wiser than my enemies,
for they are ever with me.
I have more insight than all my teachers,
for I meditate on your statutes.
I have more understanding than the elders,
for I obey your precepts.
I have kept my feet from every evil path
so that I might obey your word.
I have not departed from your laws,
for you yourself have taught me.
How sweet are your words to my taste,
sweeter than honey to my mouth!
I gain understanding from your precepts;
therefore I hate every wrong path.

PSALM 119:97–104

Guided prayer:

Dear Lord, I love your law. I recognize the importance of meditating upon it
all day long. Your commands make me wiser. As I meditate on your statutes, I

will gain insight beyond my years. Lord, I want to choose the righteous path of obedience to your Word. I want to arrive at that place where your Word is truly sweeter to me than all the junk food in the world combined. I want to become the kind of person who feeds on your Word—and allows that to fill my spirit, rather than trying to fill myself with food and other things that can never satisfy. Teach me to feast upon your Word, O Lord. Amen.

A prayer from your heart:

_____

_____

_____

_____

Affirmation to recite:

I meditate on God's word day and night. I love to memorize Scripture!

BASED ON PSALM 119:97

Action to take:

Several years ago I was listening to a Chuck Swindoll sermon over the radio while driving in my car. The renewal was excellent, so I pulled over and jotted down his outline for Scripture memory. Here's what I wrote (my commentary is in brackets):

Scripture Memory: Memorize, Personalize, Analyze

1. Set aside fifteen minutes per day for Scripture memory.

2. Choose verses that address your weaknesses. That way, you'll have a vested interest in remembering them.

3. Read the passage aloud, over and over.

4. Break the verse down into logical parts. Learn one phrase, then two, until you've memorized the entire passage.

5. Repeat the reference often.

6. It's better to learn a few verses really well than many poorly. [That's why we're limiting ourselves to eighteen verses over the next three months.]

7. Underline difficult terms or key words. Look them up in the dictionary, a concordance, or a Bible reference book.

8. Write out the verse from memory. This is a critical step. Something about putting pen to paper makes the words more permanent.

Attitude adjustment:

> *Seven days without God's Word makes one weak.*
>
> GREG LAURIE

Scripture memory is not nearly as hard as people make it seem. Here's a strategy I have used that sounds crazy—but I promise it works! It's so effective, I even got a letter from a missionary in Brazil who is using it. She read the idea in my book *Becoming a Vessel God Can Use*. I write out the first initial of every word in the verse while looking at the passage. I set it down for a while. When I return, I try to complete the words from memory. Repeat this process several times and you'll be amazed to discover you remember that verse years later.

Diet:

☐ Drink eight ounces of hot lemon water upon rising.
☐ Take a multivitamin and Ester-C.
☐ Eat as many raw or steamed veggies as you can.

Exercise:

☐ Walk briskly for fifteen minutes.

Scripture to memorize:

> My soul finds rest in God alone;
> my salvation comes from him.
> He alone is my rock and my salvation;
> he is my fortress, I will never be shaken.

PSALM 62:1–2

Passage to read:

Two are better than one,
because they have a good return for their work:
If one falls down,
his friend can help him up.
But pity the man who falls
and has no one to help him up!
Also, if two lie down together, they will keep warm.
But how can one keep warm alone?
Though one may be overpowered,
two can defend themselves.
A cord of three strands is not quickly broken.

ECCLESIASTES 4:9–12

Guided prayer:

Dear Lord, you have said human beings are better off in pairs. You've created us to need one another. Forgive me for thinking I know more than you do! Forgive me for thinking I can go it alone. I remember too well the times I have fallen because no one was there to warn me I was heading down the wrong path. I recognize that if I try to make lifestyle changes on my own, I am likely to stumble and give up.

I am asking you for wisdom as I consider asking someone to be my *accountability partner. I'll need all the help I can get for those times when the pull of the world—and my own sinful nature and entrenched habits—threaten to overpower my best intentions. With your help and the help of a partner, I know I have the best possible chance of being all you've created me to be. Amen.*

A prayer from your heart:

_____

_____

_____

_____

Affirmation to recite:

I am blessed because I look to God's Word for advice and direction. As I live by the principles of God's Word, I will be blessed and bear fruit.

BASED ON PSALM 1

Action to take:

Find an accountability partner, someone who will work through this ninety-day renewal along with you. If you are doing this study as part of a small group, ask one of the women in your class to partner with you in a special way. If you are not part of a group, call someone today. You might even call several women and get a small group going. It doesn't have to be formal. Just keep in touch and keep each other moving in a positive direction.

Whom will you call? _____

Attitude adjustment:

I did it my way.

SUNG BY FRANK SINATRA

Americans take great pride in our independent spirit. We can do it our way and we don't need any help, thank you very much. But the Bible says people need one another. It says we are to bear one another's burdens and share one another's joys. These aren't suggestions. They are commands. Your best hope for completing this ninety-day renewal is to join forces with at least one other woman who shares your desire to become all she can be. Don't put it off! Don't wait until you've fallen and you can't get up. Find a partner now, while your enthusiasm is still high and your hope for success is at its best.

Diet:
☐ Free day—eat whatever you like.

Exercise:
☐ Rest.

Week 2

Scripture to memorize:

My soul finds rest in God alone;
my salvation comes from him.
He alone is my rock and my salvation;
he is my fortress, I will never be shaken.

PSALM 62:1–2

Passage to read:

Have nothing to do with godless myths and old wives' tales; rather, train yourself to be godly. For physical training is of some value, but godliness has value for all things, holding promise for both the present life and the life to come.

1 TIMOTHY 4:7–8

Guided prayer:

Dear Lord, you have commanded me not to waste my time on foolish talk or foolish ideas. Instead, I am to train myself to be godly. That tells me that godliness will require hard work and self-discipline on my part. My salvation is a free gift, but what I do with that gift is up to me. Thank you for telling us plainly that physical training is of some value. Exercise is important to you. You care what I do with my body. By undertaking this renewal, I have committed myself to pursuing physical training. But let me not forget that my outward appearance is not more important than the condition of my heart or the substance of my character. Help me to keep a healthy balance between caring for my spirit, soul, and body. Amen.

A prayer from your heart:

_____

_____

_____

_____

Affirmation to recite:

I actively strive for health in my spirit, soul, and body. I seek healing whenever needed so that my spirit, soul, and body may be kept blameless.

BASED ON 1 THESSALONIANS 5:23–24

Action to take:

Find at least one walking partner. Write his or her name here.

_____

Buy new sneakers if you need them. Don't try to save money. Instead, go to a store that specializes in sports footwear and buy the best you can afford. Be certain to buy the right shoes for your chosen exercise. For example, walking shoes and running shoes are quite different. This will minimize your risk of injury. Your health is worth the investment!

Attitude adjustment:

A journey of a thousand miles begins with a single step.

CHINESE PROVERB

The cornerstone of the exercise portion of your ninety-day renewal is plain old ordinary walking. (Those of you who can bounce should do that *in addition* to walking, not instead of it!) You just can't beat walking for achieving overall fitness goals with a minimum of time and expense. No special equipment is required other than a good pair of sneakers (which are an absolute must). Janet Holm McHenry, author of *Prayerwalk,* lists some of the benefits of walking:[1]

- Walking burns about the same number of calories per mile as running—but is easier on the joints and has a much lower risk of injury.
- A study by a Boston hospital, published in the *New England Journal of Medicine,* shows that brisk walking is associated with substantial declines in the incidence of coronary problems in women.
- The American Heart Association reports that regular exercise can reduce or eliminate high blood pressure. It can also increase levels of HDL (good cholesterol), reducing the risk of coronary artery disease.
- A Harvard study found that women who take a brisk walk each day can cut their risk of developing Type II diabetes *in half.*
- The American Medical Association reports that walking can strengthen bones. They recommend a minimum of three brisk three-mile walks per week.
- A study reported by the Women's Health Information Center shows that women between the ages of thirty and fifty-five can reduce breast cancer risk by 20 percent by exercising one hour each day. When the exercise is cut in half, the reduction of risk is also cut in half.
- According to the Centers for Disease Control and Prevention, regular physical exercise performed most days of the week will: reduce your risk of dying prematurely, reduce high blood pressure, and reduce your risk of developing colon cancer.

But perhaps the greatest benefits of walking are not physical but spiritual and emotional:

- Walking is a great time for praying and communing with God.
- Walking is a great time to review your Scripture memory verses. Just jot them down on Post-it notes or index cards and carry them with you.
- Walking boosts endorphins—neurotransmitters that elevate your mood and overall sense of well-being. They also improve your ability to respond appropriately to stressful situations.
- You'll have increased energy to go about your daily tasks.
- You'll save lots of time getting dressed in the morning because all your clothes will fit and look great.

---

[1]Janet Holm McHenry, *Prayerwalk: Becoming a Woman of Prayer, Strength, and Discipline* (Colorado Springs, CO: Waterbrook, 2001), 41–46.

Diet:
- ☐ Drink eight ounces of hot lemon water upon rising.
- ☐ Take a multivitamin and Ester-C.
- ☐ Drink sixty-four ounces of water throughout the day (see page 18).
- ☐ Eat two eggs sometime today.[2] (If you have a cholesterol problem, do not eat the yolks when eggs are listed as part of the diet.)
- ☐ Eat as many raw or steamed veggies as you can.

Exercise:
- ☐ Bounce for three to four minutes.
- ☐ Walk briskly for twenty minutes.

Day Nine	Today's Date

Scripture to memorize:
My soul finds rest in God alone;
my salvation comes from him.
He alone is my rock and my salvation;
he is my fortress, I will never be shaken.

PSALM 62:1–2

Passage to read:
Go to the ant, you sluggard;
consider its ways and be wise!
It has no commander,

---

[2]If you are wondering why I'm including eggs, see Day 55, page 191, for an explanation.

no overseer or ruler,
yet it stores its provisions in summer
and gathers its food at harvest.
How long will you lie there, you sluggard?
When will you get up from your sleep?
A little sleep, a little slumber,
a little folding of the hands to rest—
and poverty will come on you like a bandit
and scarcity like an armed man.

PROVERBS 6:6–11

Guided prayer:

Dear Lord, I acknowledge that sometimes I'm not quite as smart as the ant. I don't always plan ahead the way I should; then I end up running around half crazy, not to mention driving everyone around me crazy. Forgive me and cleanse me of the laziness and procrastination that hold me back from doing what needs to be done in an orderly and timely fashion. I thank you for creating an orderly world governed by basic principles. Thank you for the laws of sowing and reaping. When I look at my life right now and see things I'm dissatisfied with, I realize that for the most part I am reaping what I've sown. The encouraging news is that I firmly believe that as I begin to sow differently, I will reap differently. Lord, right now is a season of sowing for me. I'm planting new attitudes and actions. I know it will take a while before those seeds are ready to harvest, so help me to be patient.

A prayer from your heart:

_____

_____

_____

_____

Affirmation to recite:

I've made it my goal to be steadfast, unmovable, always abounding in the work of the Lord.

BASED ON 1 CORINTHIANS 15:58

Action to take:

Last week I encouraged you to envision the kind of person you hope to become in spirit, soul, and body. In order to close the gap between who you are now and who you hope to become, take a few minutes to honestly evaluate yourself. For each category, indicate how fully you are experiencing God's best, using 1 (meaning not at all, because you are in flat-out disobedience in this area and your life reflects it) to 10 (meaning you are walking in obedience in this area and enjoying tremendous blessings as a result).

Spiritual

Consistent quiet time	1 – – – – 5 – – – – 10
Prayerful (practice the presence of God)	1 – – – – 5 – – – – 10
Increasing in knowledge of the Scriptures	1 – – – – 5 – – – – 10
Routinely memorize and meditate on Scripture	1 – – – – 5 – – – – 10

Mental

Maintain a positive attitude	1 – – – – 5 – – – – 10
Read uplifting material	1 – – – – 5 – – – – 10
Regulate TV viewing	1 – – – – 5 – – – – 10
Learn something new on a regular basis	1 – – – – 5 – – – – 10

Emotional

Moods are stable, rather than up and down	1 – – – – 5 – – – – 10
Able to express and receive love	1 – – – – 5 – – – – 10
Listen carefully when others speak	1 – – – – 5 – – – – 10

Physical

Overall health is good	1 – – – – 5 – – – – 10

Weight is appropriate	1 – – – – 5 – – – – 10
Eating habits are well-balanced	1 – – – – 5 – – – – 10
Personal appearance is appealing	1 – – – – 5 – – – – 10

Relational
(evaluate the quality of each that is applicable)

Spouse	1 – – – – 5 – – – – 10
Children	1 – – – – 5 – – – – 10
Extended family	1 – – – – 5 – – – – 10
Church family	1 – – – – 5 – – – – 10
Neighbors	1 – – – – 5 – – – – 10
Friends	1 – – – – 5 – – – – 10
Co-workers	1 – – – – 5 – – – – 10
Strangers	1 – – – – 5 – – – – 10

Practical

Home is in good order	1 – – – – 5 – – – – 10
Car is in good order	1 – – – – 5 – – – – 10
Bills are paid on time	1 – – – – 5 – – – – 10
Obligations fulfilled on time (no procrastination)	1 – – – – 5 – – – – 10

Attitude adjustment:

It won't happen overnight, but it will happen.

PANTENE SHAMPOO COMMERCIAL

Sometimes we like to tell ourselves that our various predicaments are random acts of an unjust universe. Or that God must have "allowed" such and such to happen as a way to test our character. In reality, most of our lives are a direct reflection of the life choices we've made (and continue to make). I know that's a hard pill to swallow, but if you can get it down, your life will begin to improve dramatically. Not overnight, mind you! But as you begin to sow differently, eventually you will reap differently. As you incorporate gradual dietary changes, you will gradually begin to look and feel better. You won't lose ten pounds this weekend. But then again, you won't gain back those ten pounds on Monday. You won't become a Bible scholar in the next twelve weeks, but you will master many scriptures relating to the well-being of your spirit, soul, and body. And you will have developed habits that can benefit you for a lifetime. Stay the course. It won't happen overnight, but it will happen. night, but it will happen. Soon the woman you want to be will begin to emerge.

Diet:
- ☐ Drink eight ounces of hot lemon water upon rising.
- ☐ Take a multivitamin and Ester-C.
- ☐ Drink sixty-four ounces of water throughout the day.
- ☐ Eat two eggs sometime today.
- ☐ Eat as many raw or steamed veggies as you can.

Exercise:
- ☐ Bounce three to four minutes.
- ☐ Walk briskly for twenty minutes.

Day Ten	Today's Date

Scripture to memorize:
My soul finds rest in God alone;
my salvation comes from him.
He alone is my rock and my salvation;
he is my fortress, I will never be shaken.

PSALM 62:1–2

Passage to read:
Your beauty should not come from outward adornment, such as braided hair and the wearing of gold jewelry and fine clothes. Instead, it should be that of your inner self, the unfading beauty of a gentle and quiet spirit, which is of

great worth in God's sight. For this is the way the holy women of the past who put their hope in God used to make themselves beautiful.

1 PETER 3:3–5

Guided prayer:

Dear Lord, as I travel this ninety-day journey, help me to remember that it's not about weight loss (although you know I wouldn't mind dropping a few pounds!). I want to represent you well—to look like the daughter of the King. I want to care for my body as the temple of your Holy Spirit, but I don't want to become obsessed. As I look at the pictures on magazine covers, it's easy to feel inferior. Help me not to get so caught up worrying about my dress size that I forget it's the size of my heart that matters most. Holy Spirit, I need wisdom to find the delicate balance in the area of caring for my body without caring too much about how other people perceive and evaluate it. I desire to cultivate a gentle, quiet spirit, and I believe that inner peace will make me a more beautiful person from the inside out. Help me to place the highest value on the things you value most. Amen.

A prayer from your heart:

_____

_____

_____

_____

Affirmation to recite:

I diligently guard my body, because it is the only living sacrifice I have to offer God. But I am even more diligent in guarding my heart because I know out of it flow the issues of life.

BASED ON PROVERBS 4:23

Action to take:

Evaluate where you currently are in terms of God's best for your physical being and set some specific goals for the remainder of this ninety-day journey.

Tangible Goals

Current weight: _____   Goal weight: _____
Current clothing size: _____ Goal clothing size: _____
Number of days per week you exercised prior to starting renewal: _____
Goal for number of exercise days per week: _____

Intangible Goals

Write out a brief goal statement describing the woman you want to be in terms of your spiritual, physical, mental, and emotional well-being:

_____

_____

_____

Attitude Adjustment:

Those who do not find time for exercise will have to find time for illness.

Earl of Derby

It's important to find a healthy balance between caring too much and too little about your body. Some women obsess over their personal appearance and go into emotional meltdown if they are ten pounds overweight. (I should know!) Other women completely neglect their appearance, saying such concerns are "unspiritual." Of course, this argument would hold weight (pun intended) if these women devoted *all* of their time to spiritual pursuits rather than exercising for thirty minutes per day. But we know that's not the case. It's just an excuse.

I'm convinced this ninety-day renewal offers that healthy balance by requiring you to devote approximately an hour per day to your body. If you are too busy to devote an hour a day to the care of God's temple, is it possible that you are busier than God wants you to be? I'm not trying to make anyone feel bad here, sisters. I'm just challenging you to prayerfully consider whether or not you need to re-prioritize your life.

Diet:
- ☐ Drink eight ounces of hot lemon water upon rising.
- ☐ Take a multivitamin and Ester-C.
- ☐ Drink sixty-four ounces of water throughout the day.
- ☐ Eat two eggs sometime today.
- ☐ Eat as many raw or steamed veggies as you can.

Exercise:
- ☐ Bounce three to four minutes.
- ☐ Walk briskly for twenty minutes.

DAY ELEVEN	TODAY'S DATE

Scripture to memorize:
> *Since we have these promises, dear friends, let us purify ourselves from everything that contaminates body and spirit, perfecting holiness out of reverence for God.*

2 CORINTHIANS 7:1

Passage to read:
How lovely is your dwelling place,
O Lord Almighty!
My soul yearns, even faints,
for the courts of the Lord;

my heart and my flesh cry out
for the living God.

PSALM 84:1–2

Guided prayer:

Dear Lord, I thank you for a world filled with lovely places and beautiful things for me to enjoy. Yet I know nothing can compare with your dwelling place. And to think that someday I will live with you there! What an amazing future awaits me in eternity. Lord, may the words of the psalmist be true of me: that my soul yearns for you. Help me to recognize that I often eat for emotional reasons. To see and understand that what "feels" like physical hunger is often really the cry of the soul. A hot fudge sundae is not what I really want. What my heart really needs is to draw near to you, to taste and see that you are good. Your love is the only thing that can truly satisfy my hungry heart. Fill me and I will be filled. Amen.

A prayer from your heart:

_____

_____

_____

_____

Affirmation to recite:

I don't overeat because I know food can never satisfy me. My soul is satisfied with the things of God.

BASED ON PSALM 84:1–2

Action to take:

Set aside your usual prayer list for today. Instead, take a moment to pray for the billions of people on this earth who have never even heard the message of salvation. Think about nations that are currently in turmoil. Pray for them. Think about the nations we consider our enemies. Pray for them. When you stop to think about it, it is not the nations that have been blessed with the light of the gospel that are in greatest turmoil. Although all nations face difficulties, countries without Christ are probably in greatest need of our prayer support. Pray for them. You might want to purchase the book *Operation World*, by Patrick Johnstone, which is a guide to praying for the nations of the world.

Attitude adjustment:

> *Some wish to live within the sound of a chapel bell; I wish to run a rescue mission within a yard of hell.*
>
> C.T. STUDD

Do you really believe the Bible when it says *no one* comes to the Father except through Jesus? Do you believe *no one* will be declared righteous in God's sight unless they accept Jesus as their Savior? Once upon a time, these truths were basic tenets of Christianity—that's why missionaries risked their lives journeying to the ends of the earth. Now these beliefs seem passé in many circles. If you truly believed billions of people are on their way to eternity in hell, I wonder if you would live your life any differently? Would your priorities change? At the very least, your prayer list would change a little.

Diet:

- [ ] Drink eight ounces of hot lemon water upon rising.
- [ ] Take a multivitamin and Ester-C.
- [ ] Drink sixty-four ounces of water throughout the day.
- [ ] Eat two eggs sometime today.
- [ ] Eat as many raw or steamed veggies as you can.

Exercise:

- [ ] Bounce three to four minutes.
- [ ] Walk briskly for twenty minutes.

DAY TWELVE	TODAY'S DATE

Scripture to memorize:

*Since we have these promises, dear friends, let us purify
ourselves from everything that contaminates body and
spirit, perfecting holiness out of reverence for God.*

2 CORINTHIANS 7:1

Passage to read:

*You are forgiving and good, O Lord,
abounding in love to all who call to you.
Hear my prayer, O Lord;
listen to my cry for mercy.
In the day of my trouble I will call to you,
for you will answer me.*

PSALM 86:5–7

Guided prayer:

Dear Lord, I thank you that you are a forgiving God. Sometimes I picture
you up in heaven recounting my sins or rolling your eyes when I make the same
mistakes over and over again. But, Lord, your Word says that when I confess a
sin you remove it as far as the east is from the west. You choose not to hold my
sin against me. I thank you that you are not an exasperated parent. You don't
roll your eyes at me the way I do when I'm exasperated with my children or
other people in my life. I thank you that you abound in love—you have plenty
to give and your supply can never run dry. I know sometimes I wear my loved
ones out reciting my litany of woes. God, help me to become more positive in
my communication with others. Knowing that you never weary of hearing my
prayers and listening to my cries for help gives me a wonderful outlet. I don't
have to lay my burdens down at the feet of my family and friends; I can lay them
all down at your feet. Lord, help me to remember to call on you, rather than

calling on people, in my times of trouble. I know you will always answer me. And the answer you give will be just the right answer: filled with wisdom, love, and compassion. Thank you, Lord. Amen.

A prayer from your heart:

_____

_____

_____

_____

Affirmation to recite:

Any hardships I face in this world are nothing compared to the glory that will be revealed in me.

BASED ON ROMANS 8:18

Action to take:

Many women (myself included) have an inordinate need to tell everyone about our latest ordeal. We certainly like to talk about how our recent diet failed us, how fat we're getting, and how we can't stand to look in the mirror, etc. One of my all-time favorite topics is how much I hate my disproportionately large thighs. My friends must tire of hearing it!

As women age, they become increasingly fond of talking about their aches and pains or the latest medical procedure they have to undergo. None of them seem to realize that this is *not* a fascinating or uplifting topic of conversation. Fortunately, you are reading this book and I'm telling it to you straight. No one—no matter how saintly, no matter how much they love you—wants to hear about it. Wait. There is someone! Your heavenly Father.

So, right now, go ahead and list all your physical woes, from the rolls of fat on your stomach to your elevated cholesterol level. Tell God . . . then ask him to seal your lips!

_____   _____

_____   _____

_____   _____

Attitude adjustment:

If you don't have something nice to say, don't say anything.

MOTHERS EVERYWHERE

One of the best ways to "seal your lips" on the topics of weight gain, aches, and pains is to determine that only positive words will come out of your mouth. That automatically eliminates this whole line of conversation, doesn't it? Our moms all told us the solution when we were growing up, but we don't always put it into practice. If you don't have something positive to report, better to keep silent. That doesn't mean you can't make your prayer requests known to those who are likely to pray for you. You certainly should. But the grocery store clerk probably isn't going to add you to her prayer list (unless she's known throughout the town as a prayer warrior). Therefore, she doesn't need to know all about your upcoming angioplasty. Make your requests known primarily *to God,* then to your circle of influence. For everyone else, put a smile on your face and share the good things God is doing in your life!

Diet:
☐ Drink eight ounces of hot lemon water upon rising.
☐ Take a multivitamin and Ester-C.
☐ Drink sixty-four ounces of water throughout the day.
☐ Eat two eggs sometime today.
☐ Eat as many raw or steamed veggies as you can.

Exercise:
☐ Walk briskly for twenty minutes.

DAY THIRTEEN	TODAY'S DATE

Scripture to memorize:

Since we have these promises, dear friends, let us purify
ourselves from everything that contaminates body and
spirit, perfecting holiness out of reverence for God.

2 CORINTHIANS 7:1

Passage to read:

You were taught, with regard to your former way of life, to put off your old
self, which is being corrupted by its deceitful desires; to be made new in the atti-
tude of your minds; and to put on the new self, created to be like God in true
righteousness and holiness.

EPHESIANS 4:22–24

Guided prayer:

Dear Lord, my heart's desire is to leave the past behind and press on toward
all the wonderful things you have planned for my future. But you know better
than I know myself how old habits often trip me up. Habits of thinking, feeling,
and behaving. Today, this moment, I put off my old self, which is corrupted by
deceitful desires. Like the desire to always have everything go my way. Lord, I
know that is a deception. In the real world, we all face disappointments and
inconveniences. Help me not to take them so personally or to turn every minor
difficulty into an ordeal. Deliver me from the desire to lead a comfortable life,
free from suffering. God, I know that into every life a little suffering must come,
but deliver me from those attitudes and actions that bring needless suffering upon
my own head.

Lord, I am sitting here at your feet, asking you to make me new in the atti-
tude of my mind by the power of your Word and Spirit. Help me to become a
grateful person who always sees the glass as half full rather than half empty. Help
me to develop the habit of counting my blessings every day. I know there is good

in every person and every situation. Help me to see it. Let me view the world through spiritual eyes so that I can correctly discern the lessons and growth opportunities that come my way. I want to become more and more like you. More and more filled with the fruit of the Holy Spirit, so I might live a life characterized—not by grumbling and complaining—but by righteousness and holiness. Amen

A prayer from your heart:

_____

_____

_____

_____

Affirmation to recite:
I am persuaded that nothing can separate me from the love of God.

BASED ON ROMANS 8:38–39

Action to take:
In the spirit of "out with the old and in with the new," make a list of five uplifting conversation topics. These can replace your old discussions about your weight gain, aches, and pains! Make it a point to bring up these topics with the next person you encounter.

1. _____

2. _____

3. _____

4. _____

5. _____

Attitude adjustment:

No news is good news.

UNKNOWN

Have you ever noticed how much of the nightly news is devoted to bad news? Both nationally and locally, it seems the only thing worth broadcasting is disasters and criminal behavior. I've decided that I don't need to know about every car accident in the city of Phoenix. Nor do I need intimate details about the latest national scandal. My church keeps me informed of opportunities to help people who've been impacted by a crisis. I subscribe to a national Christian magazine that keeps me posted on major political events and provides specific advice on steps I can take to make the world a better place. I find that's all I really need to know. The rest just clutters my mind with negative topics of conversation. If you're looking to turn your conversation in a more upbeat direction, maybe turning off the evening news is a good place to start.

Diet:

☐ Drink eight ounces of hot lemon water upon rising.
☐ Take a multivitamin and Ester-C.
☐ Drink sixty-four ounces of water throughout the day.
☐ Eat two eggs sometime today.
☐ Eat as many raw or steamed veggies as you can.
☐ Prepare to fast tomorrow. (See page 19 for suggestions.)

Exercise:

☐ Bounce three to four minutes.
☐ Walk briskly for twenty minutes.

DAY FOURTEEN	TODAY'S DATE

Scripture to memorize:

Since we have these promises, dear friends, let us purify
ourselves from everything that contaminates body and
spirit, perfecting holiness out of reverence for God.

2 CORINTHIANS 7:1

Passage to read:

In the same way, the Spirit helps us in our weakness. We do not know what
we ought to pray for, but the Spirit himself intercedes for us with groans that
words cannot express. And he who searches our hearts knows the mind of the
Spirit, because the Spirit intercedes for the saints in accordance with God's will.

ROMANS 8:26–27

Guided prayer:

Holy Spirit, today I ask you to help me in my weakness. You know I have
my prayer list, but are my requests what I ought to pray for . . . or just what I
want to pray for? When I'm honest, I must confess that many of my prayers
boil down to, "God, please set my life up so perfectly that I no longer need
you or anyone else." Maybe that's not the kind of prayer I ought to be praying!
Maybe what I need to be praying is, "God, please change my heart so that
when life inevitably falls far short of perfection, I am not shaken. Help me to
lean on you, moment by moment." Holy Spirit, you know what I ought to
pray. Please intercede for me now. Search my heart. See my areas of need. Set
about the work of transforming me from the inside out so that I will learn to
pray and live according to God's will rather than my own. Amen.

A prayer from your heart:

_____

_____

_____

_____

Affirmation to recite:

I know nothing is impossible with God. He is able to transform my life from the inside out.

BASED ON LUKE 1:37

Action to take:

One way to focus your prayer time is to eliminate other distractions, like eating! Today will be the first of several fasts you will undertake during your ninety-day journey to a new you. If you have health concerns, consult your doctor before beginning. If you are unable to fast from food, please ask the Lord to show you a different form of fasting. For example, you can fast from words (or at least unnecessary words); you can fast from media consumption or surfing the Internet; anything that's important to you can be offered to God as an acceptable sacrifice. Just pray and God will show you the way. The important thing is to honor the day of fasting, one way or another.

Attitude adjustment:

When you take control of your physical appetite, you develop strength to take control of your emotional appetite.

ELMER TOWNS

Fasting presents a wonderful opportunity to practice something most of us need to do more often: saying "No" to our flesh. Our body says, "Give me a doughnut," so we drop everything we're doing and rush to the nearest bakery. Isn't that a little bit ridiculous? You can and should say no to your appetites on a routine basis. And the more you do it, the easier it will become. Today, if the temptation to eat begins to overtake you, say these words aloud (you can even shout them if you feel so inclined): "I'm a big girl. I won't be ruled by tiny little taste buds!"

Diet:
☐ Fast today (see page 19 for guidelines).

Exercise:
☐ Do only light stretching exercises. Do not overexert yourself while fasting.

Week 3

Scripture to memorize:

> *Since we have these promises, dear friends, let us purify ourselves*
> *from everything that contaminates body and*
> *spirit, perfecting holiness out of reverence for God.*

2 CORINTHIANS 7:1

Passage to read:

To you, O Lord, I lift up my soul;
in you I trust, O my God.
Do not let me be put to shame,
nor let my enemies triumph over me.
No one whose hope is in you
will ever be put to shame,
but they will be put to shame
who are treacherous without excuse.
Show me your ways, O Lord,
teach me your paths;
guide me in your truth and teach me,
for you are God my Savior,
and my hope is in you all day long.
Remember, O Lord, your great mercy and love,
for they are from of old.
Remember not the sins of my youth
and my rebellious ways;
according to your love remember me,
for you are good, O Lord.

PSALM 25:1–7

Guided prayer:

Dear Lord, I lift my mind to you today. Even though no one else can read my thoughts, I want them to be pleasing in your sight. I lift my will to you as well and, once again, renew my determination to live a life that honors you—yes, even when it's difficult. I lift my emotions to you and desire to bring them under the Lordship of Christ. I want to be ruled by your truth, love, and grace, not by my feelings. God, you know all about my enemies—those people who oppose me and try to drag me down. I leave them in your hands. I'm not going to think about them, talk about them, or give them one more moment of my mental time or emotional energy. Instead, I am determined to focus my attention on you.

Teach me your paths. Guide me into the truth. Thank you for the incredible gift of salvation and the forgiveness of my sins. I realize that without your mercy I would be eternally lost. Thank you for choosing to forget the sins of my youth and all the foolishness of my younger days. Lord, you know I still have some foolish days! That's why I'm so grateful that you remember me—not according to my performance, but according to your love. You are good! Amen.

A prayer from your heart:

Dear Lord, please help me to remember your love and grace that you have for me; that I can use it to love others by and share your strong love.

Affirmation to recite:

I don't let negative people in my life drag me down; instead, I strive to be a positive, loving influence on everyone I meet.

BASED ON 1 JOHN 5:4

Action to take:

List two people you might consider "enemies" (or those who are difficult to get along with). Ask God to show you, specifically, how to pray for each one. In some cases, pray from your own experience. For example, if your co-worker Joan is difficult because she gossips about you, pray that God would reveal his love to her so she won't have to build herself up by tearing others down.

Person	Prayer

Attitude adjustment:

Not forgiving is like drinking rat poison and waiting for the rat to die.

ANNE LAMOTT

My dear friend Rachel had been profoundly hurt by her mother-in-law. When Rachel's husband died of a drug overdose at the age of thirty-seven, his mother blamed Rachel. This, of course, was ridiculous because Rachel was powerless to stop her husband's drug abuse. And few people suffered more from his addiction than Rachel and her two small children. Nevertheless, her mother-in-law hired attorneys to rob Rachel and her children of the inheritance that was due to them. She did everything in her power to make their lives more difficult.

One day as Rachel was sharing the latest cruel action taken by this woman, I said, "She sounds like she's in a lot of pain. She doesn't want to face the truth about her son. I think you should pray for her."

That was five years ago. Recently Rachel told me that was the best advice anyone had ever given her. Praying really changed her heart toward her mother-in-law *even though* it didn't change her mother-in-law's behavior. The woman is now dying, so Rachel took the children to visit her. They were able to speak kindly to their grandmother, viewing her through their mother's eyes of compassion. Most importantly, Rachel felt wonderful because she did not let this negative person drag her down.

Diet:

- ☐ Drink eight ounces of hot lemon water upon rising.
- ☐ Take a multivitamin and Ester-C.
- ☐ Drink sixty-four ounces of water throughout the day.
- ☐ Eat two eggs sometime today.
- ☐ Have a salad with your lunch.
- ☐ Eat as many raw or steamed veggies as you can.

Exercise:

- ☐ Bounce for four minutes.
- ☐ Walk briskly for twenty minutes.

DAY SIXTEEN	TODAY'S DATE

Scripture to memorize:

Create in me a pure heart, O God,
and renew a steadfast spirit within me.
Do not cast me from your presence
or take your Holy Spirit from me.
Restore to me the joy of your salvation
and grant me a willing spirit, to sustain me.

PSALM 51:10–12

Passage to read:

Just as you used to offer the parts of your body in slavery to impurity and to ever-increasing wickedness, so now offer them in slavery to righteousness leading to holiness. When you were slaves to sin, you were free from the control of

71

righteousness. What benefit did you reap at that time from the things you are now ashamed of? Those things result in death! But now that you have been set free from sin and have become slaves to God, the benefit you reap leads to holiness, and the result is eternal life. For the wages of sin is death, but the gift of God is eternal life in Christ Jesus our Lord.

ROMANS 6:19–23

Guided prayer:

Dear Lord, I have my share of things I'm ashamed of from my past. I thank you for forgiving those actions that are now a distant memory. Surely I received no direct benefit from my sin, though I am grateful for the lessons learned. I also acknowledge that at times, even now, I live as someone free from the control of righteousness. I act like I don't know any better or like "I just can't help myself," when in truth, I do know better and I can "help myself" by the power of your Spirit at work within me.

Sometimes I almost wish you didn't give me so much freedom. I almost wish this Christian walk wasn't so filled with daily choices that only I can make. Yet you have designed us for freedom. Then, in an ironic twist, you invite us to become "voluntary slaves" to righteousness. Lord, the older I get the more obvious it becomes that every one of your commands is for my benefit. Not one of them is burdensome. Not one of them is capricious. The guidelines you have set forth in your Word are a precious gift designed to protect me from heartache on earth and eternal death in the world to come. Thank you for the gift of eternal life in Christ. Amen.

A prayer from your heart:

_____

_____

_____

_____

Affirmation to recite:

I am a slave to righteousness. I am no longer free to live however I please.

BASED ON ROMANS 6:19–23

Action to take:

Is there something you are enslaved to? It could be anything from diet soda to gossip! Ask God to show you what He wants you to surrender to him today.

_____   _____

_____   _____

Attitude adjustment:

I surrender all. I surrender all. All to Thee,
my blessed Savior, I surrender all.

JUDSON W. VAN DE VENTER

We Christians are a funny bunch, aren't we? We'll stand in church, swaying to the music, singing with all our hearts, "I surrender all." But then the mere thought of surrendering something as simple as a Twinkie is unbearable. Fasting? Forget about it! We're sure we'll die if we surrender our food for twenty-four hours. Christians all around the world surrender their rights—and many surrender their lives—to follow Christ. I think we can muster the courage to surrender the chocolate chip cookies. What is God challenging you to surrender?

Diet:

- ☐ Drink eight ounces of hot lemon water upon rising.
- ☐ Take a multivitamin and Ester-C.
- ☐ Drink sixty-four ounces of water throughout the day.
- ☐ Eat two eggs sometime today.
- ☐ Have a salad with your lunch.
- ☐ Eat as many raw or steamed veggies as you can.

Exercise:

- ☐ Walk briskly for twenty minutes.

DAY SEVENTEEN	TODAY'S DATE

Scripture to memorize:

Create in me a pure heart, O God,
and renew a steadfast spirit within me.
Do not cast me from your presence
or take your Holy Spirit from me.
Restore to me the joy of your salvation
and grant me a willing spirit, to sustain me.

PSALM 51:10–12

Passage to read:

I pray that out of his glorious riches he may strengthen you with power through his Spirit in your inner being, so that Christ may dwell in your hearts through faith. And I pray that you, being rooted and established in love, may have power, together with all the saints, to grasp how wide and long and high

*and deep is the love of Christ, and to know this love that surpasses knowledge—
that you may be filled to the measure of all the fullness of God.*

EPHESIANS 3:16–19

Guided prayer:

Dear Lord, I ask you to strengthen me with power. Oh, how I need power in
my life! When I look at entrenched habits—even simple things like eating my
favorite junk foods or failing to think before I speak—I feel powerless to change.
That's how I feel, but your Word says my feelings are wrong. Right now, I choose
to believe your Word rather than my feelings. Your Spirit living within me can
empower my inner being. Lord, I desire to be rooted and established in love, so
that all of my thoughts, words, and actions flow not from my personal insecuri-
ties but from the love that flows from your throne. More than anything, I need
to grasp how incredible your love for me really is. I know that I won't fully
understand until that glorious day when I finally see you face-to-face. But my
heart's desire is to become increasingly aware of your love for me, even as I go
about my daily routine. I want to be filled to the measure of all the fullness of
God. Amen.

A prayer from your heart:

_____

_____

_____

_____

Affirmation to recite:

I know God is able to do exceedingly abundantly above all that I could possibly ask or imagine.

BASED ON EPHESIANS 3:20

Action to take:

Today, make it a point to think about what you're thinking about! What are the top five topics that usually occupy your mind? You can do a before-and-after study. List what you *think* you think about. Then pay attention to what you actually think about!

	Think	Actual
1.	_____	_____
2.	_____	_____
3.	_____	_____
4.	_____	_____
5.	_____	_____

Attitude adjustment:

A man is what he thinks about all day long.

RALPH WALDO EMERSON

According to Dr. John H. Sklare, moderator of the Emotional Support Center at *ediets.com,* the average person ruminates on the same handful of topics day after day. We are creatures of habit, even in our thinking patterns. You can work this fact in your favor! The key is to choose the right "handful of topics" to focus your repeated attention on. You just can't go wrong thinking about: God's love, mercy, grace, kindness, and bountiful provision!

Diet:
☐ Free day—eat whatever you can today.

Exercise:
☐ Bounce four minutes.
☐ Walk briskly for twenty minutes.

DAY EIGHTEEN	TODAY'S DATE

Scripture to memorize:

> Create in me a pure heart, O God,
> and renew a steadfast spirit within me.
> Do not cast me from your presence
> or take your Holy Spirit from me.
> Restore to me the joy of your salvation
> and grant me a willing spirit, to sustain me.

PSALM 51:10–12

Passage to read:

Therefore, I urge you, brothers, in view of God's mercy, to offer your bodies as living sacrifices, holy and pleasing to God—this is your spiritual act of worship. Do not conform any longer to the pattern of this world, but be transformed by the renewing of your mind. Then you will be able to test and approve what God's will is—his good, pleasing and perfect will.

ROMANS 12:1–2

Guided prayer:

Dear Lord, in view of your mercy, I want to offer my body as a living sacrifice to you. I want to use my body in ways that are holy and pleasing to you, as a spiritual act of worship. You have left my body on the earth for one purpose—to serve you. Even Jesus needed an earthly body to accomplish his mission of securing salvation for mankind. He made the ultimate sacrifice of laying down his life for us; it is a small thing you have asked me to do, sacrificing what I "feel like" eating and doing with my body. If I'm going to serve you effectively, I need all the strength and energy this body can muster. I need to take care of myself. Lord, I don't want to conform to the world's way of thinking about the body. I want your perspective. Amen.

A prayer from your heart:

_____

_____

_____

Affirmation to recite:

My body belongs to God—he bought and paid for it. I have no right to treat God's temple like a trash can, filling it with junk food and abusing it through neglect. Instead, I have an obligation to take care of myself.

BASED ON ROMANS 12:1–2

Action to take:

Did you know that bathing is important for the body? A cleansing bath can purify your body from the toxins that have built up in your body. Mix 1 cup Dead Sea salts, 1 cup Epsom salts, 1 cup regular sea salt, 1 cup baking soda, and a few drops of lavender oil. Alternatively, you can use 2 pounds of sea salt and 2 pounds of baking soda (a bit simpler, but less elegant!). Begin with the bath water hot and soak until the water turns cold. Do not remain longer than thirty minutes. Be aware that you may feel dizzy when you emerge. That means the bath did its job! This process draws out the toxins and enables your body's digestive system to function more efficiently. You may want to incorporate a cleansing bath into your weekly routine. It's a simple, pleasant way to care for your body, God's temple. Light an aromatic candle, put on some relaxing praise music, and it will simultaneously do wonders for your soul and spirit.

Attitude adjustment:

If I had known I was going to live this long, I would have taken better care of myself.

EUBIE BLAKE, ON REACHING THE AGE OF 100

If you ask most people why they don't take better care of their bodies, they will use the old "I don't have enough time" excuse. Sometimes life is incredibly hectic and we feel overwhelmed. The thought of undertaking some grand exercise renewal or elaborate diet seems impossible. That's why this book advocates small, incremental changes. One simple thing you can easily do, no matter how crazy your life gets, is to start your day with a cleansing drink. This takes only a few minutes and jump-starts your body's digestive process, thus maximizing the efficiency with which it burns calories.

For the first three weeks, lemon is the cleansing tonic of choice. Lemon juice is widely recognized as a natural cleanser and is considered "ideal for removing toxic materials from the body."[1] It is also a mild diuretic, which will help if you tend to retain fluids and will do no harm if you do not.

Diet:
☐ Drink eight ounces of hot lemon water upon rising.
☐ Take a multivitamin and Ester-C.
☐ Drink sixty-four ounces of water throughout the day.
☐ Eat two eggs sometime today.
☐ Have a salad with your lunch.
☐ Eat as many raw or steamed veggies as you can.

Exercise:
☐ Walk briskly for twenty minutes.

---

[1]Cheryl Townsley, *Food Smart!: Eat Your Way to Better Health* (Colorado Springs: Pinon Press, 1994), 173.

Scripture to memorize:

Create in me a pure heart, O God,
and renew a steadfast spirit within me.
Do not cast me from your presence
or take your Holy Spirit from me.
Restore to me the joy of your salvation
and grant me a willing spirit, to sustain me.

PSALM 51:10–12

Passage to read:

So if you faithfully obey the commands I am giving you today—to love the Lord your God and to serve him with all your heart and with all your soul— then I will send rain on your land in its season, both autumn and spring rains, so that you may gather in your grain, new wine and oil. I will provide grass in the fields for your cattle, and you will eat and be satisfied.

DEUTERONOMY 11:13–15

Guided prayer:

Dear Lord, I desire to live according to your commands. I desire to love and serve you with all my heart and soul. I thank you that you have promised to send rain in due season—to send just what I need exactly when I need it. I know I can rest securely in your faithful provision. Therefore, I don't have to worry about my bills, my job, my relationships, or any other details of my life. I am satisfied with the life you have given me and the circumstances that surround me. I trust you and I thank you, Lord. Amen.

A prayer from your heart:

_____

_____

_____

_____

Affirmation to recite:

I lay up for myself treasures in heaven. I do not store treasure here on earth. I realize that where my treasure is, there my heart will also be.

BASED ON MATTHEW 6:19–21

Action to take:

Think of one occasion in the past when you were in need and God provided for you in a very special way. Perhaps your husband was unemployed and God sent "rain" in the form of a gift certificate to dinner, given to you by a friend. Or you were pregnant and someone came over to clean your house. Maybe you were stressed out and a neighbor offered to take *all* the kids to the park so that you could take a nap. Describe.

_____

_____

_____

Now do the same thing (or something similar) for someone else. If you don't know someone facing a similar circumstance, call your pastor or women's ministry director. I guarantee they do!

Note the name of the person you plan to help:_____

What you plan to do:_____

When you plan to do it:_____

Attitude adjustment:

> *More things are wrought by prayer than this world dreams of.*
>
> ALFRED, LORD TENNYSON

Several years ago one of my neighbors was in a severe car crash. She had to undergo extensive physical rehabilitation. Often the exercises were extremely painful. So she decided, in advance, that while in therapy, she wouldn't pray for herself (although she had made her request known to others). Instead, she was ready with a prayer list filled with the needs of others. She said it did wonders for her body, soul, and spirit, as it forced her to keep her mind off of herself and her own troubles. What a great strategy! Why not try it? Pick a time of day you will set aside to pray not for yourself but for others!

Diet:
- [ ] Drink eight ounces of hot lemon water upon rising.
- [ ] Take a multivitamin and Ester-C.
- [ ] Drink sixty-four ounces of water throughout the day.
- [ ] Eat two eggs sometime today.
- [ ] Have a salad with your lunch.
- [ ] Eat as many raw or steamed veggies as you can.

Exercise:
- [ ] Bounce four minutes.
- [ ] Walk briskly for twenty minutes.

Scripture to memorize:

> Create in me a pure heart, O God,
> and renew a steadfast spirit within me.
> Do not cast me from your presence
> or take your Holy Spirit from me.
> Restore to me the joy of your salvation
> and grant me a willing spirit, to sustain me.

PSALM 51:10–12

Passage to read:

Good and upright is the Lord;
therefore he instructs sinners in his ways.
He guides the humble in what is right
and teaches them his way.
All the ways of the Lord are loving and faithful
for those who keep the demands of his covenant.
For the sake of your name, O Lord,
forgive my iniquity, though it is great.
Who, then, is the man that fears the Lord?
He will instruct him in the way chosen for him.
He will spend his days in prosperity,
and his descendants will inherit the land.
The Lord confides in those who fear him;
he makes his covenant known to them.
My eyes are ever on the Lord,
for only he will release my feet from the snare.

PSALM 25:8–15

Guided prayer:

Dear Lord, thank you for declaring me righteous in your sight. I thank you that I am the righteousness of God in Christ. Indeed, your Word says I am—in some mysterious way I don't completely understand—already seated with you in heavenly places (Ephesians 2:6). Yet as long as I live on earth, I still battle against my sinful inclinations each and every day. Thank you for forgiveness that is new every morning.

Lord, instruct me. Teach me your way. I know that your Word includes general instructions for all believers. I desire the wisdom to understand them better and the will to obey them more faithfully. In addition, there is a way "chosen for me." For me, specifically. And I ask you today for specific instruction concerning the way you have chosen for me so that I might walk in it and be blessed. Amen.

A prayer from your heart:

_____

_____

_____

_____

Affirmation to recite:

I am confident that God will reward me as I diligently seek him. I don't know what form the reward will take, but I know it will be awesome.

BASED ON HEBREWS 11:6

Action to take:

Is there a specific area of your life where you are in need of God's instruction? What is it? God wants to instruct you and lead you in the way you should go. In fact, he has been leading you all through your life (not that you've always followed, of course!). Stop and think! Recall three occasions when you had clear instruction from the Lord. Note them below:

1. _____

2. _____

3. _____

What can you glean about your future by pondering God's instructions from your past?

Attitude adjustment:

Change your thoughts and you change your world.

NORMAN VINCENT PEALE

I'm not sure why, but for some reason I always associated "positive thinking" with airheads, bimbos, and simpletons. It might be my East Coast roots, but I always equated negativity with sophistication and intellect. Miserable people were the only ones smart enough to recognize how messed up the world was; the rest were too blind to see the truth. But the older I get, the more convinced I am that the "positive thinkers" were smarter than I thought.

Many of our thoughts—whether negative or positive—become like self-fulfilling prophecies. If I'm going to predict something for my future, wouldn't I be better off predicting something good? God is the original positive thinker. No matter how many times we've blown it in the past, God continues teaching, guiding, and giving us more opportunities to learn and grow. I'm positive I feel positive about *that*!

Diet:

- [ ] Drink eight ounces of hot lemon water upon rising.
- [ ] Take a multivitamin and Ester-C.
- [ ] Drink sixty-four ounces of water throughout the day.
- [ ] Eat two eggs sometime today.
- [ ] Have a salad with your lunch.
- [ ] Eat as many raw or steamed veggies as you can.
- [ ] Tomorrow you will begin a two-day fast. Be prepared!

Exercise:

☐ Walk briskly for twenty minutes.

DAY TWENTY-ONE	TODAY'S DATE

Scripture to memorize:

Let the morning bring me word of your unfailing love,
for I have put my trust in you.
Show me the way I should go,
for to you I lift up my soul.

PSALM 143:8

Passage to read:

You will keep in perfect peace
him whose mind is steadfast,
because he trusts in you.

ISAIAH 26:3

Guided prayer:

Dear Lord, I come before you today seeking peace. Yes, I would love peace in my outer world. And I do pray for peace on the earth. God, grant wisdom to the world's leaders and especially to our president. Comfort those who are torn apart by the countless wars that are raging around the earth. I pray for peace within my local church. Holy Spirit, bring conviction upon those who are causing strife. Lord, I seek peace in my home. You know how chaotic it can be sometimes, with everyone running in a thousand different directions at once. The noise from within and the intrusions from without are sometimes more than I can bear. But, Lord, more than anything, I desire a peace within that remains strong no matter what is happening around me. I want my mind to remain steadfast, unmovable, unshaken in every situation. Lord, I ask you for the ability to see and respond to situations with a clear head. I know the key to a steady mind is *a steady faith, a faith that trusts in you through all of life's ups and downs. Lord, I trust you. Help me to trust you more. Amen.*

A prayer from your heart:

_____

_____

_____

_____

Affirmation to recite:

I remain calm no matter what happens. I keep a clear head in all situations because I trust God to provide for my every need.

BASED ON ISAIAH 26:3

Action to take:

The next time you are in the midst of a chaotic situation (if your life is anything like mine, you won't have to wait very long), stop and ask God to enable you to think clearly. See what a difference this simple request can make.

Attitude adjustment:

She has a good head on her shoulders.

SOMEONE REFERRING TO SOMEONE OTHER THAN ME :)

When life starts getting crazy, do you start getting even crazier? When you're faced with a crisis, do you shift into crisis mode? When situations start to spiral out of control, does your behavior get out of control? Your behavior should be determined by your relationship with God, not by your outward circumstances. The degree to which you respond with calmness and confidence is a measure of your trust in God. How much do you trust him?

If your answer is "Not nearly enough," the solution is found in keeping your mind steadfastly focused on the goodness of God.

Diet:

☐ Today, begin a two-day fast. Your advance preparations may require a bit more attention, as you'll want to keep your family well fed without spending an excessive amount of time around food (for obvious reasons). The bottled forty-eight-hour fasting juices are designed for a two-day fast and are a good option if you need some sustenance. I've found that I'm typically less hungry and more energetic on the second day. Just be sure to drink plenty of water and, if possible, maintain a lighter-than-usual schedule.

Exercise:

☐ Do only light stretching exercises. Do not overexert yourself while fasting.

Week 4

Scripture to memorize:

> *Let the morning bring me word of your unfailing love,*
> *for I have put my trust in you.*
> *Show me the way I should go,*
> *for to you I lift up my soul.*

PSALM 143:8

Passage to read:

The Lord your God commands you this day to follow these decrees and laws; carefully observe them with all your heart and with all your soul. You have declared this day that the Lord is your God and that you will walk in his ways, that you will keep his decrees, commands and laws, and that you will obey him. And the Lord has declared this day that you are his people, his treasured possession as he promised, and that you are to keep all his commands. He has declared that he will set you in praise, fame and honor high above all the nations he has made and that you will be a people holy to the Lord your God, as he promised.

DEUTERONOMY 26:16–19

Guided prayer:

Dear Lord, I declare today that you are God and I will walk in your ways. I will keep your decrees and commands. I will obey you. Lord, I thank you for declaring that I am one of your chosen people. You handpicked me to be your own. What unfathomable love! Lord, you say I am your treasured possession. You say I am infinitely valuable. So valuable that you sent your Son to redeem me. Thank you, Father. Help me to base my worth on your estimation of me, not my own estimate—and certainly not the world's! Lord, you have declared that your people will receive praise, fame, and honor high above all the nations. I believe that promise will one day be fulfilled when Jesus returns for his bride. Meanwhile, I rejoice to be one of your holy people. Amen.

A prayer from your heart:

_____

_____

_____

_____

Affirmation to recite:

I am one of God's treasured possessions. He handpicked me to be his own.

BASED ON DEUTERONOMY 26:16–19

Action to take:

List three of your most prominent habits—things you do every day without even thinking about them.

1. _____

2. _____

3. _____

Now make a list of "holy habits" (i.e., spiritual disciplines) you would like to acquire. If possible, link these to the old habits so they will more easily become part of your life. For example, you always walk your dog in the morning, but you haven't gotten in the habit of memorizing Scripture. Link the two activities. Print your Bible memory verses on Post-it notes or index cards and carry them in one hand while you walk the dog. Of course, if all your old habits are truly wretched (like watching soap operas and eating doughnuts), then this idea won't work!

	New habit	Link to old habit
1.	_____	_____
2.	_____	_____
3.	_____	_____

Attitude adjustment:

> *It is not too much to say that "habit is ten natures." We have lost sight of the fact that habit is to life what [railroad tracks] are to [trains]. It follows that lines of habit must be laid down toward given ends and after careful survey, or the joltings and delays of life become insupportable. More, habit is inevitable. If we fail to ease life by laying down habits of right thinking and right acting, habits of wrong thinking and wrong acting fix themselves of their own accord.*
>
> CHARLOTTE MASON[1]

We are all creatures of habit. Since habits are inevitable, why not make them work in your favor? Develop new, holy habits to replace your old, self-destructive habits. Then each day will—out of simple habit—bring you closer and closer to becoming the woman you want to be. Not to mention closer and closer to God.

Diet:

☐ Fast again today. Pray for extra grace as you end your fast tomorrow morning. You may be tempted to binge on all your favorite foods, but you will feel so much better if you ease back into eating. Perhaps start with some fresh fruit and whole-grain toast for breakfast. Continue drinking plenty of water, especially the first day back to normal eating.

Exercise:

☐ Do only light stretching exercises. Do not overexert yourself while fasting.

---

[1]Charlotte Mason, *A Philosophy of Education* (Wheaton, Il.: Tyndale House, 1989), 101.

Spirit

Scripture to memorize:

Let the morning bring me word of your unfailing love,
    for I have put my trust in you.
Show me the way I should go,
    for to you I lift up my soul.

PSALM 143:8

Passage to read:

If your right eye causes you to sin, gouge it out and throw it away. It is better for you to lose one part of your body than for your whole body to be thrown into hell. And if your right hand causes you to sin, cut it off and throw it away. It is better for you to lose one part of your body than for your whole body to go into hell.

MATTHEW 5:29–30

Guided prayer:

Dear Lord, I confess to you that I have often placed the demands of my body above your commands. My body has led me into sin and I've allowed it. I'm too soft on my body, letting it dictate how I live my life and set my daily priorities. I don't want to go to extremes, but, Jesus, you made your point clearly. We are to do whatever it takes to put to death the misdeeds of the body. If my tongue is causing me to sin, I need to take tough action to tame it. If my mind is leading me astray, I must aggressively renew it. If my head wants to remain on the pillow or my buns want to remain on the couch, I need to be tough enough to say, "Get up!" Empower me to take dominion over my own body. To be faithful in that small thing so you can entrust me with greater things for your kingdom's sake. Amen.

A prayer from your heart:

_____

_____

_____

_____

Affirmation to recite:

I take dominion over my body; I don't allow my body to have dominion over me.

BASED ON MATTHEW 5:29–30

Action to take:

Identify the body part that most often leads you into sin. Aggressively take dominion over it. Ask God exactly what that will involve.

Attitude adjustment:

Probably nothing you do to control your weight is as important as keeping your liver healthy.

ANN LOUISE GITTLEMAN

Nearly a decade ago I stumbled upon an article in a woman's magazine advocating detoxification of the liver. Since it recommended eating God's food and made intuitive sense to me, I undertook my first detox and instantly felt better. Ever since, I have periodically detoxified my body. That's why I was intrigued to discover Anne Louise Gittleman's book *The Fat Flush Plan,* a diet based on the principles of liver detoxification. I have incorporated several of her recommendations into the diet portion of our renewal, including her use of cranberry juice as a morning tonic. Gittleman calls cranberry juice her "secret weapon against cellulite." It has the ability to "emulsify any fatty globules in the lymphatic system that haven't been processed by the liver before they are stored in fat cells."[2] She combines cranberry juice with psyllium to digest fatty globules in the lymph system, block the absorption of fat, increase fat excretion, and bind toxins so they are not reabsorbed into the body.

The incorporation of psyllium is especially vital since most Americans consume only half of the recommended daily fiber. "Without adequate fiber, up to 90 percent of cholesterol and bile acids will be reabsorbed and recirculated to the liver. This taxes your liver and reduces its fat-burning abilities. No matter what the cause, a sluggish, overworked liver does a poor job metabolizing fat, and you gain weight."[3]

The other component of Gittleman's diet that I have adapted is her recommendation of EFAs, or Essential Fatty Acids, because an estimated 80 percent of Americans eat a diet deficient in EFAs. Omega–3 fatty acids "have been clinically proven to help regulate insulin, the body's fat-storage hormone. Flaxseed oil binds to oil-soluble poisons and carries them out of your system. Studies have shown that Omega–3s also increase your metabolism and reduce hunger by as much as 20%."[4] The human body needs fat to survive. So when we are deficient in good fat (EFAs), our body craves *any* fat it can get. That's why the low-fat craze has left Americans fatter than ever. Your body can only survive so long before it *screams* for fat. Unfortunately, you respond by giving it the wrong kind of fat—like greasy French fries!

Take a trip to your local health food store to obtain EFA capsules or liquid. I hope you will be pleasantly surprised by how dramatically your fat cravings reduce within a relatively short period of time.

Diet:

- ☐ Upon rising, drink 8 oz. water mixed with 1.5 oz. unsweetened cranberry juice and 1 t. psyllium husk.
- ☐ Take a multivitamin and Ester-C, and EFAs.[5]
- ☐ Drink sixty-four ounces of water throughout the day.

---

[2]Gittleman, *The Fat Flush Plan*, 18.
[3]Ibid.
[4]Ibid.
[5]Essential Fatty Acids. Available at your local health food store in capsule or liquid form.

- [ ] Eat two eggs sometime today.
- [ ] Have a salad with your lunch.
- [ ] Eat as many raw or steamed veggies as you can.

Exercise: ,

- [ ] Bounce five minutes.
- [ ] Walk briskly for thirty minutes.

DAY TWENTY-FOUR   TODAY'S DATE

Scripture to memorize:

> *Let the morning bring me word of your unfailing love,*
> *for I have put my trust in you.*
> *Show me the way I should go,*
> *for to you I lift up my soul.*

PSALM 143:8

Passage to read:

My soul glorifies the Lord
and my spirit rejoices in God my Savior,
for he has been mindful
of the humble state of his servant.
From now on all generations will call me blessed,
for the Mighty One has done great things for me—
holy is his name.
His mercy extends to those who fear him,
from generation to generation.
He has performed mighty deeds with his arm;
he has scattered those who are proud in their inmost thoughts.
He has brought down rulers from their thrones
but has lifted up the humble.

LUKE 1:46–52

Guided prayer:

Dear Lord, I want my soul to glorify you—to show the world an accurate reflection of who you are. I want people to look at my life and know, with certainty, that you take good care of your children. Not that I am free from difficulties, but that difficulties do not overwhelm me. I want to glorify you in my mind—by focusing on your unfailing goodness at all times. I want to glorify you in my will—by choosing to do the right thing, even when I'm tempted to take the easy way out. And I want to glorify you in my emotions—by responding to those around me in love. Lord, I want my life to be remembered as blessed. I realize the need to continually point out your many blessings to my loved ones so that when I am gone, they will remember all the mighty works you've done. I ask you to extend your mercy to the generations who will come after me, that they, too, would know your goodness. Amen.

A prayer from your heart:

_____

_____

_____

_____

Affirmation to recite:

I am a blessing to God when I choose to be grateful and hopeful, no matter how difficult my circumstances.

BASED ON LUKE 1:46–52

Action to take:

Count your blessings. List five things you can be grateful for and choose to focus on them today. Then go a step further and remind your family and friends how blessed they are, too.

1. _____
2. _____
3. _____
4. _____
5. _____

Attitude adjustment:

A man's life is what his thoughts make it.

MARCUS AURELIUS

Every moment of every day has good and bad in it. Every person we meet has strengths and weaknesses. Every situation has pros and cons. Every event contains both the handiwork of God and the counterattack of the enemy. The question is: what will you choose to magnify? It's entirely up to you. Keep in mind: whatever you focus your magnifying glass on will appear larger than everything else. When we choose to magnify the bad, it appears larger than it really is. But when we choose to magnify God, we begin to get a clearer picture of reality. You can focus on what's wrong with your life and be miserable, or you can focus on your many blessings and be joyful. The choice is yours.

Diet:
☐ Free day—eat whatever you like.

Exercise:
☐ Walk briskly for thirty minutes.

Scripture to memorize:

> Let the morning bring me word of your unfailing love,
> for I have put my trust in you.
> Show me the way I should go,
> for to you I lift up my soul.

PSALM 143:8

Passage to read:

I will give them an undivided heart and put a new spirit in them; I will remove from them their heart of stone and give them a heart of flesh. Then they will follow my decrees and be careful to keep my laws. They will be my people, and I will be their God.

EZEKIEL 11:19–20

Guided Prayer:

Dear Lord, I confess that my heart is often divided. In my spirit, I yearn to be near you, to become more like you. I desire to be the woman you envisioned when you fashioned me in my mother's womb. Yet my body and soul tear me in other directions. My eyes see material things I long to have and I chase after them. My ears hear gossip and though I know I shouldn't fill my mind with such thoughts, I savor the "morsels" I can gather. My taste buds demand satisfaction and command way too much of my attention.

Lord, I ask you to give me an undivided heart—one that is fixed on pursuing you. Give me a new spirit—one that is more sensitive to the things of heaven than the things of earth. As you transform me from the inside out, then and only then will I become all I'm meant to be. I leave myself in your hands. Mold and fashion me into your image. Amen.

A prayer from your heart:

_____

_____

_____

_____

Affirmation to recite:

I remember all God's benefits: He forgives me, heals me, and surrounds me with loving-kindness. He has rescued me from an eternity in hell and has blessed me in this life as well.

Based on Psalm 103:1–5

Action to take:

Today you have the option to begin a weight-training renewal. See page 21 for recommendations, but you can use any workout video that incorporates weight training. The video you choose will recommend specific equipment. In general, you can expect to purchase dumbbells in three weights if you don't have them already. (See page 21 for suggestions on how to choose the correct weights.) You may also want to purchase weight-lifting gloves.

Attitude Adjustment:

For good health, we'd like to see you pick up a few pounds.

Susan Moores

Muscle burns more calories than fat. Muscle even burns calories while you watch television, which is why physically fit people can consume far more calories than sedentary people without gaining weight. Conversely, this physiological fact also explains how people who "hardly eat anything" continue gaining weight if they are inactive. What's worse, as we age, our body's muscle mass steadily decreases unless we intervene. According to medical research, we lose about 10 percent of our muscle per decade, or a half-pound of muscle every year. By age seventy, our natural strength has decreased at least 40 percent, so even simple everyday chores can become Herculean tasks.

The only way to stop muscle loss and build new muscle tissue is resistance or strength training. Strength training even reverses some of the changes normally associated with old age, such as decreased stamina, energy, and balance. "Strength training . . . helps lower blood pressure and cholesterol levels; heightens your insulin sensitivity, which keeps blood sugar levels normal; and improves blood flow. . . . A study at Tufts University's Center on Aging found that women who participated in strength training not only stopped losing bone density, but actually *gained* bone mass over a year's time."[6]

Diet:

- ☐ Upon rising, drink 8 oz. water mixed with 1.5 oz. unsweetened cranberry juice and 1 t. psyllium husk.
- ☐ Take multivitamin, Ester-C, and EFAs.
- ☐ Drink sixty-four ounces of water throughout the day.
- ☐ Eat two eggs sometime today.
- ☐ Have a salad with your lunch.
- ☐ Eat as many raw or steamed veggies as you can.

Exercise:

- ☐ Bounce five minutes.
- ☐ Walk briskly for thirty minutes.
- ☐ Optional: strength training.

---

[6] Susan Moores, "Give me Strength," *http://www.tops601.com/Feature0203.html*.

Scripture to memorize:

*Do you not know that your body is a temple of the Holy Spirit, who
is in you, whom you have received from God? You are not your own;
you were bought at a price. Therefore honor God with your body.*

1 CORINTHIANS 6:19–20

Passage to read:

*A wise man's heart guides his mouth,
and his lips promote instruction.
Pleasant words are a honeycomb,
sweet to the soul and healing to the bones.*

PROVERBS 16:23–24

Guided prayer:

*Dear Lord, I know my body is the temple of your Holy Spirit. I don't always
act on that knowledge, but it remains true, nevertheless. Lord, I acknowledge
that I am not my own. You bought me at a price and I am yours. I want to honor
you with my body. Lord, forgive me for dishonoring you by filling your temple
with junk food. I also corrupt your temple with unpleasant words and negative
thoughts. Lord, if I take nothing else away from this renewal, let me be transformed in my habits of thinking and speaking. Lord, your Word says pleasant
words are sweet to the soul and can actually bring healing to my bones. Because
you have said it, I believe it. Amen.*

A prayer from your heart:

_____

_____

_____

_____

Affirmation to recite:

My faith makes me whole in spirit, soul, and body. Jesus offers me the same healing he offered others when he walked the earth.

BASED ON MARK 5:34

Action to take:

Read the labels on some of the foods you routinely eat and think about the list of ingredients. Hint: If you can't pronounce half the words or if they end in -ose or -tol, it's trash food. (Of course, the best foods don't really have labels, do they?) List the foods in the appropriate category below.

Promotes a healthy temple   Treats the temple like a garbage can

_____   _____

_____   _____

_____   _____

Here's some food for thought: Maybe the foods in Column B belong in your trash can rather than in your body.

Attitude adjustment:

I have long been a proponent of the Mediterranean diet. This is a diet low in red meats, hydrogenated oils, and processed foods, and high in fiber, nuts, fish, fruits, vegetables, and olive oil—all of which are also mentioned in the Bible.

REGINALD B. CHERRY, M.D., IN *GOD'S PATHWAY TO HEALING, HEART*

Diet:
- [ ] Upon rising, drink 8 oz. water mixed with 1.5 oz. unsweetened cranberry juice and 1 t. psyllium husk.
- [ ] Take multivitamin, Ester-C, and EFAs.
- [ ] Drink sixty-four ounces of water throughout the day.
- [ ] Eat two eggs sometime today.
- [ ] Have a salad with your lunch.
- [ ] Eat as many raw or steamed veggies as you can.

Exercise:
- [ ] Bounce five minutes.
- [ ] Walk briskly for thirty minutes.
- [ ] Optional: strength training.

Day Twenty-seven	Today's Date

Scripture to memorize:

Do you not know that your body is a temple of the Holy Spirit, who is in you, whom you have received from God? You are not your own; you were bought at a price. Therefore honor God with your body.

1 Corinthians 6:19–20

Passage to read:

Dear friends, I urge you, as aliens and strangers in the world, to abstain from sinful desires, which war against your soul. Live such good lives among the pagans that, though they accuse you of doing wrong, they may see your good deeds and glorify God on the day he visits us.

1 Peter 2:11–12

Guided prayer:

Dear Lord, I confess that my own sinful desires war against my soul. My mind desires to feast on gossip, though I know "what goes around comes around." I often find myself trying to get away with something—trying to violate the basic rules of the universe without reaping the consequences. I want to eat Oreos and wear a size 6. I want to sit on the couch watching television yet become a spiritual leader in my church. I let my mind linger too long upon the handsome men who pass me by. I neglect the things I know I ought to do, and I do those things I know I should avoid. Truly there is a battle within me! Yet, on too many days, I sit on the sidelines of the war and lose by default.

I know you have called me to get up and fight against my own sinful desires. You ask me to fight and win, not only for my own good, but for your glory. When those around me begin to see progress in my life—when they no longer have a basis to accuse me of wrongdoing—your name will be glorified. This day, I desire to get up and fight. I know that by the power of your Holy Spirit at work within me, I can win. In my life, Lord, be glorified! Amen.

A prayer from your heart:

_____

_____

_____

_____

Affirmation to recite:
   My life is a life of contribution. I am making a positive difference in this world and for eternity.

BASED ON 1 PETER 2:11–12

Action to take:
   Choose one area—in terms of your spirit, soul, or body—that is a battleground for you. Determine that, at least for this week, you will obtain the victory! List the battleground and the strategy below. For example, getting up early enough for your quiet time may be the battleground, and asking a friend to call to wake you up every day this week, rather than relying on your alarm clock, may be the strategy. Or the battleground may be overeating junk food. Your strategy may be to throw it out.

   Battleground: _____

   Strategy: _____

Attitude adjustment:
   We cannot expect to make steady progress on our spiritual journey if we insist on taking little side trips away from the highway of holiness.

CYNTHIA HEALD

105

The spiritual life really is a journey and you must travel it one moment at a time. Each choice you make represents a step on your journey. It's either a step in the right direction . . . or the wrong direction. Before you take any action, make it a habit to ask yourself: Will this bring me closer to God? Will it bring me closer to becoming the woman I want to be? If the answer is no, change direction in a hurry.

Diet:

- ☐ Upon rising, drink 8 oz. water mixed with 1.5 oz. unsweetened cranberry juice and 1 t. psyllium husk.
- ☐ Take multivitamin, Ester-C, and EFAs.
- ☐ Drink sixty-four ounces of water throughout the day.
- ☐ Eat two eggs sometime today.
- ☐ Have a salad with your lunch.
- ☐ Eat as many raw or steamed veggies as you can.

Exercise:

- ☐ Bounce six minutes.
- ☐ Walk briskly for thirty minutes.
- ☐ Optional: strength training.

DAY TWENTY-EIGHT	TODAY'S DATE

Scripture to memorize:

Do you not know that your body is a temple of the Holy Spirit, who is in you, whom you have received from God? You are not your own; you were bought at a price. Therefore honor God with your body.

1 CORINTHIANS 6:19–20

Passage to read:
The law of the Lord is perfect,
reviving the soul.
The statutes of the Lord are trustworthy,
making wise the simple.
The precepts of the Lord are right,
giving joy to the heart.
The commands of the Lord are radiant,
giving light to the eyes.

PSALM 19:7–8

Guided prayer:
Dear Lord, your law is perfect. Meditating upon your Word revives my soul. Thank you that the Bible is completely trustworthy. You've given me clear guidance. I don't have to rely on other people's opinions or worry about conflicting advice from so-called experts. I don't need a Ph.D. in psychology to know how to conduct my personal life. Studying your Word will make me wise and give joy to my heart. In a world filled with so much confusion, I thank you for your commands. I don't have to wander around clueless in the dark; your Word gives light to my eyes and makes everything clear. Amen.

A prayer from your heart:

_____

_____

_____

_____

Affirmation to recite:
When my emotions go haywire, I turn to God's Word and it revives my soul.

BASED ON PSALM 19:7–8

107

Action to take:

Get a pack of Post-it notes. Set a timer for fifteen to thirty minutes. Write out as many Bible verses as you can in the time allotted. You may choose your memory verses or some of the selected passages. Now stick the Post-it notes all over your house where you can see them. If your family asks what happened, tell them you're doing it for your health.

Attitude adjustment:

How can I give you healing for your body while there is anxiety in your mind? So long as there is dis-ease in your thoughts, there shall be disease in your body. You have need of many things, but one thing in particular you must develop for your own preservation, and that is an absolute confidence in my loving care.

FRANCES ROBERTS[7]

If you were to write out your health prescription, what would it read? Take two pills and call a friend to complain in the morning? If I were writing out a prescription for someone I loved who was sick, I would write: "Develop absolute confidence in God's loving care." Then, just to make it authentic, I'd scribble my name illegibly in true physician fashion. It strikes me as perfectly logical that someone who doesn't trust God, who allows herself to worry and fret and fuss, will get sick a lot more often than someone whose mind is kept in perfect peace, focusing on the goodness of God. That's just common sense—and it makes medical sense too. Is it a proven cure? Can it prevent all illness? Well, I don't know, but it's got to yield better results than the alternative. Try the prescription and e-mail me in ninety days.

Diet:
☐ Free day—eat whatever you like.

Exercise:
☐ Rest.

---

[7]Frances Roberts, *Come Away My Beloved* (Uhrichsville, OH: Promise Press, 2002), 92.

Week 5

Scripture to memorize:

Do you not know that your body is a temple of the Holy Spirit, who is in you, whom you have received from God? You are not your own; you were bought at a price. Therefore honor God with your body.

1 CORINTHIANS 6:19–20

Passage to read:

Beloved, I pray that you may prosper in every way and [that your body] may keep well, even as [I know] your soul keeps well and prospers.

3 JOHN 2 AMP

Guided prayer:

Dear Lord, thank you for desiring that I may prosper in every way and that my body may keep well. I recognize my responsibility to care for my spirit, soul, and body so that I can enjoy your richest blessings. Thank you for making it possible for my soul to prosper as I meditate upon your Word. Amen.

A prayer from your heart:

_____

_____

_____

_____

Affirmation to recite:

I firmly believe God desires for me to prosper and enjoy good health.

BASED ON 3 JOHN 2

Action to take:

Tomorrow you will be exactly one-third of the way through your ninety-day renewal. Take a moment to evaluate your progress to date in the following areas. For each category, indicate how fully you are experiencing God's best, from 1 (meaning not at all, because you are in flat-out disobedience in this area and your life reflects it) to 10 (meaning you are walking in obedience in this area and enjoying tremendous blessings as a result).

Spiritual

Consistent quiet time	1 – – – – – 5 – – – – – 10
Prayerful (practice the presence of God)	1 – – – – – 5 – – – – – 10
Increasing in knowledge of the Scriptures	1 – – – – – 5 – – – – – 10
Routinely memorize and meditate on Scripture	1 – – – – – 5 – – – – – 10

Mental

Maintain a positive attitude	1 – – – – – 5 – – – – – 10
Read uplifting material	1 – – – – – 5 – – – – – 10
Regulate TV viewing	1 – – – – – 5 – – – – – 10
Learn something new on a regular basis	1 – – – – – 5 – – – – – 10

Emotional

Moods are stable, rather than up and down	1 – – – – – 5 – – – – – 10
Able to express and receive love	1 – – – – – 5 – – – – – 10
Listen carefully when others speak	1 – – – – – 5 – – – – – 10

Physical

Overall health is good	1 – – – – – 5 – – – – – 10
Weight is appropriate	1 – – – – – 5 – – – – – 10
Eating habits are well-balanced	1 – – – – – 5 – – – – – 10

Personal appearance is appealing	1 – – – – 5 – – – – 10

Relational
(evaluate the quality of each that is applicable)

Spouse	1 – – – – 5 – – – – 10
Children	1 – – – – 5 – – – – 10
Extended family	1 – – – – 5 – – – – 10
Church family	1 – – – – 5 – – – – 10
Neighbors	1 – – – – 5 – – – – 10
Friends	1 – – – – 5 – – – – 10
Co-workers	1 – – – – 5 – – – – 10
Strangers	1 – – – – 5 – – – – 10

Practical

Home is in good order	1 – – – – 5 – – – – 10
Car is in good order	1 – – – – 5 – – – – 10
Bills are paid on time	1 – – – – 5 – – – – 10
Obligations fulfilled on time (no procrastination)	1 – – – – 5 – – – – 10

Attitude adjustment:

"Come unto Me," it is written, "all ye that labor and are heavy-laden, and I will give you rest" (Matt.11:28). Only when your mind is at rest can your body build health. Worry is an actively destructive force. Anxiety produces tension, and tension is the road to pain. Fear is devastating to the physical well-being of the body. Anger throws poison into the system that no antibiotic ever can counteract. Ten minutes of unbridled temper can waste enough strength to do a half-day of wholesome work.

FRANCES ROBERTS[1]

Poor diet, lack of exercise, and a lousy mental outlook account for a wide range of common ailments. Many people neglect their physical body, then blame God or the devil when they become ill. It's not enough to pray for healing. You have to modify your behavior *and* your attitude.

---

[1]Roberts, *Come Away My Beloved*, 92–93.

Diet:

- ☐ Upon rising, drink 8 oz. water mixed with 1.5 oz. unsweetened cranberry juice and 1 t. psyllium husk.
- ☐ Take multivitamin, Ester-C, and EFAs.
- ☐ Drink sixty-four ounces of water throughout the day.
- ☐ Drink a protein shake, with 1 cup of frozen raspberries or strawberries mixed in, for breakfast.
- ☐ Have a salad with your lunch.
- ☐ Eat as many raw or steamed veggies as you can.
- ☐ Before retiring for the evening, drink 8 oz. water mixed with 1.5 oz. unsweetened cranberry juice and 1 t. psyllium husk.

Exercise:

- ☐ Bounce six minutes.
- ☐ Walk briskly for thirty minutes.
- ☐ Optional: strength training.

Day Thirty	Today's Date

Scripture to memorize:

Do you not know that your body is a temple of the Holy Spirit, who is in you, whom you have received from God? You are not your own; you were bought at a price. Therefore honor God with your body.

1 CORINTHIANS 6:19–20

Passage to read:

For we know that our old self was crucified with him so that the body of sin might be done away with, that we should no longer be slaves to sin—because anyone who has died has been freed from sin.

ROMANS 6:6–7

Guided prayer:

Dear Lord, my old self continually tries to jump off that cross. I know my old self was crucified, but it wants to come to life again. I want my body of sin to be done away with. I don't want to live as a slave to sin. Dead people don't sin, because temptation holds no sway over them. Lord, may I be as a dead woman over whom the pleasures of this world no longer have power. Amen.

A prayer from your heart:

_____

_____

_____

_____

Affirmation to recite:

I trust in God and he shows me the way I should go.

BASED ON PSALM 143:8

Action to take:

If you are like most people, your tongue is a major battleground. It's a place where many believers allow "sin to reign in [their] mortal body." My problem is twofold: what goes in my mouth (junk food) and what comes out (junk words). Since this renewal incorporates fasting from food, today let's declare a fast from junk words.

Attitude adjustment:

We must stop expecting God to pour out blessings on us while we pour out of our mouths curses on others.

JOYCE MEYER

In her outstanding book *Me and My Big Mouth,* Joyce Meyer shares the concept of fasting your words. Since she has a very forceful, outgoing personality, she says it often happens that she talks from the moment she wakes up until she falls asleep at night. She reports, "By that time I have talked so much that my insides are rattled and my brain is mincemeat. I am just physically and mentally exhausted. Do you know what the Lord told me about that? He said, 'The reason you are so tired all the time is because you talk too much!'"[2]

Today, practice keeping quiet. Only speak if absolutely necessary. (Don't take this to the extreme and annoy people!) Just try to maintain a quiet spirit. See if you don't feel energized by the end of the day.

Several years ago I spent three days enjoying a "silent retreat" at a Franciscan renewal center. No phone. No TV. No music. No conversation. Not even a clock! At mealtimes, one of the monks would ring a bell and we would gather in the dining hall, where I sat in total silence. It was one of the most powerful experiences of my life. If there is a convent, monastery, or Christian retreat center near you, ask if they will allow you to use their facilities for a silent retreat. I guarantee your extended fast-from-words will be an incredible blessing.

Diet:

- ☐ Upon rising, drink 8 oz. water mixed with 1.5 oz. unsweetened cranberry juice and 1 t. psyllium husk.
- ☐ Take multivitamin, Ester-C, and EFAs.
- ☐ Drink sixty-four ounces of water throughout the day.
- ☐ Drink a protein shake, with 1 cup of frozen raspberries or strawberries mixed in, for breakfast.
- ☐ Have a salad with your lunch.
- ☐ Eat as many raw or steamed veggies as you can.

---

[2]Joyce Meyer, *Me and My Big Mouth: Your Answer Is Right Under Your Nose* (Tulsa, OK: Harrison House, 1997), 150.

☐ Before retiring for the evening, drink 8 oz. water mixed with 1.5 oz. unsweetened cranberry juice and 1 t. psyllium husk.

Exercise:
☐ Walk briskly for thirty minutes.
☐ Optional: strength training.

DAY THIRTY-ONE   TODAY'S DATE

Scripture to memorize:

> For God did not give us a spirit of timidity, but
> a spirit of power, of love and of self-discipline.

2 TIMOTHY 1:7

Passage to read:

The Spirit of the Sovereign Lord is on me,
because the Lord has anointed me
to preach good news to the poor.
He has sent me to bind up the brokenhearted,
to proclaim freedom for the captives
and release from darkness for the prisoners,
to proclaim the year of the Lord's favor
and the day of vengeance of our God,
to comfort all who mourn,
and provide for those who grieve in Zion—
to bestow on them a crown of beauty
instead of ashes,
the oil of gladness
instead of mourning,
and a garment of praise
instead of a spirit of despair.
They will be called oaks of righteousness,

a planting of the Lord
for the display of his splendor.

ISAIAH 61:1–3

Guided prayer:

Dear Lord, I thank you that you did not give me a spirit of timidity, fear, or weakness. Instead, you have given me a spirit of power, love, and self-discipline. Lord, I set my will toward your service. Never again will I say, "I don't know what God wants me to do." Father, your Word is perfectly clear that all of your children, like your Son, are to be about your business. I know you have called me and anointed me to preach good news to the poor, to bind up the broken-hearted and proclaim freedom to the captives. I am to proclaim release from darkness to those who are imprisoned by the lies of the enemy and the false promises of this world. Lord, it's my job—not someone else's—to offer people the opportunity, now while the day of your favor is here. And to warn all who will listen that a day of vengeance is indeed coming upon the earth. That's not a message people want to hear, and it probably won't make me particularly popular. But people need to hear it nonetheless. Give me wisdom to share it in a way that others will hear.

Lord, you've called me to comfort the grieving. My natural desire is to flee the grief-stricken, but you are telling me to draw near and bestow upon them a crown of beauty. Put your words in my mouth, Father, that I might be able to offer them beauty for their ashes, the oil of gladness to replace their mourning, and a garment of praise instead of a spirit of despair. That's a mighty tall job description. I know that apart from your Spirit's power I cannot fulfill even one iota of this assignment. But in your power it is possible.

Lord, I want to be an oak of righteousness to display your splendor on this earth. Strengthen me that I might bring honor to your name. Amen.

A prayer from your heart:

_____

_____

_____

_____

Affirmation to recite:

God has called me to serve others. I fulfill that call enthusiastically in the power of the Holy Spirit.

BASED ON ISAIAH 61:1–3

Action to take:

Reach out to an unbelieving friend, perhaps sharing with her a special book that's been particularly meaningful to you and which addresses a specific need in her life. Or you may invite her to dinner or perform an act of service designed to make her life a bit easier.

Attitude Adjustment:

God never asked a cat to plow a field.

MY FRIEND CAROL'S GRANDMOTHER

In Isaiah 61:1–3 we read Christ's job description and, I do believe, in a very real sense, the job description for each and every one of us as his followers. However, God knows that you are *not* Jesus . . . although your goal is to become more and more like him. Believers function as a body—no single one of us is gifted in all of the areas described, as Jesus was. Some of us are better at comforting those who mourn, while others are more equipped at setting captives free. Yet when the church functions as God designed, with the eye guiding the hand and the foot following the will, then we have all accomplished whatever even one has accomplished. You may be the eye who sees the need and reports it to the hand so it may reach out. No job is more important than another, and none dare be neglected.

Diet:

- ☐ Upon rising, drink 8 oz. water mixed with 1.5 oz. unsweetened cranberry juice and 1 t. psyllium husk.
- ☐ Take multivitamin, Ester-C, and EFAs.
- ☐ Drink sixty-four ounces of water throughout the day.
- ☐ Drink a protein shake, with 1 cup of frozen raspberries or strawberries mixed in, for breakfast.
- ☐ Have a salad with your lunch.
- ☐ Eat as many raw or steamed veggies as you can.
- ☐ Before retiring for the evening, drink 8 oz. water mixed with 1.5 oz. unsweetened cranberry juice and 1 t. psyllium husk.

Exercise:

- ☐ Bounce seven minutes.
- ☐ Walk briskly for thirty minutes.
- ☐ Optional: strength training.

DAY THIRTY-TWO	TODAY'S DATE

Scripture to memorize:

For God did not give us a spirit of timidity, but a spirit of power, of love and of self-discipline.

2 TIMOTHY 1:7

Passage to read:

So be strong, show yourself a man, and observe what the Lord your God requires: Walk in his ways, and keep his decrees and commands, his laws and requirements, as written in the Law of Moses, so that you may prosper in all you do and wherever you go.

1 KINGS 2:2–3

Guided prayer:

Dear Lord, I know you desire for me to be strong. To demonstrate to the world that I am a person of fortitude, courage, and conviction. With so many hypocrites and phonies walking the earth, I want to be genuine. I want to walk the walk, not just talk the talk. Help me to live what I believe on Monday through Saturday, not just talk about it on Sunday. I desire to live my life in a spirit of prayer, practicing your presence throughout each day. I want to stand firm upon your Word—upon the values and principles you have set forth—so that people will know I march to the beat of a different drum. That drum is the heartbeat of the Holy Spirit.

Lord, you ask me to walk in your ways not because you want to make my life more difficult, but so that I may prosper in all I do and wherever I go. Help me to remember that, especially when disregarding your law or compromising my standards seems like a more certain way to my desired ends. You have promised to prosper me as I obey you, and I trust you to be true to your Word. Amen.

A prayer from your heart:

_____

_____

_____

_____

Affirmation to recite:

As a follower of God, I am automatically in a position of leadership in this world. I take that responsibility seriously and always seek to set a good example.

BASED ON 1 KINGS 2:2–3

Action to take:

Think about three people who look to you as a leader or role model. Then note one way you might set a better example in each of those relationships.

1. _____

2. _____

3. _____

Attitude adjustment:

Lead, follow, or get out of the way.

LEE IACOCCA

Young people today are crying out for leadership. You might be very surprised to know how many are looking to you as a role model. I hope you take that obligation seriously, because Jesus said if anyone causes a little one to stumble, they'd be better off thrown into the ocean with a millstone tied around their necks. You don't have to hand a kid drugs to make him stumble; just be one of the church gossips who condemns and shuns his family when they face a crisis and are most in need of loving support. I can't tell you how many adults I've known who walked away from the Lord and shipwrecked their lives *because of their negative perception of church-goers.* You might say, "That's just an excuse."

Okay, don't give anyone an excuse to accuse you. Be above reproach. Be a role model. Be a leader.

Diet:

- [ ] Upon rising, drink 8 oz. water mixed with 1.5 oz. unsweetened cranberry juice and 1 t. psyllium husk.
- [ ] Take multivitamin, Ester-C, and EFAs.
- [ ] Drink sixty-four ounces of water throughout the day.
- [ ] Drink a protein shake, with 1 cup of frozen raspberries or strawberries mixed in, for breakfast.
- [ ] Have a salad with your lunch.
- [ ] Eat as many raw or steamed veggies as you can.
- [ ] Before retiring for the evening, drink 8 oz. water mixed with 1.5 oz. unsweetened cranberry juice and 1 t. psyllium husk.

Exercise:

- [ ] Walk briskly for thirty minutes.
- [ ] Optional: strength training.

DAY THIRTY-THREE	TODAY'S DATE

Scripture to memorize:

For God did not give us a spirit of timidity, but a spirit of power, of love and of self-discipline.

2 TIMOTHY 1:7

Passage to read:

This is what the Lord says:
"Heaven is my throne,

and the earth is my footstool.
Where is the house you will build for me?
Where will my resting place be?
Has not my hand made all these things,
and so they came into being?"
declares the Lord.
"This is the one I esteem:
he who is humble and contrite in spirit,
and trembles at my word."

ISAIAH 66:1–2

Guided prayer:

Dear Lord, I come before you acknowledging your majesty. Heaven is your throne and the earth is your footstool. You have created all things. Lord, I know there is nothing I can add to your greatness by my human effort. You do not esteem those who try to accomplish great things for you. Instead, you esteem the one who is humble and contrite in spirit. God, I humble myself before you, realizing apart from you I can do nothing of eternal significance. Yet I make myself available to you as your vessel. Use me. Work through my life to accomplish all the good pleasure of your will here on earth. Amen.

A prayer from your heart:

_____

_____

_____

_____

Affirmation to recite:

I walk in love and humility. I am patient and kind in every situation.

BASED ON 1 CORINTHIANS 13

Action to take:

Do something nice for someone, but do it anonymously. Don't tell anyone about what you've done. Ideally, not even the recipient of your kindness will know whom to thank. (That's not always possible, but see if you can pull it off!)

Attitude adjustment:

Humility is the proper estimate of oneself.

CHARLES SPURGEON

I used to confuse humility with self-loathing. But humility is not the same as beating yourself up or letting other people tear you down. Humility is not the same as low self-esteem and it's not the opposite of confidence. In fact, the truly humble person walks with absolute confidence, knowing that we are simply empty vessels through whom God wants to accomplish his work. When we understand true humility, we understand that it's not about us at all. It's about God. That's a tremendously freeing realization, so grab hold of it and serve him with confidence . . . in humility.

Diet:

- [ ] Upon rising, drink 8 oz. water mixed with 1.5 oz. unsweetened cranberry juice and 1 t. psyllium husk.
- [ ] Take multivitamin, Ester-C, and EFAs.
- [ ] Drink sixty-four ounces of water throughout the day.
- [ ] Drink a protein shake, with 1 cup of frozen raspberries or strawberries mixed in, for breakfast.
- [ ] Have a salad with your lunch.
- [ ] Eat as many raw or steamed veggies as you can.
- [ ] Before retiring for the evening, drink 8 oz. water mixed with 1.5 oz. unsweetened cranberry juice and 1 t. psyllium husk.

Exercise:

- [ ] Bounce seven minutes.
- [ ] Walk briskly for thirty minutes.
- [ ] Optional: strength training.

DAY THIRTY-FOUR	TODAY'S DATE

Scripture to memorize:

> For God did not give us a spirit of timidity, but
> a spirit of power, of love and of self-discipline.

2 TIMOTHY 1:7

Passage to read:

Is this the kind of fast I have chosen,
only a day for a man to humble himself?
Is it only for bowing one's head like a reed
and for lying on sackcloth and ashes?
Is that what you call a fast,
a day acceptable to the Lord?
"Is not this the kind of fasting I have chosen:
to loose the chains of injustice
and untie the cords of the yoke,
to set the oppressed free
and break every yoke?
Is it not to share your food with the hungry
and to provide the poor wanderer with shelter—
when you see the naked, to clothe him,
and not to turn away from your own flesh and blood?
Then your light will break forth like the dawn,
and your healing will quickly appear;
then your righteousness will go before you,
and the glory of the Lord will be your rear guard.
Then you will call, and the Lord will answer;
you will cry for help, and he will say: Here am I."

ISAIAH 58:5–9

Guided prayer:

Dear Lord, I know you have called me to the spiritual discipline of fasting. When Jesus spoke to the disciples, he didn't say if *you fast, he said* when. *You have brought this renewal plan into my life at this time for a reason, and perhaps part of the purpose is that I might discover the power of fasting. As I prepare for my fast, help me not to think about superficial concerns, like how hungry I am or will I lose weight. Help me not to congratulate myself for being such a spiritual giant . . . or berate myself if I fail to complete my fast. I know you aren't nearly as concerned about my stomach as you are about the condition of my heart. Help me to focus my attention on you and the needs of others. As I set aside my usual tasks, open my eyes to see people around me who are in need of my help. Show me, in ways small and large, how I can make a difference in my corner of the world. Amen.*

A prayer from your heart:

_____

_____

_____

_____

Affirmation to recite:

I spend more time praying than grumbling, therefore I have less to grumble about.

BASED ON PHILIPPIANS 2:14

Action to take:

Prepare for your upcoming fast, which begins tomorrow.

Attitude adjustment:

If Christians spent as much time praying as they do grumbling, they would soon have nothing to grumble about.

UNKNOWN

Fasting is presented as a vital spiritual discipline throughout Scripture and has been considered so throughout church history. Yet it is often neglected by Christians today. Why? Because we, especially in America, place the demands of our stomach above all other demands. And if your stomach is anything like mine, it is always demanding something! This is actually good news, because it will give you the opportunity to practice saying "no" to your flesh. When your stomach starts grumbling and demanding its way (Feed me, Feed me, Feed me NOW), that's your cue to turn to prayer and find the strength to say, "No, you can't have an Oreo. I'm busy right now." Each time you say "No," it becomes easier to say "No" the next time. So be encouraged when your stomach grumbles. Turn to prayer and you'll soon have much less to grumble about.

Diet:

- ☐ Upon rising, drink 8 oz. water mixed with 1.5 oz. unsweetened cranberry juice and 1 t. psyllium husk.
- ☐ Take multivitamin, Ester-C, and EFAs.
- ☐ Drink sixty-four ounces of water throughout the day.
- ☐ Drink a protein shake, with 1 cup of frozen raspberries or strawberries mixed in, for breakfast.
- ☐ Have a salad with your lunch.
- ☐ Eat as many raw or steamed veggies as you can.
- ☐ Before retiring for the evening, drink 8 oz. water mixed with 1.5 oz. unsweetened cranberry juice and 1 t. psyllium husk.
- ☐ Be prepared: tomorrow is a fast.

Exercise:

- ☐ Bounce eight minutes.
- ☐ Walk briskly for thirty minutes.
- ☐ Optional: strength training.

DAY THIRTY-FIVE	TODAY'S DATE

Scripture to memorize:

*For God did not give us a spirit of timidity, but
a spirit of power, of love and of self-discipline.*

2 TIMOTHY 1:7

Passage to read:

*I will extol the Lord at all times;
his praise will always be on my lips.
My soul will boast in the Lord;
let the afflicted hear and rejoice.
Glorify the Lord with me;
let us exalt his name together.
I sought the Lord, and he answered me;
he delivered me from all my fears.
Those who look to him are radiant;
their faces are never covered with shame.*

PSALM 34:1–5

Guided prayer:

*Dear Lord, I extol you and declare you are larger than all of my problems
combined. I praise you for who you are, quite apart from everything you've done
for me. Lord, I want to glorify you with my life, so those around me will know
who you are—just by looking at your dealings with me. Lord, I know you
answer me when I seek you. I thank you for answered prayer. God, you are daily
delivering me from all my foolish fears and worries. Thank you, Lord. Lord, I
look to you that my face may be radiant. I want to glow with the kind of beauty
that works its way outward from the core of my being. There's no shame on me!
Only forgiveness, righteousness, and one fresh start after another. Hallelujah!
Amen.*

A prayer from your heart:

_____

_____

_____

_____

Soul

Affirmation to recite:

I don't have to rely on cosmetics to make me beautiful. I look to the Lord, so my face is radiant. He makes me beautiful from the inside out.

BASED ON PSALM 34:1–5

Action to take:

Determine that you will devote as much time each day to cultivating inner beauty as you do to outer beauty. Calculate how much time you spend grooming; then, if necessary, reorganize your daily routine to allow you to devote at least that much time to spiritual disciplines. (For most of us, it is approximately one hour.)

Attitude Adjustment:

Peace within makes beauty without.

ENGLISH PROVERB

I'll never forget the day I stumbled upon this passage in Psalm 34. I'd probably read it dozens of times, but it never hit me like it did that day on an airplane, flying from coast to coast. Like many middle-aged women, I have purchased my share of facial lotions, all promising to "restore the radiance of youth." (Although come to think of it, I wasted my youth hanging my head in shame . . . but let's not go there.) Radiance is a major buzzword in the cosmetics industry these days, in case you haven't noticed. Yet God's Word says if we look to *him*, our faces will be radiant. As I thought about it, I recalled seeing certain older Christian women who had an incredible aura about them. Not that fake plastic surgery look—but an appeal that defied magazine covers. That's the kind of authentic, from-the-inside beauty I want to have. And it's not available in a bottle. You can only get it on your knees.

Diet:
☐ Fast today.

Exercise:
☐ Do only light stretching exercises. Do not overexert yourself while fasting.

Week 6

Scripture to memorize:

> I will be glad and rejoice in your love,
> for you saw my affliction
> and knew the anguish of my soul.
> You have not handed me over to the enemy
> but have set my feet in a spacious place.

PSALM 31:7–8

Passage to read:

Then he returned to his disciples and found them sleeping. "Could you men not keep watch with me for one hour?" he asked Peter. "Watch and pray so that you will not fall into temptation. The spirit is willing, but the body is weak."

MATTHEW 26:40–41

Guided prayer:

Dear Lord, my spirit is indeed willing, but my body is weak. Tempted though I am to judge the disciples for falling asleep when Jesus needed them to be steadfast in prayer, I have to admit I would often rather sleep than pray. I would prefer not to set the alarm an hour earlier in order to meet with you in prayer. Holy Spirit, I invite you to show me all the areas of my spiritual walk that are being hindered because my body is weak. I want to cooperate with you in the process of strengthening my body. Amen.

A prayer from your heart:

Dear Father, help me to be strong, to train with you to be a great Christian! To work out my spirit, soul, mind & body for your purpose. Amen

Soul

Affirmation to recite:

I build myself up through wisdom. Through increasing knowledge, I fill my life with blessings and every good thing.

BASED ON PROVERBS 24:3–4

Action to take:

List ways in which your body's weakness (i.e., desire for ease and comfort) is hindering your spiritual walk. Ask God to show you specific ways you can battle the demands of your body. Some of us sleep too much; many more don't get enough sleep. Some struggle with laziness; others must battle busyness and the never-ending urge to run at breakneck speed. Some don't exercise enough; others may be addicted to exercise. It is unhealthy to overeat, but many in our society do not eat enough or have fallen into the traps of anorexia or bulimia. As always, if you are unclear about what action to take, ask God and he will surely answer.

Demands of Your Body	Needs of Your Spirit	Strategy to Ensure the Spirit Wins
more exercise	think clearly	1/2 hr exercise + Bible reading each day
more self-discipline	read Bible	
less sugar	do for others	helping others is sweeter

131

Attitude Adjustment:

Prayer is better than sleep.

MUSLIM RALLYING CRY IN RESPONSE TO THE DAILY 5 A.M. CALL TO PRAYER

When I first learned that all devout Muslims were expected to wake up at five in the morning to pray, I hung my head. Very few Christians show that type of spiritual fervor. I know I certainly don't. You've got to admire their zeal and devotion. Do you truly believe prayer is better than sleep? Or do you think sleep is more important than prayer? Examine your heart, mind, and soul to see what you truly believe. Then examine those beliefs to see if they line up with God's Word. You might be surprised at your ultimate answers.

Diet:

☐ Free day—eat whatever you like.

Exercise:

☐ Walk briskly for thirty minutes.
☐ Optional: strength training.

DAY THIRTY-SEVEN	TODAY'S DATE

Scripture to memorize:

I will be glad and rejoice in your love,
for you saw my affliction
and knew the anguish of my soul.
You have not handed me over to the enemy
but have set my feet in a spacious place.

PSALM 31:7–8

Passage to read:

Very early in the morning, while it was still dark, Jesus got up, left the house and went off to a solitary place, where he prayed. Simon and his companions went to look for him, and when they found him, they exclaimed: "Everyone is looking for you!"

MARK 1:35–37

Guided prayer:

Dear heavenly Father, if Jesus felt the need to wake up very early in the morning to spend time alone with you, how much more do I need to do the same? Forgive me for those times when I cling to the false belief that sleep is better than prayer. How foolish of me to think anything I might devote my time to would yield more benefit than time spent with you. Lord, help me to find a solitary place, away from my house, suitable for meeting with you. A special place I can go to from time to time when the pressures of life are crowding out my eternal perspective. Help me to remember that just because "everyone is looking for [me]" doesn't mean I should skip my time with you to meet their demands. I know I'll be far better equipped to serve my family and the world after I've spent time with you. Help me to remember that. Amen.

A prayer from your heart:

Help me to take the time out each day to be with you - undivided - for at least 1/2 hr. Help me to start with this small bit of time to get working on my purpose for You!

Affirmation to recite:

Nothing I have to do today is more important than spending time in prayer. My day goes more smoothly when I begin it on my knees.

BASED ON MARK 1.35–37

Action to take:

Take a moment to think about your neighborhood. If necessary, hop in the car and take a drive around. Locate a "solitary place" you can go to meet with God. If you are reading this during a season of inclement weather, try a hotel lobby. These can often serve as a quiet oasis in the early morning hours, and if you order a cup of herbal tea, no one will object to your presence. A small café or roadside diner may serve the same purpose. Set your alarm early for tomorrow to allow time to sneak out of the house and spend a full hour alone with God. Describe your experience and how you feel when you return to the house. It just might feel so terrific you'll make this a regular practice.

_____

_____

_____

Attitude adjustment:

> *I have so much to do today that I shall spend the*
> *first three hours in prayer.*

MARTIN LUTHER

Every once in a while, I sit and think about how illogical my own behavior is. (I should probably think such thoughts more often.) Do I honestly believe my day will go more smoothly and I'll get more accomplished by skipping time with God? When I put it in writing, it is obviously irrational. But let me turn the tables for a minute: do *you* honestly believe you can get ahead of the game by jumping right into the demands of your day, bypassing your quiet time with God? Your logic is fatally flawed, my friend. Jesus had people constantly demanding his time and attention. The disciples said "everyone" was looking for him. (People always exaggerate the urgency of the matter, don't they?) By his actions, Jesus said "everyone" can wait; my Father comes first. Your actions should communicate the same message to your loved ones. They may act frustrated at the moment, when you won't drop everything and give in to their demands. Ultimately, they will respect you for it. Stand your ground . . . on your knees.

Diet:

- ☐ Upon rising, drink 8 oz. water mixed with 1.5 oz. unsweetened cranberry juice and 1 t. psyllium husk.
- ☐ Take multivitamin, Ester-C, EFAs.
- ☐ Drink sixty-four ounces of water throughout the day.
- ☐ Drink a protein shake, with 1 cup of frozen raspberries or strawberries mixed in, for breakfast.
- ☐ For lunch, have a salad with a palm-sized portion of healthy protein such as fish, poultry, lean beef, or tofu. Even all-natural peanut butter will do!
- ☐ Eat as many raw or steamed veggies as you can.
- ☐ Before retiring for the evening, drink 8 oz. water mixed with 1.5 oz. unsweetened cranberry juice and 1 t. psyllium husk.

Exercise:

- ☐ Bounce eight minutes.
- ☐ Walk briskly for thirty minutes.
- ☐ Optional: strength training.

DAY THIRTY-EIGHT   TODAY'S DATE

Scripture to memorize:

I will be glad and rejoice in your love,
for you saw my affliction
and knew the anguish of my soul.
You have not handed me over to the enemy
but have set my feet in a spacious place.

PSALM 31:7–8

Passage to read:

When all these blessings and curses I have set before you come upon you and you take them to heart wherever the Lord your God disperses you among the nations, and when you and your children return to the Lord your God and obey him with all your heart and with all your soul according to everything I command you today, then the Lord your God will restore your fortunes and have compassion on you and gather you again from all the nations where he scattered you. Even if you have been banished to the most distant land under the heavens, from there the Lord your God will gather you and bring you back. He will bring you to the land that belonged to your fathers, and you will take possession of it. He will make you more prosperous and numerous than your fathers. The Lord your God will circumcise your hearts and the hearts of your descendants, so that you may love him with all your heart and with all your soul, and live. The Lord your God will put all these curses on your enemies who hate and persecute you. You will again obey the Lord and follow all his commands I am giving you today. Then the Lord your God will make you most prosperous in all the work of your hands and in the fruit of your womb, the young of your livestock and the crops of your land. The Lord will again delight in you and make you prosperous, just as he delighted in your fathers, if you obey the Lord your God and keep his commands and decrees that are written in this Book of the Law and turn to the Lord your God with all your heart and with all your soul.

DEUTERONOMY 30:1–10

Guided prayer:

Dear Lord, I thank you for the freedom to choose my path. You have set before me blessings and curses, making the consequences of disobedience clear. I'm grateful the option of returning to obedience is always before me. Thank you for drawing me back to you with compassion. This moment, I choose your way. I desire to follow your commands, so I can enjoy fellowship with you and enjoy prosperity. I turn to you now with all my heart and with all my soul. Amen.

A prayer from your heart:

_____

_____

_____

_____

Affirmation to recite:

I reject negative thinking patterns, focusing instead on the positive promises of God. When negative thoughts come, I stop them in their tracks and take them captive.

BASED ON 2 CORINTHIANS 10:5

Action to take:

Practice catching negative thoughts today. At the end of the day, make a note of those you captured:

_____

_____

_____

_____

Attitude adjustment:

God's love is unconditional, but his promises are not.

CHARLES SWINDOLL

Throughout Scripture, God clearly states we get to choose between blessings and curses. God tells us exactly what we need to do and how we need to live if we want to enjoy his best for our lives. He will love us whether or not we choose wisely, but he will not alter the logical consequences of our choices.

If we want:	*Then we must:*
Love	Be loving
Find our life purpose	Lose our lives *by loving others*
Power	Pray
Peace	Trust
Wisdom	Study God's Word
Spiritual growth	Cultivate spiritual disciplines
Emotional healing	Forgive others and repent of our sin
Joy	Be grateful
Health	Care for our body
Financial security	Tithe, save, and stay out of debt
Victory over sin	Establish accountability and actively fight temptation
Abundant life	Walk in obedience

You can't get Column A without Column B. They go hand in hand. So choose wisely.

Body

Diet:

- [ ] Upon rising, drink 8 oz. water mixed with 1.5 oz. unsweetened cranberry juice and 1 t. psyllium husk.
- [ ] Take multivitamin, Ester-C, and EFAs.
- [ ] Drink sixty-four ounces of water throughout the day.
- [ ] Drink a protein shake, with 1 cup of frozen raspberries or strawberries mixed in, for breakfast.
- [ ] For lunch, have a salad with a palm-sized portion of healthy protein.
- [ ] Eat as many raw or steamed veggies as you can.
- [ ] Before retiring for the evening, drink 8 oz. water mixed with 1.5 oz. unsweetened cranberry juice and 1 t. psyllium husk.

Exercise:

- [ ] Bounce nine minutes.

☐ Walk briskly for thirty minutes.
☐ Optional: strength training.

Scripture to memorize:

I will be glad and rejoice in your love,
for you saw my affliction
and knew the anguish of my soul.
You have not handed me over to the enemy
but have set my feet in a spacious place.

PSALM 31:7–8

Passage to read:

I remember my affliction and my wandering,
the bitterness and the gall.
I well remember them,
and my soul is downcast within me.
Yet this I call to mind
and therefore I have hope:
Because of the Lord's great love we are not consumed,
for his compassions never fail.
They are new every morning;
great is your faithfulness.
I say to myself, "The Lord is my portion;
therefore I will wait for him."
The Lord is good to those whose hope is in him,
to the one who seeks him.

LAMENTATIONS 3:19–25

Guided prayer:

Dear Lord, when I remember the tough times in my life and the people who've hurt me, I feel bitterness welling up within. Today, I choose to bring to mind your great love and compassion. I recall that I have hurt others, just as I have been hurt. And if it weren't for your compassion and unfailing love, I would be forever lost. Help me to extend that same compassion toward others. Lord, you are my portion, so I don't need to fuss about getting my fair share in this world. I believe you when you say you will not withhold any good thing from me. So even though I may feel disappointed at times, I will continue to wait for you and your timing. My hope is in you, because I know you are good to me. I have committed my life to continually seeking you. You have said I will find you when I seek you with all my heart. I am seeking, Lord. Meet me here today. Amen.

A prayer from your heart:

_____

_____

_____

_____

Affirmation to recite:

I keep my mind at peace by focusing on God's goodness, rather than striving after my fair share.

BASED ON ISAIAH 26:3

Action to take:

Call to mind a situation that tends to make you feel bitter. Perhaps a job you were fired from. Or a church you walked away from with hurt feelings. Now recall some of the people involved. Jot down names if you like. Begin to pray for them, inviting God to give them the same second chance he has given you. Pray that they, too, would experience God's compassion in a fresh way this morning.

_____   _____

_____   _____

Attitude adjustment:

Tomorrow is a brand-new day with no mistakes in it.

LUCY MAUD MONTGOMERY, ANNE OF GREEN GABLES

Most of us frail humans manage to make a mistake or two every single day. And sometimes we make colossal mistakes. Or we find ourselves swept away in the backwash of someone else's sin. It's easy for regret, bitterness, or despair to overtake us. That's when it helps to remember that our God is the God of fresh starts and second chances. No matter what happened in your past, no matter what happened yesterday or even today, remember: tomorrow is a brand-new day with no mistakes in it. God's compassions are new every single morning. So get a good night's sleep tonight and wake up early!

Diet:

- [ ] Upon rising, drink 8 oz. water mixed with 1.5 oz. unsweetened cranberry juice and 1 t. psyllium husk.
- [ ] Take multivitamin, Ester-C, EFAs.
- [ ] Drink sixty-four ounces of water throughout the day.
- [ ] Drink a protein shake, with 1 cup of frozen raspberries or strawberries mixed in, for breakfast.
- [ ] For lunch, have a salad with a palm-sized portion of healthy protein.
- [ ] Eat as many raw or steamed veggies as you can.
- [ ] Before retiring for the evening, drink 8 oz. water mixed with 1.5 oz. unsweetened cranberry juice and 1 t. psyllium husk.

Exercise:

- [ ] Bounce nine minutes.
- [ ] Walk briskly for thirty minutes.
- [ ] Optional: strength training.

DAY FORTY	TODAY'S DATE

Scripture to memorize:

I will be glad and rejoice in your love,
for you saw my affliction
and knew the anguish of my soul.
You have not handed me over to the enemy
but have set my feet in a spacious place.

PSALM 31:7–8

Passage to read:

This poor man called, and the Lord heard him;
he saved him out of all his troubles.
The angel of the Lord encamps around those who fear him,
and he delivers them.
Taste and see that the Lord is good;
blessed is the man who takes refuge in him.
Fear the Lord, you his saints,
for those who fear him lack nothing.
The lions may grow weak and hungry,
but those who seek the Lord lack no good thing.

PSALM 34:6–10

Guided prayer:

Dear Lord, thank you for hearing me when I call out to you. Thank you for creating angels and sending them for our protection. Lord, you alone know the tragedies that didn't happen in my life. I can only imagine how many times I have been spared from harm—car accidents, home fires, criminal attacks. I believe angels are all around me every day and I thank you for it. Sometimes I get so focused on the hardships that come my way, I lose sight of your goodness. I am richly blessed because I have taken refuge in you. I lack no good thing. I *have all the essentials of life: food, clothing, shelter. That's much more than many people around the world can say. And not only are they suffering in this life, they will suffer in the life to come unless someone tells them about Jesus. Lord, give me your heart of compassion, so that I'll be more concerned about what others lack than I am about what I lack. The truth is, compared to the joy of spending eternity with you, I lack nothing. Thank you, Father. Amen.*

A prayer from your heart:

_____

_____

_____

_____

Affirmation to recite:

When someone asks me how I am, I say, "I am richly blessed," because that is always true—no matter what else is happening in my life.

BASED ON PROVERBS 28:20

Action to take:

Think of someone less fortunate than you—someone who lacks many of the things you take for granted. Determine how you can help . . . and take action. You might consider sponsoring a child through Compassion International or World Vision. Without your help, there is a child somewhere in the world who will continue to lack many good things.

Attitude adjustment:

Let my heart be broken with the things that break God's heart.

BOB PIERCE, WORLD VISION FOUNDER

As you move closer to your upcoming two-day fast, you will do well to remember that people throughout the world face starvation every day. Did you know that, as of this writing, an estimated twenty million people in the southern African countries of Malawi, Zimbabwe, Lesotho, Zambia, Mozambique, and Swaziland face starvation in the coming months if sufficient outside food is not supplied?[1] Perhaps you can make these nations part of your prayer focus this week.

Diet:

- [ ] Upon rising, drink 8 oz. water mixed with 1.5 oz. unsweetened cranberry juice and 1 t. psyllium husk.
- [ ] Take multivitamin, Ester-C, EFAs.
- [ ] Drink sixty-four ounces of water throughout the day.
- [ ] Drink a protein shake, with 1 cup of frozen raspberries or strawberries mixed in, for breakfast.
- [ ] For lunch, have a salad with a palm-sized portion of healthy protein.
- [ ] Eat as many raw or steamed veggies as you can.
- [ ] Before retiring for the evening, drink 8 oz. water mixed with 1.5 oz. unsweetened cranberry juice and 1 t. psyllium husk.

Exercise:

- [ ] Walk briskly for thirty minutes.
- [ ] Optional: strength training.

---

[1]According to United Nations World Food Program e-mail bulletin (July 2002).

Scripture to memorize:

Do you not know that in a race all the runners run, but only one gets the prize? Run in such a way as to get the prize. Everyone who competes in the games goes into strict training. They do it to get a crown that will not last; but we do it to get a crown that will last forever.

1 CORINTHIANS 9:24–25

Passage to read:

Therefore do not let sin reign in your mortal body so that you obey its evil desires. Do not offer the parts of your body to sin, as instruments of wickedness, but rather offer yourselves to God, as those who have been brought from death to life; and offer the parts of your body to him as instruments of righteousness. For sin shall not be your master, because you are not under law, but under grace.

ROMANS 6:12–14

Guided prayer:

Dear Lord, your commands are clear. I am not to let sin reign in my body. It's up to me to resist evil desires. God, I offer my body to you, rather than offering it to sin. I want to be an instrument of righteousness. Sin is not my master. I am no longer a slave to my impulses. I live my life by faith through the grace of God. Amen.

A prayer from your heart:

_____

_____

_____

_____

Affirmation to recite:

I protect my body by keeping my mind at peace. The more confidence I have in God's loving care for me, the more my mind will remain at peace.

BASED ON ISAIAH 26:3

Action to take:

Identify an area where your body leads you away from righteousness. Just for today, make a determined effort not to yield to that temptation (whether it's over-eating, resting when you should be working, etc.).

Attitude Adjustment:

Your physical energy is a gift from God, entrusted to you to be
employed for His glory. It is a sin to take His gift and dissipate it
through the trap doors of the evil emotions of the disposition.
Look not upon others and condemn them for jeopardizing
their health by harmful habits and wasting energies on vain pursuits
while you yourself undermine your health by unworthy emotions
and take time which by keeping your mind in an attitude of praise
and faith could be constructively employed, but instead you allow this
time to be a period of destructive action by entertaining such things

146

time to be a period of destructive action by entertaining such things
as self-pity and remorse and evil-surmisings.

FRANCES ROBERTS[2]

Most of us Christians like to congratulate ourselves because we don't carouse like the world. We're not out there drinking, smoking, gambling, doing drugs, or fooling around. At the same time, many of us do something just as damaging to our spirit, soul, and body: we feel sorry for ourselves. Self-pity is one of the most destructive forces in America today. It can eat you up, physically, emotionally, and spiritually. It is a serious enemy. Actively fight against it. How? By focusing on the goodness of God.

Diet:

- ☐ Upon rising, drink 8 oz. water mixed with 1.5 oz. unsweetened cranberry juice and 1 t. psyllium husk.
- ☐ Take multivitamin, Ester-C, EFAs
- ☐ Drink sixty-four ounces of water throughout the day.
- ☐ Drink a protein shake, with 1 cup of frozen raspberries or strawberries mixed in, for breakfast.
- ☐ For lunch, have a salad with a palm-sized portion of healthy protein.
- ☐ Eat as many raw or steamed veggies as you can.
- ☐ Before retiring for the evening, drink 8 oz. water mixed with 1.5 oz. unsweetened cranberry juice and 1 t. psyllium husk.
- ☐ Prepare to start a two-day fast tomorrow.

Exercise:

- ☐ Bounce ten minutes.
- ☐ Walk briskly for thirty minutes.
- ☐ Optional: strength training.

---

[2]Roberts, *Come Away My Beloved*, 93.

Scripture to memorize:

Do you not know that in a race all the runners run,
but only one gets the prize? Run in such a way as to get
the prize. Everyone who competes in the games goes into
strict training. They do it to get a crown that will not
last; but we do it to get a crown that will last forever.

1 CORINTHIANS 9:24–25

Passage to read:

Teach me your way, O Lord,
and I will walk in your truth;
give me an undivided heart,
that I may fear your name.
I will praise you, O Lord my God, with all my heart;
I will glorify your name forever.
For great is your love toward me;
you have delivered me from the depths of the grave.

PSALM 86:11–13

Guided prayer:

Dear Lord, you have called me to run the race of life. You created me for a purpose. I want to run the race in such a way as to get the prize. I know that will mean going into strict training, and I commit myself, here and now, to take my life mission seriously. Olympic athletes don't sleep late, eat whatever they feel like, and lounge around watching television. They wake up each day with a plan. They go about their daily routine with vigor. They exercise, eat right, and stay on task. All of that for what? A gold medal and a cereal endorsement? Lord, you have called me to pursue a heavenly prize! You have a crown waiting for me that

I will proudly wear for all eternity. It's high time I got into strict training. Lord, with you as my personal trainer, I am ready to get serious today. Amen.

A prayer from your heart:

_____

_____

_____

_____

Affirmation to recite:

I am in strict training as a disciple of Christ and I work hard. But I don't drive myself to exhaustion trying to prove I'm worth something. I know I am worthwhile because I am a child of God.

BASED ON 1 JOHN 3:1

Action to take:

Conduct yourself like a person in strict training. Go watch a local sports team during its daily workout and observe the intensity. (The next time the Olympics roll around, watch one of the documentaries on the athletes' training regimens. It will boggle your mind.) Or rent a movie like *Chariots of Fire* that shows how hard athletes must train. Make a big poster that says *In Training* and put it up somewhere in your house. Run to get the prize.

Attitude adjustment:

Let me exhort you: Examine yourselves. Let each of you discover where your true chance of greatness lies. . . . Seize this chance, rejoice in it, and let no power or persuasion deter you in your task.

MASTER OF CAIUS COLLEGE, FROM THE MOVIE CHARIOTS OF FIRE

Have you seen the classic movie *Chariots of Fire*? It recounts the true story of 1924 Olympic gold medalist Eric Liddell. You may recall the scene in the movie where Eric and his sister are walking along a cliff in Scotland on a windy afternoon. His sister is trying to persuade him to forget all this frivolous nonsense about running and devote himself to missionary work. Eric responds with one of the most unforgettable lines. He says, "I know God made me for a purpose. But he made me fast, too. And when I run, I feel God's pleasure."

Is there something you do that, when you do it, you feel God's pleasure? You feel "the smile of God" upon your life? You sense that "Yes, this is it! This is what he created me to do!" I firmly believe that God has a unique calling upon the life of every woman reading this today. He has a role for each of you to fill in your home, in your church, and in your world. And we'll never be fully alive until we put on our running shoes and begin to run the race God has set before us.

Diet:
☐ Today you will begin your second two-day fast.

Exercise:
☐ Do only light stretching exercises. Do not overexert yourself while fasting.

Week 7

Scripture to memorize:

Do you not know that in a race all the runners run, but only one gets the prize? Run in such a way as to get the prize. Everyone who competes in the games goes into strict training. They do it to get a crown that will not last; but we do it to get a crown that will last forever.

1 CORINTHIANS 9:24–25

Passage to read:

After a long time had passed and the Lord had given Israel rest from all their enemies around them, Joshua, by then old and well advanced in years, summoned all Israel—their elders, leaders, judges and officials—and said to them: "I am old and well advanced in years. . . .

"Now I am about to go the way of all the earth. You know with all your heart and soul that not one of all the good promises the Lord your God gave you has failed. Every promise has been fulfilled; not one has failed."

JOSHUA 23:1–2, 14

Guided prayer:

Dear Lord, each day I am getting older and some day, if you don't take me home suddenly, I will reach the stage Joshua did. That point where I am able to look back over my lifetime and declare to all who will listen: "Not one of all the good promises the Lord my God gave me has failed." What a moment that will be. I know your promises are not unconditional; they are contingent upon my faithfulness. I desire to be a faithful servant, so I can enjoy the full benefits of a life spent in service to you. I want my life to be an inspiration and a positive example to all who come after me. Holy Spirit, remind me of the big picture on a routine basis. Amen.

A prayer from your heart:

Dear Father - I pray that I will please you each day, resist temptation, so that you may mold me and fill me with your everlasting blessings. Thank you so much for the amazing blessings you have already trusted me with. Please help me to treat your rewards with respect - Amen

Affirmation to recite:

I don't get worked up when things don't turn out the way I had hoped. I simply adjust to circumstances as they unfold, trusting that God has a better plan in mind.

BASED ON JEREMIAH 29:11

Action to take:

Imagine you are at your own eightieth birthday party, organized as a tribute to your life. What would you like each of the following people to say about you?[1]

Name	Tribute Statement
Sage - always had time for me	
From your family	
Krista - positive, caring & thoughtful & generous	
From your friends	
loving, forgiving - always tries to be like Jesus	
From your church	
good ambassador, giving	
From your community	
good role model, goes that "extra mile"	
From your working life	

[1]Adapted from *The Franklin Covey Planner*.

Attitude adjustment:

Live your life in such a way that you wouldn't be embarrassed to sell your pet parrot to the town gossip.

WILL ROGERS

It's not enough to think about your eightieth birthday, hoping for the best. You have to live in such a way that you will be remembered as you hope. Use today's exercise as a lifelong planning tool. For example, I wrote that I want my daughter Leah to say, "My mom put us first. She never lost sight of what matters most. She taught us to love and live with passion—to love God, ourselves, and others." I want my neighbors to say, "Donna treated everyone with love and generosity. She was gracious at all times, even under pressure." Obviously, if I expect people to say those things, I'm going to have to live them out first. That will require prayer, planning, and action. I'll have to substitute what I know I should do for what "I feel like" doing. You'll have to do the same.

Diet:
☐ Fast again today.

Exercise:
☐ Do only light stretching exercises. Do not overexert yourself while fasting.

Scripture to memorize:

*Do you not know that in a race all the runners run,
but only one gets the prize? Run in such a way as to get
the prize. Everyone who competes in the games goes into
strict training. They do it to get a crown that will not
last; but we do it to get a crown that will last forever.*

1 CORINTHIANS 9:24–25

Passage to read:

*How can I repay the Lord
for all his goodness to me?
I will lift up the cup of salvation
and call on the name of the Lord.
I will fulfill my vows to the Lord
in the presence of all his people.*

PSALM 116:12–14

Guided prayer:

Dear Lord, I recognize I have done nothing to earn your love. You bestow it freely. My salvation is a free gift. Let me never take it for granted! Lord, it is impossible for me to repay all of your goodness to me. Yet one way I can show my gratitude is through service to others—even the simple service of praying for them. Lord, I have made many vows during my lifetime. Even during the first half of this journey, there are many things I have purposed in my heart to do. Others I have written out and committed myself to. Holy Spirit, I invite you to remind me of these vows as I spend time in prayer. I want to fulfill my vows, not for your sake, but for my own. Amen.

A prayer from your heart:

_____

_____

_____

_____

Affirmation to recite:

I am not shaken by tough times, because I am confident God will bring something good out of every circumstance, even if I don't understand the how, when, or why.

BASED ON ROMANS 8:28

Action to take:

Write out your typical daily food consumption prior to starting this renewal. Now calculate how many grams of carbohydrates you consumed in a typical day. Be sure to check cereal and pasta boxes, bread and snack packages, plus milk and juice cartons. Check everything you put in your mouth, including the creamer you put in your coffee and the ketchup you put on your favorite French fries. Fruits and vegetables also contain carbohydrates, although these contain healthier complex carbohydrates. If you want to be exact, you can even calculate the carbs in your produce (see *www.atkinsnutritionals.com*). Now determine the total number of daily carbs:

Food   Number of Carbs

_____   _____

_____   _____

_____   _____

_____   _____

_____   _____

_____   _____
_____   _____
_____   _____

Attitude adjustment:

The typical American now consumes 152 pounds of sugar and high fructose corn syrup a year.

DR. ROBERT C. ATKINS[2]

An increasing body of evidence conclusively demonstrates the damaging effects of refined carbohydrates.[3] If it comes in a box, chances are it's filled with refined carbohydrates. Be especially wary if the label says "Low Fat" or "No Fat." The American people insist on good-tasting food. If manufacturers take out the fat, they've got to replace it with something tasty. Guess what that replacement is? You guessed it. Sugar in one form or another. Now for the real catch. Sugar is almost instantly converted into fat in your body. So fat-free frozen yogurt is actually very fattening indeed. In fact, it's probably worse for you than good old-fashioned ice cream. And if you ask me, it doesn't taste half as good. Pretty crazy, huh? Is it any wonder so many Americans are overweight? Don't be fooled by manufacturers' fake food. Eat real food made by *the* manufacturer: God himself. Here's a vow all of us should make: From this day forward, I will choose God's food over man's food.

Diet:

☐ Upon rising, drink 8 oz. water mixed with 1.5 oz. unsweetened cranberry juice and 1 t. psyllium husk.

☐ Take multivitamin, Ester-C, EFAs.

☐ Drink sixty-four ounces of water throughout the day.

☐ Drink a protein shake, with 1 cup of frozen raspberries or strawberries mixed in, for breakfast.

---

[2]*www.atkins.com/Archive/2002/12/17–622198.html.*
[3]Gary Taubes, "What if it's all been a big fat lie?" *The New York Times Magazine,* as reprinted at *www.atkinscenter.com.*

☐ For lunch, have a salad with a palm-sized portion of healthy protein.
☐ Eat as many raw or steamed veggies as you can.
☐ Before retiring for the evening, drink 8 oz. water mixed with 1.5 oz. unsweetened cranberry juice and 1 t. psyllium husk.

Exercise:
☐ Walk briskly for thirty minutes.
☐ Optional: strength training.

DAY FORTY-FIVE	TODAY'S DATE

Scripture to memorize:

Do you not know that in a race all the runners run,
but only one gets the prize? Run in such a way as to get
the prize. Everyone who competes in the games goes into
strict training. They do it to get a crown that will not
last; but we do it to get a crown that will last forever.

1 CORINTHIANS 9:24–25

Passage to read:
Come, my children, listen to me;
I will teach you the fear of the Lord.
Whoever of you loves life
and desires to see many good days,
keep your tongue from evil
and your lips from speaking lies.
Turn from evil and do good;
seek peace and pursue it.

PSALM 34:11–14

Guided prayer:
Dear Lord, thank you again for the gift of life. For lungs that breathe and a heart that beats. Thank you for the beauty that surrounds me every day, from the

157

blue skies overhead to the grass below my feet. Thank you for loved ones who bring joy to my life. Lord, I've had my share of bad days like everyone else. My desire is to see many good days. I recognize I have a part to play in making that happen. Holy Spirit, set a guard over my tongue. Make me mindful of the words I speak . . . and even the words that pass through my head. Words are powerful. Lord, I want to be a peacemaker in all of my relationships. I desire and work toward peace within and around me. Empower me to cultivate harmony in all my relationships by being gracious, no matter how difficult the circumstances. Amen.

A prayer from your heart:

_____

_____

_____

_____

Affirmation to recite:

I desire and work toward peace within and around me. I cultivate harmony in all my relationships by being gracious, no matter how difficult the circumstances.

BASED ON PSALM 34:11–14

Action to take:

Congratulations! You've made it halfway through your ninety-day renewal. Take a moment to evaluate your progress. For each category, indicate how fully you are experiencing God's best, from 1 (meaning not at all, because you are in flat-out disobedience in this area and your life reflects it) to 10 (meaning you are walking in obedience in this area and enjoying tremendous blessings as a result).

Spiritual

Consistent quiet time	1 – – – – – 5 – – – – – 10
Prayerful (practice the presence of God)	1 – – – – – 5 – – – – – 10
Increasing in knowledge of the Scriptures	1 – – – – – 5 – – – – – 10
Routinely memorize and meditate on Scripture	1 – – – – – 5 – – – – – 10

Mental

Maintain a positive attitude	1 – – – – – 5 – – – – – 10
Read uplifting material	1 – – – – – 5 – – – – – 10
Regulate TV viewing	1 – – – – – 5 – – – – – 10
Learn something new on a regular basis	1 – – – – – 5 – – – – – 10

Emotional

Moods are stable, rather than up and down	1 – – – – – 5 – – – – – 10
Able to express and receive love	1 – – – – – 5 – – – – – 10
Listen carefully when others speak	1 – – – – – 5 – – – – – 10

Physical

Overall health is good	1 – – – – – 5 – – – – – 10
Weight is appropriate	1 – – – – – 5 – – – – – 10
Eating habits are well-balanced	1 – – – – – 5 – – – – – 10
Personal appearance is appealing	1 – – – – – 5 – – – – – 10

Relational

(evaluate the quality of each that is applicable)

Spouse	1 – – – – – 5 – – – – – 10
Children	1 – – – – – 5 – – – – – 10
Extended family	1 – – – – – 5 – – – – – 10
Church family	1 – – – – – 5 – – – – – 10
Neighbors	1 – – – – – 5 – – – – – 10
Friends	1 – – – – – 5 – – – – – 10
Co-workers	1 – – – – – 5 – – – – – 10
Strangers	1 – – – – – 5 – – – – – 10

Practical

Home is in good order	1 – – – – – 5 – – – – – 10
Car is in good order	1 – – – – – 5 – – – – – 10
Bills are paid on time	1 – – – – – 5 – – – – – 10
Obligations fulfilled on time (no procrastination)	1 – – – – – 5 – – – – – 10

Attitude adjustment:

This habit of uselessly wasting time is the whole difficulty; it is vastly important to you, and still more so to your children, that you should break the habit. It is more important to them, because they have longer to live, and can keep out of an idle habit before they are in it, easier than they can get out after they are in.

ABRAHAM LINCOLN

If you've made it this far, you are well on your way to establishing a whole new set of positive habits. These will benefit you and your children for years to come. Keep up the good work. We're almost there.

Diet:

☐ Upon rising, drink 8 oz. water mixed with 1.5 oz. unsweetened cranberry juice and 1 t. psyllium husk.

☐ Take multivitamin, Ester-C, EFAs.

☐ Drink sixty-four ounces of water throughout the day.

☐ Drink a protein shake, with 1 cup of frozen raspberries or strawberries mixed in, for breakfast.

☐ For lunch, have a salad with a palm-sized portion of healthy protein.

☐ Eat as many raw or steamed veggies as you can.

☐ Before retiring for the evening, drink 8 oz. water mixed with 1.5 oz. unsweetened cranberry juice and 1 t. psyllium husk.

Exercise:

☐ Bounce ten minutes.

☐ Walk briskly for thirty minutes.

☐ Optional: strength training.

Day Forty-six   Today's Date

Scripture to memorize:

> Therefore I do not run like a man running aimlessly;
> I do not fight like a man beating the air. No, I beat
> my body and make it my slave so that after I have preached
> to others, I myself will not be disqualified for the prize.

1 Corinthians 9:26–27

Passage to Read:

He does not treat us as our sins deserve
or repay us according to our iniquities.
For as high as the heavens are above the earth,
so great is his love for those who fear him;
as far as the east is from the west,
so far has he removed our transgressions from us.
As a father has compassion on his children,
so the Lord has compassion on those who fear him;
for he knows how we are formed,
he remembers that we are dust.
As for man, his days are like grass,
he flourishes like a flower of the field;
the wind blows over it and it is gone,
and its place remembers it no more.
But from everlasting to everlasting
the Lord's love is with those who fear him,
and his righteousness with their children's children—
with those who keep his covenant
and remember to obey his precepts.

Psalm 103:10–18

Guided prayer:

Dear Lord, I know that my time here on earth is brief, so I want to make the most of it. I thank you for your great love toward me. Help me to use my time wisely, so I can demonstrate that love to others. I want to care for my body, so I will have enough strength to teach and serve throughout my lifetime. I especially want my loved ones to remember me as an energetic example of how great a life spent serving God can be. I pray that my right choices would be a blessing to my children's children. I dream of the day when my grandchildren will come to know you and I will know I had a part in that. What a blessing!

Opportunities to make a difference surround me—at home, in my community, and around the world. Help me to keep my eyes off myself so I can see the needs of others. Lord, I dedicate myself to keeping your covenant and obeying your precepts. I know my obedience will bring joy to you and blessings to me and those I love. Thank you for your faithfulness. Amen.

A prayer from your heart:

_____

_____

_____

_____

Affirmation to recite:

I fill my mind with loving, positive thoughts concerning my family rather than mentally rehearsing their faults.

BASED ON PHILIPPIANS 4:8

Action to take:

If you have grandchildren, do something today to promote their spiritual growth. (Receiving a simple postcard in the mail, with a Bible verse included, will thrill most small children.) If you don't have grandchildren of your own, do something for someone else's grandchild.

Name of the child: _____

What you plan to do: _____

When you plan to do it: _____

Attitude adjustment:

> *Our obedience opens the door for God to lavish us*
> *with His boundless blessings.*

JAN MCCRAY

As you are faithful in the small things, like showing concern for others and seeking to promote the well-being of those in your circle of influence, you begin a cycle of blessing that takes on a life of its own. God is standing ready to shower you with blessings. One of those blessings is the joy of learning that you don't have to "get" anything to be blessed. Your greatest blessings may come simply from the realization that you are a blessing to others. The prosperity the Bible speaks of has little to do with cars and houses, and everything to do with your overall sense of happiness and well-being. That can come regardless of your material condition, as you focus your attention on God and others.

Diet:

- ☐ Upon rising, drink 8 oz. water mixed with 1.5 oz. unsweetened cranberry juice and 1 t. psyllium husk.
- ☐ Take multivitamin, Ester-C, EFAs.
- ☐ Drink sixty-four ounces of water throughout the day.
- ☐ Drink a protein shake, with 1 cup of frozen raspberries or strawberries mixed in, for breakfast.
- ☐ Eat two eggs sometime today.
- ☐ For lunch, have a salad with a palm-sized portion of healthy protein.
- ☐ Eat as many raw or steamed veggies as you can.
- ☐ Before retiring for the evening, drink 8 oz. water mixed with 1.5 oz. unsweetened cranberry juice and 1 t. psyllium husk.

Exercise:

- ☐ Bounce eleven minutes.
- ☐ Walk briskly for thirty minutes.
- ☐ Optional: strength training.

DAY FORTY-SEVEN	TODAY'S DATE

Scripture to memorize:

*Therefore I do not run like a man running aimlessly;
I do not fight like a man beating the air. No, I beat
my body and make it my slave so that after I have preached
to others, I myself will not be disqualified for the prize.*

1 CORINTHIANS 9:26–27

Passage to read:

Finally, be strong in the Lord and in his mighty power. Put on the full armor of God so that you can take your stand against the devil's schemes. For our struggle is not against flesh and blood, but against the rulers, against the authorities, against the powers of this dark world and against the spiritual forces of evil in the heavenly realms. Therefore put on the full armor of God, so that when the day of evil comes, you may be able to stand your ground, and after you have done everything, to stand. Stand firm then, with the belt of truth buckled around your waist, with the breastplate of righteousness in place, and with your feet fitted with the readiness that comes from the gospel of peace. In addition to all this, take up the shield of faith, with which you can extinguish all the flaming arrows of the evil one. Take the helmet of salvation and the sword of the Spirit, which is the word of God. And pray in the Spirit on all occasions with all kinds of prayers and requests. With this in mind, be alert and always keep on praying for all the saints.

EPHESIANS 6:10–18

Guided prayer:

Dear Lord, thank you for providing me with your full armor so that I can be protected against the attacks of the enemy. I admit sometimes I'm so foolish, I walk out onto the battlefield with my armor left on the sidelines. Then I wonder why I'm getting beaten so badly! You have made the provision, but it's up to me to put on the armor. Right now I put on the belt of truth and the breastplate of righteousness. My feet have been fitted with the gospel of peace. I take up the shield of faith and put on the helmet of salvation. Lord, thank you for teaching me how to use your Word as the sword of the Spirit so I can defeat the enemy.

Throughout today, I invite you to bring to my remembrance all those who are in need of prayer support. I am purposing in my heart, your grace enabling me, to walk through this day in a spirit of prayer, practicing your presence at all times and in all my affairs. Amen.

A prayer from your heart:

_____

_____

_____

_____

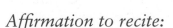

Affirmation to recite:

I live my life in a spirit of prayer, practicing the presence of God at all times and in all my affairs.

BASED ON EPHESIANS 6:10–18

Action to take:

Put on your armor today and *keep* it on! Find articles of clothing (or household items) to symbolize each piece of armor. You might want to put them on and have someone take your photograph. Then you can use it as a bookmark for this book or your Bible.

Attitude Adjustment:

> *No Christian is greater than his prayer life.*

LEONARD RAVENHILL

My friend Sandra says her mother is truly a hero. She served as a single overseas missionary in Asia until her early thirties, when she met and married Sandra's father. He passed away several years ago, and since then she has devoted herself full time to prayer. Other than basic household chores and weekly errands, she prays. Period. Sandra says that when you walk into her mother's house, the air is so thick with prayer—not to mention the power and presence of God—you can literally feel it.

What a sharp contrast this sixty-something woman is to so many others her age. I live in Arizona, so I see lots of retired folks. A depressing number of them seem to be reliving their teenage years—trying to cast off as many responsibilities as possible so they can maintain a comfortable, carefree existence. And still others sit mindlessly in front of a television set all day. Then there are the spiritual giants who—down on their knees—form the pillars of every church in America. Which type of senior citizen do you want to become? Pick your path now . . . because you are likely to stay on it. I want to be like Sandra's mom. How about you?

Diet:

- [ ] Upon rising, drink 8 oz. water mixed with 1.5 oz. unsweetened cranberry juice and 1 t. psyllium husk.
- [ ] Take multivitamin, Ester-C, EFAs.
- [ ] Drink sixty-four ounces of water throughout the day.
- [ ] Drink a protein shake, with 1 cup of frozen raspberries or strawberries mixed in, for breakfast.
- [ ] Eat two eggs sometime today.
- [ ] For lunch, have a salad with a palm-sized portion of healthy protein.
- [ ] Eat as many raw or steamed veggies as you can.

☐ Before retiring for the evening, drink 8 oz. water mixed with 1.5 oz. unsweetened cranberry juice and 1 t. psyllium husk.

Exercise:
☐ Bounce eleven minutes.
☐ Walk briskly for thirty minutes.
☐ Optional: strength training.

DAY FORTY-EIGHT	TODAY'S DATE

Scripture to memorize:
Therefore I do not run like a man running aimlessly;
I do not fight like a man beating the air. No, I beat
my body and make it my slave so that after I have preached
to others, I myself will not be disqualified for the prize.

1 CORINTHIANS 9:26–27

Passage to read:
When they saw the courage of Peter and John and realized that they were *unschooled, ordinary men, they were astonished and they took note that these men had been with Jesus.*

ACTS 4:13

Guided prayer:
Dear Lord, I want to have the courage of Peter and John. When people look at my life and realize there is nothing spectacular in me—other than the presence of the living God, that is—I want them to be astonished. I want it to be evident to all that everything good that happens in my life and through my life is because I walk with you. After I talk with people, I want them to take note that I have been with Jesus. Amen.

A prayer from your heart:

_____

_____

_____

_____

Affirmation to recite:

I am not easily provoked. Instead, I give other people the benefit of the doubt, knowing others are probably doing the best they can.

BASED ON 1 CORINTHIANS 13

Action to take:

Today as you interact with people, take note of whom you think they spend their time with. (Don't pass judgment. Just take note!) If they talk about their new boyfriend or their kids, that's whom they spend time with. If they talk about other people, they spend time with gossips. (Beware, by the way, because gossips who gossip *to* you will always gossip *about* you.) If they talk about the latest reality television show, you know they spend time with their TV. If they talk about their latest ordeal, they spend too much time with themselves! If they don't talk about the Lord, you can safely assume they're probably not spending much time with him.

Okay, now for the challenging part. Based on your conversations on a typical day, who would people conclude you spend your time with? Give an honest answer:

_____

Attitude adjustment:

Nothing betrays the condition of your heart
as readily as the words you speak.

JAN MCCRAY

168

I'm not sure if it's fair or unfair, but all a human being has to do is open his or her mouth and the whole planet instantly has a pretty good idea of what goes on in the deepest part of that person's soul. Now, if you are neglecting your soul, this is very bad news indeed. I recently read a book that said you can gauge whether or not a person's emotional health is ailing with a few simple conversational cues.[4] Although you should normally devote your conversation time listening to the other person, you might conduct a little research this next week by listening to *yourself.* You can also reflect back upon recent conversations. To gauge the condition of your soul, ask yourself the following questions:

1. Do I interrupt other people or do I allow them to finish their thoughts? Even the seemingly innocent act of "finishing other people's sentences" may actually reflect a soul that wants to show off.
2. Do you really look at people, eyeball-to-eyeball, when speaking? Or do you look everywhere else instead? My first strategy for evaluating someone's trustworthiness is whether or not he/she will look me in the eye. Most people feel the same way, although they may come to that determination subconsciously.
3. Do your conversations include a balanced flow of words back and forth? Dominating conversations *and* refusing to engage (excessive shyness) both reflect a soul that's more concerned with self than others.
4. Do you discuss a range of topics or consistently fixate on one issue? Obviously, "harping" on any negative topic is a troubling indicator. However, even talking constantly about pleasant subjects—your children or grandchildren, your favorite hobby—can indicate an unhealthy soul if it's the *only* thing you talk about.
5. While a range of topics is healthy, abruptly changing subjects is not. If your conversation partners get exhausted trying to keep up with you, that's a sure indicator that you are more concerned with amusing yourself than ministering to them.

Please don't misunderstand. I'm not saying everyone has to have the same conversational style. How boring would that be! God made each of us with a unique personality—some of us are more introverted, others are pure extroverts. There's no need to put on an act, trying to be someone you're not. However, God

---

[4]Adapted from *Date or Soul Mate?* by Neil Clark Warren (Nashville: Thomas Nelson, 2002).

will give you the grace to become more balanced, more gracious, more attentive to the needs of others. He can help you become the woman you want to be!

Diet:

- ☐ Upon rising, drink 8 oz. water mixed with 1.5 oz. unsweetened cranberry juice and 1 t. psyllium husk.
- ☐ Take multivitamin, Ester-C, EFAs.
- ☐ Drink sixty-four ounces of water throughout the day.
- ☐ Drink a protein shake, with 1 cup of frozen raspberries or strawberries mixed in, for breakfast.
- ☐ Eat two eggs sometime today.
- ☐ For lunch, have a salad with a palm-sized portion of healthy protein.
- ☐ Eat as many raw or steamed veggies as you can.
- ☐ Before retiring for the evening, drink 8 oz. water mixed with 1.5 oz. unsweetened cranberry juice and 1 t. psyllium husk.

Exercise:

- ☐ Bounce twelve minutes.
- ☐ Walk briskly for thirty minutes.
- ☐ Optional: strength training.

Scripture to memorize:

Therefore I do not run like a man running aimlessly; I do not fight like a man beating the air. No, I beat my body and make it my slave so that after I have preached to others, I myself will not be disqualified for the prize.

1 CORINTHIANS 9:26–27

Passage to read:

Find rest, O my soul, in God alone;
my hope comes from him.
He alone is my rock and my salvation;
he is my fortress, I will not be shaken.
My salvation and my honor depend on God;
he is my mighty rock, my refuge.
Trust in him at all times, O people;
pour out your hearts to him,
for God is our refuge.

PSALM 62:5–8

Guided prayer:

Dear Lord, I confess my tendency to try to figure everything out. I try to reason my way through my problems and develop my own solutions. My head spins as I try to sort through all the details and "play out" every possible outcome in my mind. Yet so often my clever ideas just make a bigger mess. I get all stressed out planning tomorrow, when all you've asked me to do is be faithful today. Help me to let it all go. To surrender forever the crazy notion that I can control my circumstances. Instead, let me rest securely in the knowledge that you are in control. I desire to leave behind emotional turmoil and find my rest in you. Lord, I want you to be my rock and my fortress. That solid place I can run to; that safe *place where nothing can harm me. I know that as I learn to trust completely in you, I will never be shaken. Amen.*

A prayer from your heart:

Dear Father, I am so thankful for your peace & grace. Help me to remember that whenever I feel that panicky feeling that means "I am out of control" that I can just give it to you and find calmness and rest in you and your amazing love! Amen!

Affirmation to recite:

I trust in the Lord with all my heart, rather than trying to figure things out for myself. I know he has everything figured out already.

BASED ON PROVERBS 3:5–6

Action to take:

Make a list of five things you cannot control but that you allow to upset you anyway. (Weather would be a good example.) One by one, surrender them to God, saying, "God, I know I am not in control of _____. I trust you with _____."

1. _____

2. _____

3. _____

4. _____

5. _____

Attitude adjustment:
He who kneels before God can stand before anyone.

UNKNOWN

My pastor began a recent sermon by announcing, "I'm not God . . . and neither are you." On the surface, that seems like an obvious statement. But if we really believed we weren't little gods, we would stop trying to rule the universe. God alone is in control. We cannot control our circumstances. We cannot control other people—not how they act or how they react to us. All we can control is ourselves—and most of us have a tough time doing that! However, as God brings wholeness to your soul, you will find it easier and easier to find contentment in any circumstance. Just *be* and let everyone else be, too!

Diet:
☐ Free day—eat whatever you can.

Exercise:
☐ Bounce twelve minutes.
☐ Walk briskly for thirty minutes.
☐ Optional: strength training.

Week 8

Scripture to memorize:

Therefore I do not run like a man running aimlessly;
I do not fight like a man beating the air. No, I beat
my body and make it my slave so that after I have preached
to others, I myself will not be disqualified for the prize.

1 CORINTHIANS 9:26–27

Passage to read:

The righteous cry out, and the Lord hears them;
he delivers them from all their troubles.
The Lord is close to the brokenhearted
and saves those who are crushed in spirit.
A righteous man may have many troubles,
but the Lord delivers him from them all;

PSALM 34:17–19

Guided prayer:

Dear Lord, I want to be a fighter in the best sense of that word. I want to be the kind of Christian who stays in the arena of life, giving it my very best shot. No matter what the Enemy may throw my way, I want to come out a winner. But I know that will involve incredible Holy Spirit-infused determination. I can't run through life aimlessly, like so many people who are in a great big hurry to get nowhere. I can't do whatever I feel like doing and expect to get the victory.

I will have to beat my body and make it my slave. That will mean setting the alarm a little earlier so I can spend time with you. It will mean forcing myself to get up and take a walk when I'd rather sit on the couch. Beating my body will mean saying a hearty "No" to potato chips and an enthusiastic "Yes" to vegetables. But, Lord, I know it will be worth it. Nothing could be worse than to preach to my friends and family about the joys of serving you . . . then crash and *burn because I neglected my body. If I get knocked out of this race for a season, I'll get back in. But I sure don't want to disqualify myself for the prize by indulging my sensual nature rather than subduing it.*

Holy Spirit, I invite you to convict me at any moment you catch me indulging myself rather than "beating my body." Remind me that my body is here to serve me; I am not here to serve my body! Amen.

A prayer from your heart:

_____

_____

_____

_____

Affirmation to recite:

I enjoy meditating on God's Word. It's such a blessing to have God's word in my mouth—to be able to speak a word in due season to those who are weary or discouraged.

BASED ON PSALM 1:2

Action to take:

Contrast what your body "feels like" doing with what it "should" be doing. Then determine to "beat your body" until it learns to do what it is supposed to be doing! Be as specific as possible, commenting on various times of day.

	Feel like	Should do
Morning	_____	_____
Lunch	_____	_____
Afternoon	_____	_____

Dinner	_____	_____
Early evening	_____	_____
Before bed	watching TV	_____

Attitude adjustment:

> *Don't believe all you hear, spend all you have or sleep all you want.*

JACKSON BROWN AND H. JACKSON BROWN, JR.

Have you ever noticed how oversleeping can leave you feeling more lethargic than not getting enough sleep? Or have you noticed how exhausted you can become just sitting, doing nothing? In contrast, think how energized you feel when you get out and *do* something. We need to recognize that our bodies don't always tell us the truth. Our bodies say, "I'm tired. I've had a tough day. Give me a doughnut and let's sit on the couch watching TV. That's all I can do." That's the moment you should fight back. "No, tired body. We're going to *get up*, drink some water, and take a walk around the block. I'm the brain in this operation, and I happen to know I'll feel a whole lot better once I get out of the house and get you moving."

Your body is a tool to serve you. Don't let your body turn into a tyrant, determining what you can and cannot do. Flesh and bone don't deserve that much power. You're supposed to be in charge, so take charge!

Diet:

- ☐ Upon rising, drink 8 oz. water mixed with 1.5 oz. unsweetened cranberry juice and 1 t. psyllium husk, followed by warm lemon water.
- ☐ Take multivitamin, Ester-C, EFAs.
- ☐ Drink sixty-four ounces of water throughout the day.
- ☐ Eat two eggs sometime today.
- ☐ Have a salad with your lunch.
- ☐ Eat as many raw or steamed veggies as you can.
- ☐ At 8 P.M. drink a cup of lemon water.

Exercise:

- ☐ Bounce thirteen minutes.

☐ Walk briskly for thirty minutes.
☐ Optional: strength training.

DAY FIFTY-ONE   **TODAY'S DATE**

Scripture to memorize:

Set your minds on things above, not on earthly things. For you died, and your life is now hidden with Christ in God. When Christ, who is your life, appears, then you also will appear with him in glory.

COLOSSIANS 3:2–4

Passage to read:

This day I call heaven and earth as witnesses against you that I have set before you life and death, blessings and curses. Now choose life, so that you and your children may live and that you may love the Lord your God, listen to his voice, and hold fast to him.

DEUTERONOMY 30:19–20

Guided prayer:

Dear Lord, thank you for giving me the power to choose. I know it is an awesome responsibility. I don't always take it seriously. Sometimes I live like I believe the right path will just drop out of heaven down onto my lap. You desire to bless me, but in order for me to receive your blessing, I must walk in obedience. Lord, you have urged me to choose wisely for my sake and the sake of my children.

My heart's desire is to love you with all my heart, listen to your voice, and hold fast to you. My spirit is completely willing, but sometimes my flesh is weak. Holy Spirit, strengthen me with power in my inner being, so that I might choose wisely and walk worthy. Amen.

A prayer from your heart:

_____

_____

_____

_____

Affirmation to recite:

I realize self-control is a marvelous fruit of the Holy Spirit, so I actively seek to cultivate it in my life. My life is so much better when I practice self-control, rather than living by impulse.

BASED ON GALATIANS 5:22–23

Action to take:

What are some choices you face every day? List the choices you should make and the choices you typically make. Ideally, you'll have two identical lists. Realistically, you'll see you have some work to do. Just to get you started, I've listed the first choice all of us must make!

Choice to be made

Stay in bed or wake up early

Typical choice

Stay in bed

_____   _____

_____   _____

_____   _____

_____   _____

_____   _____

Attitude adjustment:

The will has only one mode of action: its function is to choose, and with every choice we make we grow in force of character. "Choose ye this day," is the command that comes to each of us in every affair and on every day of our lives, and the business of the will is to choose. But choice, the effort of decision, is a heavy labor, whether it be between two lovers or two gowns. So, many people minimize this labor by following the [latest] fashion in their clothes, rooms, reading, amusements, the pictures they admire and the friends they select. We are zealous in choosing for others but shirk the responsibility of decision for ourselves.

CHARLOTTE MASON[1]

Whether you like to admit it or not, who you are right now is largely the sum of the daily choices you've been making for many years. The good news is, as you begin to make different choices, your life will begin the transformation process. The woman you want to be will begin to emerge. Be encouraged!

Diet:
- [ ] Upon rising, drink 8 oz. water mixed with 1.5 oz. unsweetened cranberry juice and 1 t. psyllium husk, followed by warm lemon water.
- [ ] Take multivitamin, Ester-C, EFAs.
- [ ] Drink sixty-four ounces of water throughout the day.
- [ ] Eat two eggs sometime today.
- [ ] Have a salad with your lunch.
- [ ] Eat as many raw or steamed veggies as you can.
- [ ] At 8 P.M. drink a cup of lemon water.

Exercise:
- [ ] Bounce thirteen minutes.
- [ ] Walk briskly for thirty minutes.
- [ ] Optional: strength training.

---

[1]Mason, *A Philosophy of Education*, 129–130.

Scripture to memorize:

Set your minds on things above, not on earthly things. For you died, and your life is now hidden with Christ in God. When Christ, who is your life, appears, then you also will appear with him in glory.

COLOSSIANS 3:2–4

Passage to read:

But you, O Lord, are a compassionate and gracious God,
slow to anger, abounding in love and faithfulness.
Turn to me and have mercy on me;
grant your strength to your servant.

PSALM 86:15–16

Guided prayer:

Dear Lord, I thank you for being a compassionate and gracious God. Where would I be if you were not slow to anger, abounding in love and faithfulness? If you counted my sins against me, I would have been cast from your presence long ago. Lord, I ask you to turn to me and have mercy toward me, as I desire to turn my heart toward you and live in the light of your mercy and grace. Grant me your strength so that I might live a life of fruitful service for your Kingdom. Amen.

A prayer from your heart:

_____

_____

_____

_____

Affirmation to recite:

   I believe God's Word rather than what I might believe by looking at my circumstances. Circumstances can deceive me, but God's Word never will.

BASED ON PROVERBS 4:20–22

Action to take:

   Review yesterday's choices and make a decision to apply the power of your will to make changes in at least one area that will significantly impact the well-being of your spirit, soul, or body. What one decision, what one change, are you absolutely committed to making? Write out your commitment and date it.

_____

_____

_____

Attitude adjustment:

   There are two services open to us all, the service of God,
   and the service of self.

CHARLOTTE MASON[2]

_____

[2]Ibid., 135.

When we say that God has "given us a free will,"[3] we are referring to that portion of our soul that is responsible for making our daily choices. The command "Choose ye this day" applies to the people you allow into your life, into your home, onto your TV and computer screens, and into your minds. It applies to the way you spend your time, the food you put into your mouth, and the way you spend your money. God sets the choices before you, but you must make the right one.

It's like taking a multiple-choice exam:

When living your life on earth, you can either:
    a. Choose life
    b. Choose death
    c. Refuse to make any choices (which is, in itself, a choice)
    d. Go back and forth between *a* and *b*.

Of course, while you're taking this particular exam, God is standing there the entire time saying, "The correct answer is *a*."

Diet:

- ☐ Upon rising, drink 8 oz. water mixed with 1.5 oz. unsweetened cranberry juice and 1 t. psyllium husk, followed by warm lemon water.
- ☐ Take multivitamin, Ester-C, EFAs.
- ☐ Drink sixty-four ounces of water throughout the day.
- ☐ Eat two eggs sometime today.
- ☐ Have a salad with your lunch.
- ☐ Eat as many raw or steamed veggies as you can.
- ☐ At 8 P.M. drink a cup of lemon water.

Exercise:

- ☐ Walk briskly for thirty minutes.
- ☐ Optional: strength training.

---

[3]This phrase does not appear anywhere in Scripture, so I use it with caution. Nevertheless, I think it is a helpful term when used in the context of accepting our personal responsibility to make wise choices.

Scripture to memorize:

Set your minds on things above, not on earthly things. For you died, and your life is now hidden with Christ in God. When Christ, who is your life, appears, then you also will appear with him in glory.

COLOSSIANS 3:2–4

Passage to read:

The earth is the Lord's, and everything in it,
    the world, and all who live in it;
for he founded it upon the seas
    and established it upon the waters.
Who may ascend the hill of the Lord?
    Who may stand in his holy place?
He who has clean hands and a pure heart,
    who does not lift up his soul to an idol
    or swear by what is false.
He will receive blessing from the Lord
    and vindication from God his Savior.
Such is the generation of those who seek him,
    who seek your face, O God of Jacob.

PSALM 24:1–6

Guided prayer:

Dear Lord, the earth is yours. It's not like you need anything I might give you. You don't need my time or money. You've created everything and everyone. But not everyone can approach you—only those whose hands and hearts have been cleansed. Thank you, for I know I have been cleansed in Jesus' name. When I stand before you, you see me arrayed in garments of salvation and righteousness—not stained with sin. I turn my mind, will, and emotions away from idols, *away from anything that might take greater importance in my life than you. I desire your blessing. I thank you for vindicating me. You set me free from shame, guilt, and suspicion; therefore I seek your face and enter your throne room with confidence. Amen.*

A prayer from your heart:

_____

_____

_____

_____

Affirmation to recite:

I love giving because I know that in the same measure I give, it will be given back to me—good measure, pressed down, shaken together, and running over.

BASED ON LUKE 6:38

Action to take:

Get a realistic handle on what size you should be wearing. Set a goal to fill your closet with that size and give everything else away. It may take you a while to get back to your ideal weight, but once you've achieved it, ask God for a holy determination to stay there. Giving away your wrong-size clothing—and absolutely refusing to buy the next size up—is one way to keep yourself motivated. Then use the money you would have spent on a multiple-size wardrobe and give it to people who don't even have a one-size wardrobe.

According to Carrie Carter, M.D., "Since women come in all shapes and sizes, the ideal weight is different for every woman. Most of us have a good idea of the weight range that is right for us, but there is a more scientific way to calculate it (and some big health benefits if we stay in that healthy weight range). This scientific way to calculate our best weight is called the Body Mass Index (BMI)."[4] You can quickly calculate your BMI at the following Web site: *www. nhlbisupport.com/bmi/bmicalc.htm.*

What is your ideal size? _____   Healthy weight? _____

Attitude adjustment:

"Today Christians spend more money on dog food than missions."

LEONARD RAVENHILL

Each year, in late winter or early spring, I set out on my annual "retreat season" tour of churches around the country. By the end of spring, when my travels are over, I have inevitably put on some additional weight. (Church ladies just love to feed their guest speaker, don't you know?) Sure enough, this year was no different. By the time I finished my travels, I was ten pounds heavier than when I began. I have a small frame, so that is a significant amount of weight for me. In fact, it represents almost a two-size jump! As a result, most of my "stage clothes" no longer fit. When I mentioned this predicament to one of my girl friends, she casually suggested that I simply buy new clothes in a larger size. That's certainly a practical solution, and to be honest, like most women in America, I have some clothes in my closet in a variety of sizes. What I would have needed, however, was a whole new travel wardrobe. So I turned to my girlfriend and said, "This isn't about clothes. It's about stewardship. I used the money God entrusted to me to buy all of these clothes. Now it's my responsibility to make the most of what he's already provided."

I'm not trying to make anyone feel bad, and I do think we need to be realistic. As we age, it may be inevitable that we will wear somewhat larger sizes. It is okay to give away all those size 7/8s you wore in college. What I think is not okay is to constantly buy new clothes simply because we don't want to "beat our bodies" back into the appropriate size. Find the right size for you and stick with it, no matter what it takes.

---

[4]Carrie Carter, *Thrive!* (Minneapolis, MN: Bethany House Publishers, 2002), 86.

Body

Diet:

- ☐ Upon rising, drink 8 oz. water mixed with 1.5 oz. unsweetened cranberry juice and 1 t. psyllium husk, followed by warm lemon water.
- ☐ Take multivitamin, Ester-C, EFAs.
- ☐ Drink sixty-four ounces of water throughout the day.
- ☐ Eat two eggs sometime today.
- ☐ Have a salad with your lunch.
- ☐ Eat as many raw or steamed veggies as you can.
- ☐ At 8 P.M. drink a cup of lemon water.

Exercise:

- ☐ Bounce fourteen minutes.
- ☐ Walk briskly for thirty minutes.
- ☐ Optional: strength training.

DAY FIFTY-FOUR	TODAY'S DATE

Spirit

Scripture to memorize:

Set your minds on things above, not on earthly things. For you died, and your life is now hidden with Christ in God. When Christ, who is your life, appears, then you also will appear with him in glory.

COLOSSIANS 3:2–4

Passage to read:

Whatever is true, whatever is noble, whatever is right, whatever is pure, whatever is lovely, whatever is admirable—if anything is excellent or praiseworthy—

think about such things. Whatever you have learned or received or heard from me, or seen in me—put it into practice. And the God of peace will be with you.

PHILIPPIANS 4:8–9

Guided prayer:

Dear Lord, thank you for all the wonderful things you have brought into my life. I know there is trouble and sorrow in this world. But there is also much that is true, noble, right, pure, lovely, and admirable. When I look closely, I see much that is excellent and praiseworthy. Therefore I choose to think about such things. I will focus my energy on living as you would have me to live and let you handle the rest. Thank you for the peace that comes when I trust in you. Amen.

A prayer from your heart:

_____

_____

_____

_____

Affirmation to recite:

The more I fill my mind with "whatever is true, noble, excellent, and praiseworthy," the less room there will be in my mind for negative thoughts. Therefore I choose to think about such things.

BASED ON PHILIPPIANS 4:8–9

Action to take:

List five positive things worth thinking about:

1. _____

2. _____

3. _____

4. _____

5. _____

Attitude adjustment:

If we have a negative mind, we will have a negative life. Your life will not get straightened out until your mind does.

JOYCE MEYER

When we choose to think right thoughts, we experience God's peace. Our emotions settle down. The Amplified Bible expounds upon this passage very effectively. It says you should "fix your mind." Have you ever met someone who was fixated upon something? My older daughter is fixated upon horses. It's her only topic of discussion. Her room is filled with horse paraphernalia, from posters and statues to bedspreads and paintings. Her clothes are splattered with horses. Her school notebooks all have horses on the cover and horse bookmarks inside. Yesterday she saw an advertisement for horse towels and washcloths for her bathroom. When her birthday or Christmas rolls around, everyone knows what to give Leah: horse stuff! Well, you get the idea.

Are you *that* fixated on all that's right in your life and in the world? Or are you fixated on what's wrong? You can fixate on what's right and be happy, or you can fixate on what's wrong and be miserable. The choice is yours. Of course, the best thing to fixate on is the character and goodness of God.

The word peace in this passage means "untroubled, undisturbed well-being" (AMP). Well-being. Yes, that's our goal. Emotional well-being. Wouldn't you love to be able to say, as the hymn writer of old, "it is well with my soul"? To live a life where your emotions are untroubled and undisturbed, no matter what is happening in your outward circumstances? If you answered yes, the key is to choose your thoughts carefully.

Diet:
- ☐ Upon rising, drink 8 oz. water mixed with 1.5 oz. unsweetened cranberry juice and 1 t. psyllium husk, followed by warm lemon water.
- ☐ Take multivitamin, Ester-C, and EFAs.
- ☐ Drink sixty-four ounces of water throughout the day.
- ☐ Eat two eggs sometime today.
- ☐ Have a salad with your lunch.
- ☐ Eat as many raw or steamed veggies as you can.
- ☐ At 8 P.M. drink a cup of lemon water.

Exercise:
- ☐ Walk briskly for thirty minutes.
- ☐ Optional: strength training.

DAY FIFTY-FIVE	TODAY'S DATE

Scripture to memorize:
Set your minds on things above, not on earthly things. For you died, and your life is now hidden with Christ in God. When Christ, who is your life, appears, then you also will appear with him in glory.

COLOSSIANS 3:2–4

Passage to read:
Their destiny is destruction, their god is their stomach, and their glory is in their shame. Their mind is on earthly things.

PHILIPPIANS 3:19

Guided prayer:

Dear Lord, I confess that I have allowed my stomach to be my god in the past. It has decided my priorities. It has controlled my mood and attitude. It has had a profound effect on the way I treat my loved ones. It has hindered my ability to think clearly and function at my best. Rather than being controlled by the Spirit, as the scripture commands, I have been controlled by the demands of my stomach. Forgive me, Lord. I know the world—even the church—winks at the sin of gluttony. But you take it seriously because it causes me to be less than I am. I want to be all you created me to be. Help me to keep my mind on earthly things. Amen.

A prayer from your heart:

Help me to turn to (you) every time I think of eating sweets! Instead of craving sugar I crave You, dear Heavenly Father! Instead of filling my body with poisonous sugar I want to fill my body & soul with the goodness of your love! ♡ xoxo ♡

Affirmation to recite:

I am controlled by the Spirit, not by my taste buds.

BASED ON ROMANS 8:6

Action to take:

Select one food you truly *love.* . . . and give it up for the next ten days. Name that food: SUGAR

Dates you will "fast" from that food: From Feb. 17 '05 to Feb. 26 '05. Mark your calendar so you won't forget your commitment.

Every time I think of having a sweet I will instead pray to God for a taste of His sweetness!

190

Attitude adjustment:

*A recent study found that dieters who ate two eggs a day for six weeks
lost weight without exception, especially around the waist.*

ANN LOUISE GITTLEMAN

Did you know that the liver is your body's key organ for fat burning? That's why eating cleansing foods, designed to detoxify the liver, is the highest priority in the diet portion of your ninety-day renewal. "Among the liver's 400-plus known functions, many are crucial to maintaining a healthy weight," according to Dr. Ann Louise Gittleman. "The liver is largely responsible for breaking down fat. It also filters away impurities that cause fluid retention."[5]

An overloaded liver cannot process fat properly; therefore it stores it just under the skin. That's what causes that roll of fat at your waistline. A poorly functioning liver cannot control blood sugar, leading to hypoglycemia and intense sugar cravings. Unfiltered toxins may linger in your bloodstream, draining you of energy and promoting the appearance of cellulite.

"Eggs are the single richest source of sulfur-bearing amino acids which play a vital role in the liver's ability to produce bile, the substance that breaks down fat. A recent study found that dieters who ate two eggs a day for six weeks lost weight without exception, especially around the waist." In addition, eggs are high in protein, and protein has been found to raise the metabolism by 25 percent.[6]

Now you know why I have been encouraging you to eat a couple of eggs each day.

Diet:

- [ ] Upon rising, drink 8 oz. water mixed with 1.5 oz. unsweetened cranberry juice and 1 t. psyllium husk, followed by warm lemon water.
- [ ] Take multivitamin, Ester-C, EFAs.
- [ ] Drink sixty-four ounces of water throughout the day.
- [ ] Eat two eggs sometime today.
- [ ] Have a salad with your lunch.

---

[5]Ann Louise Gittleman, *The Fat Flush Plan,* 13.
[6]Ibid, 4.

☐ Eat as many raw or steamed veggies as you can.
☐ At 8 P.M. drink a cup of lemon water.

Exercise:
☐ Bounce fourteen minutes.
☐ Walk briskly for thirty minutes.
☐ Optional: strength training.

DAY FIFTY-SIX	TODAY'S DATE

Scripture to memorize:

I sought the Lord, and he answered me;
he delivered me from all my fears.
Those who look to him are radiant;
their faces are never covered with shame.

PSALM 34:4–5

Passage to read:

Be strong and courageous, because you will lead these people to inherit the land I swore to their forefathers to give them. Be strong and very courageous. Be careful to obey all the law my servant Moses gave you; do not turn from it to the right or to the left, that you may be successful wherever you go. Do not let this Book of the Law depart from your mouth; meditate on it day and night, so that you may be careful to do everything written in it. Then you will be prosperous and successful. Have I not commanded you? Be strong and courageous. Do not be terrified; do not be discouraged, for the Lord your God will be with you wherever you go.

JOSHUA 1:6–9

Guided prayer:

Dear Lord, you have commanded me to be strong. I confess that, many times in the past, I have allowed my spirit, soul, and body to weaken from neglect.

Thank you for never giving up on me. Thank you for giving me the strength to make it this far through my ninety-day renewal. I really am seeing the woman I want to be emerge, and it is so exciting. Lord, I want to obey your Word. It has been such a joy to practice meditating on your Word each day. I feel myself prospering in so many areas of my life. Thank you for helping me to overcome the discouragement that once dragged me down. I am encouraged and excited to move forward with the remainder of my ninety-day journey. Your grace enabling, I am going to make it! Amen.

A prayer from your heart:

Dear Father, thank you for being there for me wherever I go. I pray that I will be courageous this week and strong, without fear.

Affirmation to recite:

I am richly blessed. I am not missing out on anything. I enjoy every spiritual blessing!

BASED ON EPHESIANS 1:3

Action to Take

Did you know a significant body of nutritional evidence exists indicating that any food you eat on a daily basis may be, to *your* body at least, an allergen or addiction? According to my former neighbor, Dr. Allan Spreen—the now famous Nutrition Physician™ and Olympic diving coach—this is particularly true of various carbohydrates. The top six "offending foods" are milk, wheat, corn, eggs, citrus and sugar.[7] Another obvious addiction is caffeine in the form of soda,

---

[7]Allan Spreen, *Nutritionally Incorrect*, (Pleasant Grove, Utah: Woodland Publishing, 1999), 170.

coffee, or tea. I'm not a scientist, but the most logical explanation is that God designed our bodies to digest a wide variety of foods. When we consume too much of the same thing, day after day, year after year, our body becomes overloaded and contaminated. In essence, our body screams, "Enough already! Give me something *else* to eat." What is contaminating you? Make a list of any foods you eat *every day*. (Be sure to include coffee, tea, cereal, cookies, etc.)

sugar
coffee
dairy
wheat

Great. Now for the tough part. Dr. Spreen recommends you eliminate those items for an entire week. (If getting rid of all of them seems too drastic, pick one or two at a time to eliminate.) Don't be surprised if, at first, your body revolts in the form of cravings, headaches, irritability, etc. You may have formed an addiction to those daily food items. Be strong. Have courage. You'll live through it . . . and you might just have an eye-opening experience, toward the *end* of the week, when your mood improves and your energy level ultimately goes through the roof. You don't have to eliminate anything permanently if you don't want to; this is just an experiment to determine food items that may be contaminating you. It's possible that you'll feel so much better, you may decide to limit your intake of certain foods.

Attitude adjustment:

> *"Research tells us that fourteen out of any ten individuals like chocolate."*

SANDRA BOYNTON

You can live without all kinds of things! Did you know that? It's true. I didn't think I could live without Oreos, but let me tell you a little secret. For the past week, there has been a bag of DoubleStuf Oreos on the premises and I have not eaten even one! Anyone who knows me will tell you that's no small miracle. I am truly an Oreo addict. At one point I was actually alone in the kitchen—just me and the Oreos. Still I stood firm.

Let me tell you why I think that is so. I determined that carbohydrates of all varieties were "contaminating" me because I've been overeating them for years. So I went cold turkey. Yep, just completely eliminated them for an entire week. I

194

even went cold turkey from my coffee habit. And with each passing day, it got easier and easier to live without them. My body is breaking through the addiction. Isn't it amazing how wonderfully God created our bodies? Often they can heal themselves if we will just cooperate.

Anyway, I share that story as an encouragement to you. Purify your body and see how much better you feel.

Diet:
☐ Free day—eat whatever you like.

Exercise:
☐ Rest.

Week 9

Scripture to memorize:

I sought the Lord, and he answered me;
he delivered me from all my fears.
Those who look to him are radiant;
their faces are never covered with shame.

PSALM 34:4–5

Passage to read:

It is not good to eat too much honey, nor is it honorable to seek one's own honor. Like a city whose walls are broken down is a man who lacks self-control.

PROVERBS 25:27–28

Guided prayer:

Dear Lord, once more I offer my body as a living sacrifice to you. Thank you for providing something sweet (honey!) for my taste buds to enjoy. I confess that I've sometimes allowed my desire for sweets to spiral out of control and that I've chosen the world's cheap substitute (processed sugar) to take the place of your provision. My body has paid the price as a result. Your Word clearly says it is not good to consume too many sweets. Forgive me for my disobedience. I recognize the need to exercise self-control in this area. Otherwise, my body is unprotected. The walls of my immune system break down and disease can easily come in to wreak havoc. Lord, I ask for your mercy. Restore my body to health as I begin to obey your Word in the area of my eating habits. Holy Spirit, empower me with the fruit of self-control as I gradually incorporate lifestyle changes over the coming weeks and months. Amen.

A prayer from your heart:

_____

_____

_____

_____

Affirmation to recite:

Tough times will either make me bitter or better. I choose to learn my life lessons, rather than resenting or resisting them, so I will become a better person.

BASED ON HEBREWS 12:15

Action to take:

Today, begin a daily cleansing ritual that I hope you will continue throughout your life: drinking a small amount of apple cider vinegar.

Attitude adjustment:

Raw honey is packed with enzymes, minerals, vitamins, and other things unique to honey, many of which have been revered for centuries, much longer than most of our miracle drugs.

DR. ALLAN SPREEN

Were you aware that too much sugar breaks down your immune system? Even those statements in the Bible that appear metaphorical turn out to be literally true. If you don't exercise self-control in your consumption of sweets, your body is just like an unprotected city. The walls of your defense system are broken down, opening the way for colds and flus, not to mention hypoglycemia, diabetes, and weight gain leading to heart disease. Once again we see that every word in the Bible was written for our benefit, not to spoil our fun. You should avoid granulated processed sugar like the plague[1], turning instead to honey when a recipe requires added sweetener. The use of local honey has been demonstrated to reduce allergy symptoms, according to Dr. Spreen. Like any other immunization, your body builds up an immunity to local allergens by consuming honey created by bees who consume local pollen.

An excess of sugar in the body causes an imbalance in acid-alkaline pH levels, creating an environment overly conducive to yeast and decreasing the body's natural resistance to illness. Daily intake of apple cider vinegar can balance the acid-alkaline pH levels in the body, inhibit the growth of unfriendly bacteria in the digestive tract, and help oxygenate the blood. It aids digestion, helping to break down minerals, protein, and fats.

Ancient Egyptians, Greeks (including Hippocrates), and Romans used apple cider vinegar for a variety of medicinal benefits. It contains over ninety vitamins, minerals, amino acids, and other compounds.[2]

Beginning today, include an apple cider vinegar and local honey tonic as part of your daily routine. You may even notice that it enhances your weight-loss efforts.

Diet:

- ☐ Drink 8 oz. water mixed with 1 Tbs. Bragg's Apple Cider Vinegar (ACV) and 1 t. local honey.
- ☐ Take multivitamin, Ester-C, EFAs.
- ☐ Drink sixty-four ounces of water throughout the day.
- ☐ Eat two eggs sometime today.
- ☐ Have a salad with your lunch.
- ☐ Eat as many raw or steamed veggies as you can.
- ☐ For dinner, eat a palm-sized portion of protein with steamed or stir-fried vegetables.

---

[1]See Day 44 for more details about sugar.
[2]The compounds include lactic acid, amino acids, propionic acid, acetic acid, enzymes, potash, and apple pectin. Trace elements/minerals include phosphorous, calcium, sodium, fluorine, silicon, potassium, magnesium, iron, sulfur, chlorine, and copper. Vitamins include A, B_1, B_2, B_6, C, E; provitamin beta-carotene and bioflavonoids. Alicia McWatters, Ph.D., C.N.C, *www.brookbyherbs.co.nz.*

☐ At 8 P.M. drink hot lemon water. Brush your teeth immediately afterward.[3]

Exercise:
☐ Bounce fifteen minutes.
☐ Walk briskly for thirty minutes.
☐ Optional: strength training.

DAY FIFTY-EIGHT	TODAY'S DATE

Scripture to memorize:

I sought the Lord, and he answered me;
he delivered me from all my fears.
Those who look to him are radiant;
their faces are never covered with shame.

PSALM 34:4–5

Passage to read:
The tongue that brings healing is a tree of life,
but a deceitful tongue crushes the spirit. . . .
A happy heart makes the face cheerful,
but heartache crushes the spirit.

PROVERBS 15:4, 13

Guided prayer:
Dear Lord, I want my words to bring healing to others. Forgive me for using my tongue to speak deceit or harsh words that crush the spirit of my spouse, my children, friends, or co-workers. Help me to be more aware of the power of my words. I desire a happy heart and a cheerful face. I want to wear a smile and inspire a smile in everyone I meet. When I see those who seem depressed, help me speak just the right word to lift their spirit. Amen.

---

[3]Brushing your teeth may discourage late-night snacking.

A prayer from your heart:

_____

_____

_____

_____

Soul

Affirmation to recite:

Even before I was born, God had a specific assignment in mind for my life.
My greatest fulfillment comes as I fulfill God's plans and purposes.

BASED ON JEREMIAH 1:5

Action to take:

Today, look at people's faces. Are they cheerful or crushed in spirit? Make it
a point to ask the cheerful what they're so happy about so that you can share
their joy. Speak an encouraging word to those who look discouraged.

Attitude adjustment:

The mouth has a mind of its own.

JOYCE MEYER

If there's one thing that gets us into trouble, time after time, it is our mouths.
The words we speak have tremendous power for good or evil. We can make
someone's day or break someone's heart. One phrase can change the course of a
person's life: *You'll never amount to anything. You're so stupid. You're such a*
loser. You'll always struggle with your weight. I meet countless grown women
whose lives have been profoundly impacted by the words of a parent, teacher, or
classmate. Of course, it's up to the individual to release the lie and choose to
believe the truth about who God says we are. Nevertheless, God says he will hold

each of us accountable for every word we speak. Choose your words wisely—they can bring life or death to the people you meet today.

Diet:

- [ ] Drink 8 oz. water mixed with 1 Tbs. ACV and 1 t. local honey.
- [ ] Take multivitamin, Ester-C, EFAs.
- [ ] Drink sixty-four ounces of water throughout the day.
- [ ] Eat two eggs sometime today.
- [ ] Have a salad with your lunch.
- [ ] Eat as many raw or steamed veggies as you can.
- [ ] For dinner, eat a palm-sized portion of protein with steamed or stir-fried vegetables.
- [ ] At 8 P.M. drink hot lemon water. Brush your teeth immediately afterward.

Exercise:

- [ ] Walk briskly for thirty minutes.

DAY FIFTY-NINE	TODAY'S DATE

Scripture to memorize:

I sought the Lord, and he answered me;
he delivered me from all my fears.
Those who look to him are radiant;
their faces are never covered with shame.

PSALM 34:4–5

Passage to read:

"No weapon forged against you will prevail,
and you will refute every tongue that accuses you.

This is the heritage of the servants of the Lord,
and this is their vindication from me,"
declares the Lord.

ISAIAH 54:17

Guided prayer:

Dear Lord, thank you that no weapon forged against me will prevail. I'm so thankful that I don't need to worry about what other people think or even what they say about me. I need only to live my life before you. If the accusations made against me are true, you will lead me to repentance. If they are false, you will see to it that the lies are refuted in due course. Either way, I don't need to be concerned. Lord, thank you that I don't have to waste time vindicating myself to the world or trying to prove I'm right and everyone else is wrong. My vindication comes from you. I rest in that knowledge. Amen.

A prayer from your heart:

_____

_____

_____

_____

Affirmation to recite:

My vindication comes from God, so I don't waste time trying to prove I'm right.

BASED ON ISAIAH 54:17

Action to take:

Make a list of three unfair accusations that have been made about you. Surrender each one, then refuse to waste one more moment trying to prove you were misjudged or falsely accused. While you are at it, forgive the people involved in propagating the accusations.

1. _____

2. _____

3. _____

Attitude adjustment:

My definition of emotional health is having total peace about who you are, what you're doing, and where you're going, both individually and in relationship to those around you. It's feeling totally at peace about the past, present, and future of your life.

STORMIE OMARTIAN

Worrying about what the neighbors say is just about the most useless waste of time imaginable. Even if you've made mistakes, all you can do is ask the forgiveness of those involved and move forward. Fretting won't change a thing. People love to make accusations against one another. Nothing will change that, but you do have a choice concerning your response. Option A: You can get all upset when people say unfair or untrue things about you. Or Option B: You can retain your peace, knowing God will handle the situation and eventually the truth will prevail. For the sake of your emotional health, I would urge you to choose Option B.

Diet:
- [ ] Drink 8 oz. water mixed with 1 Tbs. Bragg's ACV and 1 t. local honey.
- [ ] Take multivitamin, Ester-C, EFAs.
- [ ] Drink sixty-four ounces of water throughout the day.
- [ ] Eat two eggs sometime today.
- [ ] Have a salad with your lunch.
- [ ] Eat as many raw or steamed veggies as you can.
- [ ] For dinner, eat a palm-sized portion of protein with steamed or stir-fried vegetables.

☐ At 8 P.M. drink hot lemon water. Brush your teeth immediately afterward.

Exercise:
☐ Bounce fifteen minutes.
☐ Walk briskly for thirty minutes.
☐ Optional: strength training.

DAY SIXTY	TODAY'S DATE

Scripture to memorize:

I sought the Lord, and he answered me;
he delivered me from all my fears.
Those who look to him are radiant;
their faces are never covered with shame.

PSALM 34:4–5

Passage to read:

For the Lord gives wisdom,
and from his mouth come knowledge and understanding.
He holds victory in store for the upright,
he is a shield to those whose walk is blameless,
for he guards the course of the just
and protects the way of his faithful ones.
Then you will understand what is right and just
and fair—every good path.
For wisdom will enter your heart,
and knowledge will be pleasant to your soul.

PROVERBS 2:6–10

Guided prayer:

Dear Lord, thank you for filling my life with good things. Thank you for wisdom, knowledge, and understanding. Thank you that you hold victory in store for me. *Even when it looks like I have been defeated and I'll never get back on track, I stand on your Word, which says victory is just around the corner. Lord, thank you for being my shield. Thank you for protecting me, day after day. Thank you for all the car accidents I have avoided. For the many times disaster has been narrowly averted—and I never even knew. Thank you for every morning I have awakened to discover my home intact and my loved ones in good health. I don't want to take your protection for granted. I'm safe only because you are a shield around me. Lord, help me to become increasingly convinced of the benefits of wisdom and knowledge so that I will pursue them with all the energy I can muster by your grace. Amen.*

A prayer from your heart:

_____

_____

_____

_____

Affirmation to recite:

My life is full of good things. All I have to do is open my eyes to see how fortunate I really am.

BASED ON MATTHEW 6:20

Action to take:

Make a list of five good things in your life. Thank God for each one. If anyone contributed to your ability to experience any of the good things listed, send that person a thank-you note.

Good thing   Who contributed

1. _____   _____

2. _____   _____

3. _____   _____

4. _____   _____

5. _____   _____

Attitude adjustment:

You Are Blessed

If you woke up this morning with more health than illness, you are more blessed than the one million people who will not survive the week.

If you have never experienced the danger of battle, the loneliness of imprisonment, the agony of torture, or the pangs of starvation, you are more blessed than five hundred million people around the world.

If you attend a church meeting without fear of harassment, arrest, torture, or death, you are more blessed than three billion people in the world.

If you have food in your refrigerator, clothes on your back, a roof over your head, and a place to sleep, you are richer than 75 percent of this world.

If you have money in the bank, in your wallet, and spare change in a dish somewhere, you are among the top 8 percent of the world's wealthy.

If you can read this message, you are more blessed than two billion people in the world who cannot read anything at all.

If you hold up your head with a smile on your face and are truly thankful, you are blessed because the majority can, but most do not.

—SOURCE UNKNOWN[4]

Your life is full of good things. Just as a small example: if you have running water, that's a very good thing. I found that out earlier this year, when my well ran dry due to drought. For six weeks we steadily had less and less water, until eventually it stopped altogether. In the midst of this crisis, I received an e-mail from a friend in South Africa who basically said: Be grateful you live in a country where running water is an option. Throughout much of Africa, most people can't even imagine having access to such a luxury. They drink from cholera-infested rivers where the hippos go poo. What a great reality check for me . . . and maybe

---

[4] I received this as an e-mail. Although I can't vouch for the accuracy of the numbers, the basic message to be thankful is certainly true!

for you, too. Today, just for the joy of it, thank God for *everything* . . . even tap water.

Diet:

- ☐ Drink 8 oz. water mixed with 1 Tbs. ACV and 1 t. local honey.
- ☐ Take multivitamin, Ester-C, EFAs.
- ☐ Drink sixty-four ounces of water throughout the day.
- ☐ Eat two eggs sometime today.
- ☐ Have a salad with your lunch.
- ☐ Eat as many raw or steamed veggies as you can.
- ☐ For dinner, eat a palm-sized portion of protein with steamed or stir-fried vegetables.
- ☐ At 8 P.M. drink hot lemon water. Brush your teeth immediately afterward.

Exercise:

- ☐ Walk briskly for thirty minutes.

DAY SIXTY-ONE   TODAY'S DATE

Scripture to memorize:

Don't you know that you yourselves are God's temple and that God's Spirit lives in you? If anyone destroys God's temple, God will destroy him; for God's temple is sacred, and you are that temple.

1 CORINTHIANS 3:16–17

Passage to read:

Now the men of Judah approached Joshua at Gilgal, and Caleb son of Jephunneh the Kenizzite said to him, "You know what the Lord said to Moses the man of God at Kadesh Barnea about you and me. I was forty years old when Moses the servant of the Lord sent me from Kadesh Barnea to explore the land. And I brought him back a report according to my convictions, but my brothers who went up with me made the hearts of the people melt with fear. I, however, followed the Lord my God wholeheartedly. So on that day Moses swore to me, 'The land on which your feet have walked will be your inheritance and that of your children forever, because you have followed the Lord my God wholeheartedly.'

"Now then, just as the Lord promised, he has kept me alive for forty-five years since the time he said this to Moses, while Israel moved about in the desert. So here I am today, eighty-five years old![5] I am still as strong today as the day Moses sent me out; I'm just as vigorous to go out to battle now as I was then. Now give me this hill country that the Lord promised me that day. You yourself heard then that the Anakites were there and their cities were large and fortified, but, the Lord helping me, I will drive them out just as he said."

Then Joshua blessed Caleb son of Jephunneh and gave him Hebron as his inheritance. So Hebron has belonged to Caleb son of Jephunneh the Kenizzite ever since, because he followed the Lord, the God of Israel, wholeheartedly.

JOSHUA 14:6–14

Guided prayer:

Dear Lord, grant me a spirit like Caleb's. When I am eighty years old, I want to be ready to go up into the hill country—up into the hard places—to fight for your kingdom. Lord, I pledge to take good care of my body so that I won't be a burden in my old age. Bless me with long life so that I can be a blessing to many. Amen.

A prayer from your heart:

_____

_____

_____

_____

---

[5]Emphasis added. Think about an eighty-five-year-old man you know; then try to imagine him asking permission to go out into battle.

Affirmation to recite:

I desire to be blessed with long life so that I can be a blessing to others.

Based on Joshua 14:6–14

Action to take:

Visit with a truly godly person in his or her eighties. If you don't know of such a person, ask your pastor. Go. Sit and listen to his or her stories of God's faithfulness.

Attitude adjustment:

Better to burn out than rust out.

Unknown

You are never too old to be a vibrant servant of God. Commenting on the life of Caleb, J. Oswald Sanders wrote: "Perhaps we, too, should remove our slippers and attack some menacing mountain in which the enemies of God are entrenched." Then he recounts some examples of people who demonstrate spiritual fervor later in life:

C.H. Nash, who founded the Melbourne Bible Institute and trained one thousand young men and women for Christian service, retired his principalship at the age of seventy. At eighty, he received assurance from the Lord that a further fruitful ministry of ten years lay ahead of him. This assurance was abundantly fulfilled. During those years he was uniquely blessed in a ministry of Bible teaching to key groups of clergy and laymen, probably the most fruitful years of his life. When he was nearly ninety, this author found him completing the reading of Volume 6 of Toynbee's monumental history as a mental exercise.

Mr. Benjamin Ryrie retired as a missionary of the China Inland Mission when he reached the age of seventy. When he was eighty, he decided to learn New Testament Greek, as he had not had the opportunity when he was younger. He became proficient in reading and teaching the Greek New Testament. At ninety, he attended a refresher course in New Testament at the Toronto Theological Seminary.[6]

What will you be doing when you're ninety years old?

Diet:
☐ Free day—eat whatever you like.

Exercise:
☐ Bounce fifteen minutes.
☐ Walk briskly for thirty minutes.
☐ Optional: strength training.

DAY SIXTY-TWO	TODAY'S DATE

Scripture to memorize:
Don't you know that you yourselves are God's temple and that God's Spirit lives in you? If anyone destroys God's temple, God will destroy him; for God's temple is sacred, and you are that temple.

1 CORINTHIANS 3:16–17

Passage to read:
My son, do not forget my teaching,
but keep my commands in your heart,
for they will prolong your life many years
and bring you prosperity.
Let love and faithfulness never leave you;

---

[6]Charles Swindoll, *A Symphony for the Soul* audiocassette, (Insight for Living, 1978).

bind them around your neck,
write them on the tablet of your heart.
Then you will win favor and a good name
in the sight of God and man.
Trust in the Lord with all your heart
and lean not on your own understanding;
in all your ways acknowledge him,
and he will make your paths straight.
Do not be wise in your own eyes;
fear the Lord and shun evil.
This will bring health to your body
and nourishment to your bones.

PROVERBS 3:1–8

Guided prayer:

Dear Lord, I choose to believe your Word, even if others choose not to. You have clearly said that if I keep your commands in my heart they will prolong my life many years and bring me prosperity. I'm not sure that means I'll be a millionaire and live until I'm 120 . . . but I know it means my life will be much better following you than it would be otherwise. You've even said that I will win favor and a good name, both in your sight and in the sight of man.

Yet I recognize that I have a part to play. My role is to trust you with all my heart and lean not on my own understanding. Lord, I firmly believe that as I acknowledge you in all my ways, you will make my paths straight. I won't have to wear myself out—physically, mentally, or emotionally—learning everything the hard way. I am convinced that a lifestyle of peace will help bring health to my body and nourishment to my bones. Thank you, Lord, that in you I have peace. Amen.

A prayer from your heart:

_____

_____

_____

_____

Affirmation to recite:

The eyes of my understanding are enlightened. I understand how powerful God is in my life—more powerful than any obstacles I face.

BASED ON EPHESIANS 1:18–19

Action to take:

Describe yourself as the healthiest, most energetic, vibrant *you* imaginable. What would you be like? How would your life be different? Paint a picture of the woman you want to be.

_____

_____

_____

_____

Attitude adjustment:

Pretty is as pretty does.

EVERYBODY'S MOTHER

Lest you're thinking your ideal self must be a size 6, here's a nice little reality check:

- There are three billion women who don't look like super models and only eight who do.
- Marilyn Monroe wore a size 14.
- If Barbie were a real woman, she'd have to walk on all fours due to her ridiculous proportions.
- The average woman weighs 144 lb. and wears between a size 12–14.

- ✣ One out of every four college-aged females has an eating disorder.
- ✣ The models in magazines are airbrushed—not perfect!
- ✣ A psychological study in 1995 found that three minutes spent looking at a fashion magazine caused 70 percent of women to feel depressed, guilty, and shameful.
- ✣ Twenty years ago, models weighed 8 percent less than the average woman. Today they weigh 23 percent less.[7]

Don't worry about living up to someone else's ideal. And for sure don't waste time contemplating the world's fictitious ideal. Take care of your body for *health* reasons . . . not mere vanity (although there's nothing wrong with wanting to look attractive). Strive to be your very best and let God handle the rest.

Diet:

- ☐ Drink 8 oz. water mixed with 1 Tbs. ACV and 1 t. local honey.
- ☐ Take multivitamin, Ester-C, EFAs.
- ☐ Drink sixty-four ounces of water throughout the day.
- ☐ Eat two eggs sometime today.
- ☐ Have a salad with your lunch.
- ☐ Eat as many raw or steamed veggies as you can.
- ☐ For dinner, eat a palm-sized portion of protein with steamed or stir-fried vegetables.
- ☐ At 8 P.M. drink hot lemon water. Brush your teeth immediately afterward.
- ☐ Prepare for a two-day fast, which starts tomorrow.

Exercise:

- ☐ Bounce fifteen minutes.
- ☐ Walk briskly for thirty minutes.

---

[7]Source unknown. I received this over the Internet. Although I can't guarantee the accuracy of its statistics, the gist is certainly true!

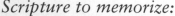

Scripture to memorize:

Don't you know that you yourselves are God's temple and that God's Spirit lives in you? If anyone destroys God's temple, God will destroy him; for God's temple is sacred, and you are that temple.

1 CORINTHIANS 3:16–17

Passage to read:

So I say, live by the Spirit, and you will not gratify the desires of the sinful nature. For the sinful nature desires what is contrary to the Spirit, and the Spirit what is contrary to the sinful nature. They are in conflict with each other, so that you do not do what you want. But if you are led by the Spirit, you are not under law.

GALATIANS 5:16–18

Guided prayer:

Dear Lord, thank you for sending the Holy Spirit as my counselor and guide. I'm so glad I don't have to try to live the Christian life in my own strength or according to man's wisdom. Thank you for empowering me to live a godly life. I recognize that my sinful nature desires what is contrary to the spirit. I also recognize that the more I feed that sinful nature, the stronger it will become. The good news is, the more I feed my spirit, the stronger it will become. Again, it comes back to choices. I can choose which part of me to feed. Today, by an act of my will, I choose to feed my spirit. I desire to live a life led by the Spirit. Amen.

A prayer from your heart:

_____

_____

_____

Affirmation to recite:
I choose to feed my spirit.

BASED ON GALATIANS 5:16–18

Action to take:
Feed your spirit! Begin reading the biography or autobiography of a Christian missionary. A few titles to check out: *William and Catherine: The Life and Legacy of the Booths, Founders of The Salvation Army,* by Trevor Yaxley; *Jesus Freaks* and *Jesus Freaks Vol. II,* by dc Talk; *Hudson Taylor,* by J. Hudson Taylor.[8]

Attitude adjustment:
*Your capacity to say "No" determines your capacity to say
"Yes" to greater things.*

E. STANLEY JONES

Many years ago, there lived in a small Eskimo village a man who owned a black dog and a white dog. Both were powerful dogs and skilled fighters. Each week the man would take his dogs into town so they could participate in the sport of dog fighting. The men of the village would place bets on which dog would prevail. Because the dogs were very evenly matched in size and experience, some weeks the black dog would win; other weeks the white dog would come out victorious. It seemed impossible to predict which dog would gain the victory on any given week. However, the villagers became suspicious when the dog's owner invariably guessed the winner correctly. Finally, they convinced him to reveal his secret. "It's simple," he said. "I take turns starving the dogs. Whichever dog I feed during the week is the one who is sure to win."

You have a black dog and a white dog within you, as well. It's your flesh and

---

[8]All from Bethany House Publishers. Available at your local bookstore.

your spirit. If you feed your flesh, your flesh will be stronger than your determination to live a godly life. If you feed your spirit, you will secure the victory. Which "dog" have you been feeding?

Diet:

☐ Today you will begin your third two-day fast.

Exercise:

☐ Do only light stretching exercises. Do not overexert yourself while fasting.

Week 10

Scripture to memorize:

Don't you know that you yourselves are God's temple and that God's Spirit lives in you? If anyone destroys God's temple, God will destroy him; for God's temple is sacred, and you are that temple.

1 CORINTHIANS 3:16–17

Passage to read:

Rejoice in the Lord always. I will say it again: Rejoice! Let your gentleness be evident to all. The Lord is near. Do not be anxious about anything, but in everything, by prayer and petition, with thanksgiving, present your requests to God. And the peace of God, which transcends all understanding, will guard your hearts and your minds in Christ Jesus.

PHILIPPIANS 4:4–7

Guided prayer:

Dear Lord, I rejoice in you. I rest in your provision, so I can be at peace. I do not strive; instead, I am gentle in all my dealings with others. Lord, I am not anxious or worried. Thank you that I can make my requests known to you, trusting you to provide everything I need. I thank you for the peace that transcends understanding—a peace that guards my heart and mind, so I can live free from emotional turmoil and stress. I know the best thing I can do for my spirit, soul, and body is to simply rejoice in all circumstances. Therefore, I choose to rejoice. Amen.

A prayer from your heart:

_____

_____

_____

_____

Affirmation to recite:

I choose to be joyful and gracious, no matter how difficult the circumstance.

BASED ON PHILIPPIANS 4:4–7

Action to take:

Set a timer for five minutes and speak out joyful words and/or songs until the timer rings.

Attitude adjustment:

Habit is overcome by habit.

DESIDERIUS ERASMUS

In the spiritual realm, as in the physical, I believe the best way to drive out the wrong stuff is to fill yourself with the right stuff. As your spiritual taste buds become accustomed to a healthier diet, you will have less desire for mental junk food. When those old cravings come calling, you will have more power to resist. Things you once consumed greedily, like women's magazines, romance novels, mindless television shows, and idle phone conversations, will lose their appeal.

But don't start by resisting. That won't work. Start by feeding yourself the *right stuff*. Read your Bible every day without fail. Then carve out time for other uplifting Christian books. Gradually, you'll notice you have lost interest in mental junk food.

Diet:
☐ Continue with the second day of your fast.

Exercise:
☐ Do only light stretching exercises. Do not overexert yourself while fasting.

DAY SIXTY-FIVE	TODAY'S DATE

Scripture to memorize:
*Don't you know that you yourselves are God's temple and that God's
Spirit lives in you? If anyone destroys God's temple, God will
destroy him; for God's temple is sacred, and you are that temple.*

1 CORINTHIANS 3:16–17

Passage to read:
*But be very careful to keep the commandment and the law that Moses the
servant of the Lord gave you: to love the Lord your God, to walk in all his ways,
to obey his commands, to hold fast to him and to serve him with all your heart
and all your soul.*

JOSHUA 22:5

Guided prayer:
*Dear Lord, you told your servant Joshua to be very careful to keep your
commandments. Obedience takes hard work for all of us, even the super saints!
No one just falls into holiness. It's a choice we all must make. Yet I thank you,
Father, because your commands aren't burdensome. All you ask is that I love*

you, obey you, hold fast to you, and serve you with my heart and soul. Lord, that's exactly the woman I want to be! I don't always live up to my highest ideals, but I'm thankful they are always before me. I love you, Lord. I declare my desire to walk in your ways and obey you. Even at this moment, I am holding fast to you. And I commit the rest of my life to serving you with all my heart and all my soul. Amen.

A prayer from your heart:

_____

_____

_____

_____

Affirmation to recite:

I have committed the rest of my life to serving God with all my heart and with all my soul.

BASED ON JOSHUA 22:5

Action to take:

Today, tell someone you've made the commitment to serve God for the rest of your life. Also, put it in writing—perhaps in the front of your Bible. Be sure to include today's date.

Attitude adjustment:

Expenditure which begins at a great rate often comes to a sudden end by bankruptcy. Begin so that you can keep on, and even rise higher.

CHARLES SPURGEON

Burnout is a catch phrase in the church today, because people get all hyped up for this or that ministry team and leap in with both feet. Unfortunately, quickly acquired zeal dissipates with equal speed. Perhaps you were moved by a sermon about the plight of the homeless and volunteered to work the soup kitchen every Saturday afternoon. Then you decided to teach Sunday school after an impassioned plea by the superintendent. Then there's hosting the Friday night youth group. Now let's get real! Can anyone keep up that pace? God will never ask you to tackle more than you can realistically handle. You are a servant of God, yes, but you are not the only servant on staff. Remember to pace yourself—the race is long.

Diet:

- [ ] Drink 8 oz. water mixed with 1 Tbs. ACV and 1 t. local honey.
- [ ] Take multivitamin, Ester-C, EFAs.
- [ ] Drink sixty-four ounces of water throughout the day.
- [ ] Eat two eggs sometime today.
- [ ] Have a salad with your lunch.
- [ ] Eat as many raw or steamed veggies as you can.
- [ ] For dinner, eat a palm-sized portion of protein with steamed or stir-fried vegetables.
- [ ] At 8 P.M.: Hot lemon water. Brush teeth. Do NOT eat again until morning.

Exercise:

- [ ] Bounce for nine minutes.
- [ ] Walk briskly for thirty minutes.
- [ ] Optional: strength training.

Scripture to memorize:

A cheerful heart is good medicine,
but a crushed spirit dries up the bones.

PROVERBS 17:22

Passage to read:

Do everything without complaining or arguing, so that you may become blameless and pure, children of God without fault in a crooked and depraved generation, in which you shine like stars in the universe.

PHILIPPIANS 2:14–15

Guided prayer:

Dear Lord, you have been so good to me. I know I am richly blessed. Forgive me for every word of complaint I have uttered. Forgive me for arguing and striving to have everything go my way. Lord, I desire to be a blameless and pure child. I want to shine for you in this crooked and depraved generation. Empower me by your Holy Spirit to rein in my tongue, so I can glorify you with my lips. Amen.

A prayer from your heart:

_____

_____

_____

_____

Affirmation to recite:

I have made a conscious decision to eliminate complaining from my life—for my sake and for the sake of everyone around me. I do everything—especially the simple, everyday tasks of life—without complaint.

BASED ON PHILIPPIANS 2:14–15

Action to take:

Go one day without uttering a single complaint. Tell your family, friends, and co-workers you will pay them a dollar for every complaint they catch you uttering. Be prepared to pay up.

Attitude adjustment:

True worship must emerge now in the context of our daily lives, for no man will worship through the great battles of tomorrow who complains in the mere skirmishes of today.

FRANCIS FRANGIPANE

Do you know God takes complaining very seriously? We may think of it as a small thing, but God certainly doesn't. When we complain, we question his goodness and reject his provision. In the Old Testament (Numbers 11), we learn that God put many Israelites to death for the sin of complaining. The cure for complaining, of course, is gratitude. Rather than focusing on what you don't have and what's going wrong, shift your attention to what you *do* have and what's going right in your life. You'll be amazed at the difference a positive attitude makes in your emotional well-being, as well as in the way others perceive you.

Body

Diet:

☐ Drink 8 oz. water mixed with 1 Tbs. ACV and 1 t. local honey.

☐ Take multivitamin, Ester-C, EFAs.

☐ Drink sixty-four ounces of water throughout the day.

☐ Eat two eggs sometime today.

☐ Have a salad with your lunch.

☐ Eat as many raw or steamed veggies as you can.

☐ For dinner, eat a palm-sized portion of protein with steamed or stir-fried vegetables.

☐ At 8 P.M.: Hot lemon water. Brush teeth. Do NOT eat again until morning.

Exercise:

☐ Walk briskly for forty-five minutes.

DAY SIXTY-SEVEN	TODAY'S DATE

Spirit

Scripture to memorize:

A cheerful heart is good medicine,
but a crushed spirit dries up the bones.

PROVERBS 17:22

Passage to read:

For in my inner being I delight in God's law; but I see another law at work in the members of my body, waging war against the law of my mind and making me a prisoner of the law of sin at work within my members. What a wretched

man I am! Who will rescue me from this body of death? Thanks be to God—
through Jesus Christ our Lord!

ROMANS 7:22–25A

Guided prayer:

Dear Lord, I thank you for creating me as a spirit who is able to commune
with you. At the deepest place, I delight in your law and desire to live it out.
That's who I really am. But I live in a body—a body that sometimes causes me
to stumble. I have a mind that wanders, a will that doesn't want to exert itself,
and emotions that do! Lord, I want to be unified in my spirit, soul, and body. I
want to live out what I know to be true. Someday I will be set free from this
mortal body. You will rescue me from this body of death! Until then, I invite you
to continue the process of sanctifying my soul and body, so that I might become
more and more like you. Amen.

A prayer from your heart:

_____

_____

_____

_____

Affirmation to recite:

God shows me the way to go. All I have to do is listen and he will tell me
which path to take.

BASED ON PROVERBS 3:5–8

Action to take:

In what ways do you see the "law of sin" at work in your body and your
mind? Describe. Then ask God for his thoughts and his strategies for delivering

you from the forces that war against you. Listen and he will show you which path to take.

_____

_____

_____

Attitude adjustment:

"The first reason why the quiet time is not attractive to most is that people do not know how to pray. Their storehouse of words is soon exhausted, and they do not know what else to say, because they forget that prayer is not a soliloquy, where everything comes from one side; it is a dialogue, where God's child listens to what the Father says, replies to it, and then makes his requests known."

ANDREW MURRAY[1]

It's amazing how much you can learn when you keep quiet. This is true even in our devotional lives. Rather than telling God our prayer requests (our ideas concerning what needs to be accomplished in our lives and in this world), we'd probably be far better off just sitting and listening. God still speaks to his children. Open your spirit and soul to listen for his voice. God has a strategy to deliver you from the forces that war against you. The silence may be, in and of itself, part of the solution.

Diet:

- ☐ Drink 8 oz. water mixed with 1 Tbs. ACV and 1 t. local honey.
- ☐ Take multivitamin, Ester-C, EFAs.
- ☐ Drink sixty-four ounces of water throughout the day.
- ☐ Eat two eggs sometime today.
- ☐ Have a salad with your lunch.
- ☐ Eat as many raw or steamed veggies as you can.
- ☐ For dinner, eat a palm-sized portion of protein with steamed or stir-fried vegetables.

[1]Andrew Murray, *Living a Prayerful Life* (Minneapolis, MN: Bethany House Publishers, 2002), 92.

☐ At 8 P.M.: Hot lemon water. Brush teeth. Do NOT eat again until morning.

Exercise:
☐ Bounce for nine minutes.
☐ Walk briskly for thirty minutes.
☐ Optional: strength training.

DAY SIXTY-EIGHT	TODAY'S DATE

Scripture to memorize:

A cheerful heart is good medicine,
but a crushed spirit dries up the bones.

PROVERBS 17:22

Passage to read:

Among the gods there is none like you, O Lord;
no deeds can compare with yours.
All the nations you have made
will come and worship before you, O Lord;
they will bring glory to your name.
For you are great and do marvelous deeds;
you alone are God.

PSALM 86:8–10

Guided prayer:

Dear Lord, I praise you today. I declare there is none like you, O Lord. None of the gods of this age can compare to you. None of the gods I've erected in my heart can take your place. You have performed mighty deeds for your people throughout history. I have seen you work miracles in my own life. Thank you, Lord. I look forward to the day when all nations will come and worship before you, for you alone are worthy of praise. You are great and your deeds are marvelous! I am grateful and my heart sings for joy. Amen.

A prayer from your heart:

_____

_____

_____

_____

Soul

Affirmation to recite:

My sinful response to the sin of others has far more destructive power than anything others can do to me. Therefore, I respond to everyone in a loving fashion no matter how they treat me.

BASED ON PROVERBS 17:22

Action to take:

Make a list of ten wonderful attributes of God. Not things he has done for you . . . but who he *is*.

1. graceful
2. faithful
3. powerful
4. loving
5. _____

6. _____
7. _____
8. _____
9. _____
10. _____

Attitude adjustment:

True praise is unconditional. It's not an attempt to manipulate God into producing the precise results we hope for. Instead, it helps us accept our situation as it is, whether or not He changes it. . . . Even in troubled circumstances, or when God does not choose to work in spectacular ways,

*praise can help us view our situation through different lenses. It can help
produce within us a restful, invigorating inner climate. And often this
change of climate within us helps transform the atmosphere around us,
for our new attitudes cause people to react differently to us and we begin
to exert a creative and uplifting influence on them.*

RUTH MYERS[2]

Precise results. If there is one thing that's thrown me into more emotional
turmoil than anything else in this world, it's setting my heart on *precise results*.
Specific prayer requests are wonderful, but they can also be problematic. When
our prayer time deteriorates into list-of-demands time, we're in deep trouble. We
need to express our concerns to God but then leave it up to him to work out the
solutions in his own way and time. I've learned to avoid outcome-based prayers
and have instead adopted an attitude that says, "Lord, here's what's bothering
me. Please share *your* perspective with me. Help me to see it through your eyes,
so that when *your* solution begins to unfold, I will recognize it, rather than resist
it."

Diet:

- [ ] Drink 8 oz. water mixed with 1 Tbs. ACV and 1 t. local honey.
- [ ] Take multivitamin, Ester-C, EFAs.
- [ ] Drink sixty-four ounces of water throughout the day.
- [ ] Eat two eggs sometime today.
- [ ] Have a salad with your lunch.
- [ ] Eat as many raw or steamed veggies as you can.
- [ ] For dinner, eat a palm-sized portion of protein with steamed or stir-fried vegetables.
- [ ] At 8 P.M.: Hot lemon water. Brush teeth. Do NOT eat again until morning.

Exercise:

- [ ] Walk briskly for forty-five minutes.

---

[2]Ruth Myers, *31 Days of Praise* (Sisters, OR: Multnomah, 1994), 120.

DAY SIXTY-NINE   TODAY'S DATE

Scripture to memorize:

A cheerful heart is good medicine,
but a crushed spirit dries up the bones.

PROVERBS 17:22

Passage to read:

For if you forgive men when they sin against you, your heavenly Father will also forgive you. But if you do not forgive men their sins, your Father will not forgive your sins.

MATTHEW 6:14–15

Guided prayer:

Dear Lord, I forgive _____ for _____. She/he hurt me because of her/his own brokenness. Amen.

A prayer from your heart:

_____

_____

_____

_____

Affirmation to recite:

I choose to forgive everyone, just as God has forgiven me. Hanging on to unforgiveness cannot benefit me in any way.

BASED ON COLOSSIANS 3:13

Action to take:

On a separate sheet of paper, make a list of people who have hurt you. Pray through to forgiving each one. Then burn the list.

Attitude adjustment:

You will know the work [of forgiveness] is complete when you can honestly say you want God's best for that person.

STORMIE OMARTIAN

I firmly believe the power to forgive is the most powerful tool—and the most precious gift—God has given us. When we extend forgiveness, I believe we are closer to the heart of God than at any other time. Colossians 3:13 says, "Bear with each other and forgive whatever grievances you may have against one another. Forgive as the Lord forgave you." How did the Lord forgive us? Unconditionally. When did the Lord forgive us? When we least deserved it. The universe makes more sense when we realize that nine times out of ten, we get what we give. This is true even in the area of forgiveness: "Forgive, and you will be forgiven" (Luke 6:37b).

The more forgiving and gracious we are to others, the more people will extend forgiveness and grace to us. As we become increasingly willing to give others the benefit of the doubt, others will do the same for us. Very few people are genuinely malicious or out to get you. Those who are need a Savior, not our condemnation or anger. The woman I want to be is gracious and forgiving.

Diet:

- ☐ Drink 8 oz. water mixed with 1 Tbs. ACV and 1 t. local honey.
- ☐ Take multivitamin, Ester-C, EFAs.
- ☐ Drink sixty-four ounces of water throughout the day.
- ☐ Eat two eggs sometime today.
- ☐ Have a salad with your lunch.
- ☐ Eat as many raw or steamed veggies as you can.
- ☐ For dinner, eat a palm-sized portion of protein with steamed or stir-fried vegetables.
- ☐ At 8 P.M.: Hot lemon water. Brush teeth. Do NOT eat again until morning.

Exercise:

- ☐ Bounce for nine minutes.
- ☐ Walk briskly for thirty minutes.
- ☐ Optional: strength training.

DAY SEVENTY	TODAY'S DATE

Scripture to memorize:

> A *cheerful heart is good medicine,*
> *but a crushed spirit dries up the bones.*
>
> PROVERBS 17:22

Passage to read:

Do not judge, or you too will be judged. For in the same way you judge others, you will be judged, and with the measure you use, it will be measured to you. Why do you look at the speck of sawdust in your brother's eye and pay no attention to the plank in your own eye? How can you say to your brother, "Let me take the speck out of your eye," when all the time there is a plank in your own eye? You hypocrite, first take the plank out of your own eye, and then you will see clearly to remove the speck from your brother's eye.

MATTHEW 7:1–5

Guided prayer:

Dear Lord, I acknowledge you as the sole judge of the universe. I surrender my right to judge. Forgive me for trying to put myself in your place as judge and jury over the universe. Forgive me for thinking I am qualified for the job. I know you take the sin of pride seriously and I don't take it seriously enough. I confess that on every point where I pass judgment on someone else, I am guilty. I know it is human nature to despise in others the weaknesses we see in ourselves. Holy Spirit, I invite you to convict me whenever that critical spirit starts rising up within me. Help me to examine myself and determine what my intense reaction to the sin of another says about my own heart condition. Help me to remove the plank from my own eye. Amen.

A prayer from your heart:

_____

_____

_____

_____

Affirmation to recite:

I don't waste my time looking for the "speck" in other people's eyes. Instead, I focus on removing the plank from my own eye—realizing the "plank" is my own critical spirit.

BASED ON MATTHEW 7:1–5

Action to take:

On a separate page, list people you have judged and what you have judged them for. Ask God to forgive you for putting yourself in his place. God alone has the right to judge human beings. Next, analyze what those judgments say about you, realizing we judge others most harshly when they reflect our own sins.

Attitude adjustment:

The lie we secretly want to believe when we criticize others is, I'm better than they are. But what we really fear is, They are better than I am.

STORMIE OMARTIAN

I recently received a series of about twelve e-mails from a woman lambasting me for everything from my theology and writing style to my personal life. No matter how many gentle responses I sent her way, she came back with harsher treatment. Fortunately, she pointed out in several of her diatribes that she was speaking up for the sake of God's Kingdom and was *not* a judgmental person. She sure could have fooled me! You can call it whatever you want. When you make it your business to point out someone else's faults, you are being judgmental. Now, you might say you are "holding them accountable," but accountability can only be exercised within the context of a loving relationship. You can't hold a total stranger accountable; you can only judge them from a distance. If you truly believe someone is straying from the straight and narrow path, you should pray for her rather than criticize her.

Here's a little self-test you can take to ensure your motives are in the right place before speaking a word of criticism to someone else in the name of accountability or "speaking the truth in love." Fast and pray for three solid days before you speak. If you don't feel strongly enough about the issue to surrender your food for three days, then you don't feel very strongly about it. The impulse is not from God. If, after three days of fasting, you still feel led to approach a sister in Christ, you will go in a more humble spirit and your rebuke will be better received.

Diet:

☐ Drink 8 oz. water mixed with 1 Tbs. ACV and 1 t. local honey.

☐ Take multivitamin, Ester-C, EFAs.

☐ Drink sixty-four ounces of water throughout the day.

☐ Eat two eggs sometime today.

☐ Have a salad with your lunch.

☐ Eat as many raw or steamed veggies as you can.

☐ For dinner, eat a palm-sized portion of protein with steamed or stir-fried vegetables.

☐ At 8 P.M.: Hot lemon water. Brush teeth. Do NOT eat again until morning.

Exercise:

☐ Bounce for nine minutes.

☐ Walk briskly for thirty minutes.

☐ Optional: strength training.

Week 11

Scripture to memorize:

The eyes of the Lord are on the righteous
and his ears are attentive to their cry.

PSALM 34:15

Passage to read:

Be very careful, then, how you live—not as unwise but as wise, making the most of every opportunity, because the days are evil. Therefore do not be foolish, but understand what the Lord's will is. Do not get drunk on wine, which leads to debauchery. Instead, be filled with the Spirit. Speak to one another with psalms, hymns and spiritual songs. Sing and make music in your heart to the Lord, always giving thanks to God the Father for everything, in the name of our Lord Jesus Christ.

EPHESIANS 5:15–20

Guided prayer:

Dear Lord, you have commanded me to live carefully. You have called me to exercise wisdom and self-control, so that I can make the most of every opportunity. Lord, I confess I have wasted opportunities to serve you more effectively because of my own laziness and self-centeredness. Lord, I don't want to be foolish. I want to understand your will and obey it. Forgive me for the sins of my flesh. I may not get drunk on wine, but I have been "drunk" on my favorite foods more times than I care to admit. Holy Spirit, fill me. Bring to my remembrance psalms, hymns, and spiritual songs. Lord, I praise you for the gift of music. Thank you for the blessing it has been to my soul. Thank you for the hymn writers and contemporary songwriters whose work blesses so many. Thank you for those people at my local church who prepare and lead the worship service, so that I might be ushered into your presence each week. Bless them and their families for the Kingdom work they are doing. Amen.

A prayer from your heart:

_____

_____

_____

_____

Affirmation to recite:

I let the peace of Christ rule in my heart by choosing to be thankful for what I do have, rather than complaining about what I don't have.

BASED ON COLOSSIANS 3:15–16

Action to take:

Go to the Christian bookstore and buy a new praise CD. Listen to it each morning as you go through your daily routine.

Write a thank-you note to your church's worship leader.

Attitude adjustment:

Jesus, Jesus, how I trust him!
How I've proved him o'er and o'er!
Jesus, Jesus, precious Jesus!
O for grace to trust Him more!

LOUISA STEAD (1850–1917)

We can praise God even in the midst of the severest trials. One day, Louisa Stead and her husband were relaxing with their four-year-old daughter on a Long Island beach when they heard a desperate child's cry. A boy was drowning so Louisa's husband tried to rescue him. In the process, however, the boy pulled Mr. Stead under the water, and both drowned as Louisa and her daughter watched.

Louisa was left with no means of support except the Lord. She and her daughter experienced dire poverty. One morning, when [she] had had neither funds nor food, she opened the front door and found that someone had left food and money on her doorstep. That day she wrote this hymn.[1]

Diet:

☐ Drink 8 oz. water mixed with 1 Tbs. ACV and 1 t. local honey.
☐ Take multivitamin, Ester-C, EFAs.
☐ Drink sixty-four ounces of water throughout the day.
☐ Eat two eggs sometime today.
☐ Eat an apple midmorning.
☐ Have a salad with your lunch.
☐ Eat as many raw or steamed veggies as you can.
☐ For dinner, eat a palm-sized portion of protein with steamed or stir-fried vegetables.
☐ At 8 P.M.: Hot lemon water. Brush teeth. Do NOT eat again until morning.

Exercise:

☐ Bounce for ten minutes.
☐ Walk briskly for thirty minutes.

DAY SEVENTY-TWO	TODAY'S DATE

Scripture to memorize:

*The eyes of the Lord are on the righteous
and his ears are attentive to their cry.*

PSALM 34:15

---

[1]Robert K. Brown and Mark R. Norton, *The One Year Book of Hymns* (Tyndale House: Wheaton, Ill., 1995), Sept. 11 entry.

Passage to read:

Therefore, as God's chosen people, holy and dearly loved, clothe yourselves with compassion, kindness, humility, gentleness and patience. Bear with each other and forgive whatever grievances you may have against one another. Forgive as the Lord forgave you. And over all these virtues put on love, which binds them all together in perfect unity.

Let the peace of Christ rule in your hearts, since as members of one body you were called to peace. And be thankful. Let the word of Christ dwell in you richly as you teach and admonish one another with all wisdom, and as you sing psalms, hymns and spiritual songs with gratitude in your hearts to God. And whatever you do, whether in word or deed, do it all in the name of the Lord Jesus, giving thanks to God the Father through him.

COLOSSIANS 3:12–17

Guided prayer:

Dear Lord, I stand amazed to be called one of your chosen people. You call me holy and dearly loved. Then, because of the love you've freely lavished upon me, you ask me in return to treat others with compassion, kindness, humility, gentleness, and patience. Isn't this the least I can do in response to your amazing love? You've called me not only to forgive but to be a forgiving person. I want to be quick to forgive and quick to release offenses and grievances.

Lord, may the peace of Christ rule in my heart. I want to live a peaceful life, one free of unnecessary strife. Lord, I am thankful. Out of that gratitude, I want to teach others your Word. May my natural inclination in every situation be praise and thanksgiving. Rather than bursting out in anger, demanding whatever I feel deprived of, I want to burst out in song in gratitude for what you have done for me. Whatever I do, whatever I say, I want to do it all in the name of Jesus. Amen.

A prayer from your heart:

_____

_____

_____

_____

Affirmation to recite:

When I choose to be thankful, I am obeying and honoring God. He, in turn, will bless my obedience.

BASED ON COLOSSIANS 3:15

Action to take:

Be determined to maintain a great attitude today. Copy the following quote from Charles Swindoll and post it in a prominent place in your home. Perhaps commit it to memory.

Attitude adjustment:

The longer I live, the more I realize the impact of attitude on life. Attitude, to me, is more important than facts. It is more important than the past, than education, than money, than circumstances, than failures, than successes, than what other people think or say or do.

It's more important than appearance, giftedness, or skill.

It will make or break a company, a church, or a home.

The remarkable thing is we have a choice, every day, regarding the attitude we will embrace for that day. We cannot change our past. We cannot change the fact that people will act in a certain way. We cannot change the inevitable. The only thing we can do is play on the one string we have, and that is our attitude. I am convinced that life is 10 percent what happens to me and 90 percent how I react to it.

We are in charge of our attitudes.

CHARLES SWINDOLL

Diet:

- [ ] Drink 8 oz. water mixed with 1 Tbs. Bragg's ACV and 1 t. local honey.
- [ ] Take multivitamin, Ester-C, EFAs.
- [ ] Drink sixty-four ounces of water throughout the day.
- [ ] Eat two eggs sometime today.
- [ ] Eat an apple midmorning.
- [ ] Have a salad with your lunch.
- [ ] Eat as many raw or steamed veggies as you can.
- [ ] For dinner, eat a palm-sized portion of protein with steamed or stir-fried vegetables.
- [ ] At 8 P.M.: Hot lemon water. Brush teeth. Do NOT eat again until morning.

Exercise:

- [ ] Walk briskly for forty-five minutes.

DAY SEVENTY-THREE	TODAY'S DATE

Scripture to memorize:

The eyes of the Lord are on the righteous
and his ears are attentive to their cry.

PSALM 34:15

Passage to read:

When you sit to dine with a ruler,
note well what is before you,
and put a knife to your throat
if you are given to gluttony.

241

...ve his delicacies,
...od is deceptive.

PROVERBS 23:1–3

Guided prayer:

Dear Lord, resisting the sin of gluttony is much tougher when eating out rather than when eating at home. Not many seem to take overeating and over-indulging seriously. But, Lord, it's clear from your Word that you do take the sin of gluttony seriously. You have said I should put a knife to my own throat rather than shoving junk food into my mouth! And it's so true. I recognize that many of the sweets I crave are silent killers. The food is deceptive. It tastes so good, but it is not good. It is destructive. I repent of the sin of gluttony and invite the Holy Spirit to continue reminding me when I am on the verge of stumbling in the area of food. Amen.

A prayer from your heart:

_____

_____

_____

_____

Affirmation to recite:

I eat to live. I don't live to eat.

BASED ON PROVERBS 23:2

Action to take:

Forewarned is forearmed. You know the places away from your home where you are most likely to eat. Prepare by calling ahead and finding out what healthy alternatives they have on the menu.

Places you are likely to eat	Healthy choices on the menu
_____	_____
_____	_____
_____	_____
_____	_____
_____	_____

Attitude adjustment:

Do you know why they call fast food fast food? Because it's better to fast than to eat the food.

SHERI ROSE SHEPHERD

How many times have you said, "Well, I have to eat *something*!" Those words are usually uttered just moments before you eat food you know is terrible for your body. But, you figure it's better than nothing. But is it? Your body might be much better off enduring a partial fast than trying to digest some of the junk that's packaged and passed off as food these days. You do have alternatives. One of the smartest is to plan and pack ahead. If you know you'll be running errands all morning, pack a snack. If you are going out to a junk-food restaurant with friends, eat something sensible before you go and just order a salad. You can make a lifestyle change, but it won't happen if you don't put forth the effort.

Diet:

- ☐ Drink 8 oz. water mixed with 1 Tbs. ACV and 1 t. local honey.
- ☐ Take multivitamin, Ester-C, EFAs.
- ☐ Drink sixty-four ounces of water throughout the day.
- ☐ Eat two eggs sometime today.
- ☐ Eat an apple midmorning.
- ☐ Have a salad with your lunch.
- ☐ Eat as many raw or steamed veggies as you can.

☐ For dinner, eat a palm-sized portion of protein with steamed or stir-fried vegetables.

☐ At 8 P.M.: Hot lemon water. Brush teeth. Do NOT eat again until morning.

Exercise:

☐ Bounce for ten minutes.

☐ Walk briskly for thirty minutes.

☐ Optional: strength training.

DAY SEVENTY-FOUR	TODAY'S DATE

Scripture to memorize:

> The eyes of the Lord are on the righteous
> and his ears are attentive to their cry.

PSALM 34:15

Passage to read:

Do not be deceived: God cannot be mocked. A man reaps what he sows. The one who sows to please his sinful nature, from that nature will reap destruction; the one who sows to please the Spirit, from the Spirit will reap eternal life. Let us not become weary in doing good, for at the proper time we will reap a harvest if we do not give up.

GALATIANS 6:7–9

Guided prayer:

Dear Lord, I thank you again for the principles of sowing and reaping. I thank you that my life is not a series of random acts. I thank you that the universe is not completely mysterious. There is some rhyme and reason. I'm grateful that my choices have consequences, even when those consequences are negative. Such experiences serve as a wake-up call to get me back on track in my walk with you.

Lord, I do not want to reap destruction; therefore I cannot afford to sow to please my sinful nature. Instead, I want to sow to please the Spirit, so I can reap eternal life. Lord, sometimes it seems like all my good seed never comes to harvest, while the bad seed shoots up like weeds! But I believe I will reap a good harvest at the proper time if I do not become weary in doing good. I look for that day eagerly. Speed its coming, Lord. Amen.

A prayer from your heart:

_____

_____

_____

_____

Affirmation to recite:

I reap what I sow. Therefore, I choose to sow wisely.

BASED ON GALATIANS 6:7–9

Action to take:

Evaluate what you are sowing and reaping in each of the following areas:

	Sowing	Reaping
Spiritual	_____	_____
	_____	_____
Physical	_____	_____
	_____	_____
Emotional	_____	_____
	_____	_____

Mental _____ _____

_____ _____

Attitude adjustment:

We reap what we sow, forgiveness not withstanding.

CHARLES SWINDOLL

Remember, it's never too late to sow a different crop. As you prayerfully consider each of the areas above, be encouraged. Just as the principles of sowing and reaping can work against you, leading to weight gain if you overeat, illness if you allow yourself to get stressed out all the time, and strained relationships if you engage in criticism and judgment, you can get the opposite results by sowing differently. As you begin to eat properly, eventually you will lose weight. As you begin to trust God more completely, you'll experience his peace even in the midst of life's most severe storms. This, in turn, will have tremendous long-term health benefits. As you begin to be more forgiving and gracious, people will welcome you into their lives. Sow differently. Reap differently. Right now, you are planting the seeds of the woman you want to be in your spirit, soul, and body.

Diet:

☐ Free day—eat whatever you like.

Exercise:

☐ Walk briskly for forty-five minutes.

Scripture to memorize:

The eyes of the Lord are on the righteous
and his ears are attentive to their cry.

PSALM 34:15

Passage to read:

Therefore, there is now no condemnation for those who are in Christ Jesus, because through Christ Jesus the law of the Spirit of life set me free from the law of sin and death. For what the law was powerless to do in that it was weakened by the sinful nature, God did by sending his own Son in the likeness of sinful man to be a sin offering. And so he condemned sin in sinful man, in order that the righteous requirements of the law might be fully met in us, who do not live according to the sinful nature but according to the Spirit.

Those who live according to the sinful nature have their minds set on what that nature desires; but those who live in accordance with the Spirit have their minds set on what the Spirit desires. The mind of sinful man is death, but the mind controlled by the Spirit is life and peace; the sinful mind is hostile to God. It does not submit to God's law, nor can it do so. Those controlled by the sinful nature cannot please God.

ROMANS 8:1–8

Guided prayer:

Dear Lord, I thank you that there is no condemnation for me, because I have accepted Christ as my savior. I thank you that I no longer have to live controlled by my sinful impulses. Sometimes I choose to surrender to them, but I have the option of walking according to the Spirit. Jesus, I thank you for coming to fulfill the law on my behalf. Thank you for dying to take the punishment my sins deserve. Lord, I confess that my mind is too often set on sinful things. Not just

247

lust, although I am surely guilty of that. But jealousy, suspicion, anger, resentment, and criticism.

Lord, I know I can never experience the abundant life as long as negative thoughts prevail. Such thinking leads only to confusion. I want my mind to be controlled by the Spirit, so I can enjoy life and peace. I want to live a life that is pleasing to you. Amen.

A prayer from your heart:

_____

_____

_____

_____

Affirmation to recite:

I enjoy life and peace, because I keep my mind fixed on the things of God. When my life lacks peace, I refocus my mind on him and watch my peace be restored.

BASED ON ISAIAH 26:3

Action to take:

Think about someone who annoys you. Someone you respond to with a barrage of sinful thought patterns like criticism, judgment, and frustration. Now prayerfully consider this fact: she (or he) is not annoying you on purpose. Depersonalize the behavior. Choose to pray, asking God to help this person overcome her negative patterns of behavior, which surely have a detrimental effect on all her relationships. Pray God will heal that place within her that is driving her to self-destructive relational patterns.

Attitude adjustment:

Our stamina is sapped, not so much through external troubles surrounding us but through problems in our thinking.

OSWALD CHAMBERS

Within the past few weeks, three people have gotten in touch with me to clear the air because they were absolutely certain I was angry with them for one reason or another. None of these people know each other, and to be honest, they don't know me particularly well, either. They are people I would describe as acquaintances on the periphery of my life. Two of the people were not only certain they had offended me, they actually claimed God had told them so. Well, the reality is, these three women couldn't have been farther from my mind. Right or wrong, I have been far too preoccupied with my own family and ministry responsibilities.

Don't get me wrong—all three are perfectly nice people and I have nothing whatsoever against them. I'm just an extremely busy person with a few close friends and a wide range of acquaintances. Yet, in their minds, there was some great conflict brewing. In their minds, there was a crisis needing immediate attention. In their minds.

The mind is very complex and it can play tricks on us. We can create problems out of thin air. Women are notorious for doing this to their husbands, especially when they have to work late at night. Don't allow your mind to spiral out of control, imagining various scenarios and offenses. Discipline your mind to focus not on what might be true but strictly on what you know to be true: God and his Word. Life is filled with enough troubles without manufacturing more in your head. Let your mind be filled with the things of the Spirit, which bring life and peace.

Diet:

☐ Drink 8 oz. water mixed with 1 Tbs. ACV and 1 t. local honey.
☐ Take multivitamin, Ester-C, EFAs.
☐ Drink sixty-four ounces of water throughout the day.
☐ Eat two eggs sometime today.
☐ Eat an apple midmorning.
☐ Have a salad with your lunch.

☐ Eat as many raw or steamed veggies as you can.

☐ For dinner, eat a palm-sized portion of protein with steamed or stir-fried vegetables.

☐ At 8 P.M.: Hot lemon water. Brush teeth. Do NOT eat again until morning.

Exercise:

☐ Bounce for ten minutes.

☐ Walk briskly for thirty minutes.

☐ Optional: strength training.

DAY SEVENTY-SIX	TODAY'S DATE

Scripture to memorize:

Praise the Lord, O my soul;
all my inmost being, praise his holy name.
Praise the Lord, O my soul,
and forget not all his benefits.

PSALM 103:1–2

Passage to read:

Praise the Lord, O my soul;
* all my inmost being, praise his holy name.*
Praise the Lord, O my soul,
* and forget not all his benefits—*
who forgives all your sins
* and heals all your diseases,*
who redeems your life from the pit
* and crowns you with love and compassion,*
who satisfies your desires with good things
* so that your youth is renewed like the eagle's.*

PSALM 103:1–5

Guided prayer:

Dear Lord, I praise your holy name. I do not forget all your benefits. Thank you for forgiving my sins and healing my diseases. Lord, you have redeemed my life from the pit and crowned me with love and compassion. Forgive me for seeking the world's solutions to my desires. You satisfy me with good things and you add no sorrow to it. Help me to live my life enthusiastically, receiving each opportunity as a gift to be celebrated. Thank you for renewing my strength and helping me envision the woman I want to be. Thank you for bringing me this far. Give me the strength to carry on through all ninety days of the journey and to incorporate permanent lifestyle changes as a result of the lessons I have learned and the decisions I have made. Amen.

A prayer from your heart:

_____

_____

_____

_____

Affirmation to recite:

I try to live every day, every moment, enthusiastically. I give thanks for every opportunity and encounter, even the challenges, because they help me grow.

BASED ON PSALM 103:1–2

Action to take:

Make a list of ten benefits you have experienced from following God through this journey to becoming the woman you want to be.

1. _____   6. _____
2. _____   7. _____
3. _____   8. _____
4. _____   9. _____
5. _____   10. _____

Attitude adjustment:

Praise can free you from wasting your energies speculating on just exactly how each circumstance in your life could be part of God's plan. Through praising and thanking God, you put your stamp of approval on His unseen purposes. You do this not because you can figure out the specific whys or hows, but because you trust His love and wisdom.

RUTH MYERS[2]

God has told us in his Word that following him has many benefits. And he has commanded us: don't forget my benefits. But it's a mistake to think we, in our finite minds, can figure out exactly what those benefits will look like. I know from personal experience: you can make yourself half crazy trying to figure out exactly why this or that happened. Did God allow it or was it his permissive will, etc.? Instead, we need to simply trust. We need to simply believe: I am better off following God than I would be walking in disobedience. Then we need to walk in obedience and leave the dispensing of benefits to God.

Body

Diet:

☐ Drink 8 oz. water mixed with 1 Tbs. ACV and 1 t. local honey.
☐ Take multivitamin, Ester-C, EFAs.
☐ Drink sixty-four ounces of water throughout the day.
☐ Eat two eggs sometime today.
☐ Eat an apple midmorning.

---

[2]Myers, *31 Days of Praise*, 140.

☐ Have a salad with your lunch.
☐ Eat as many raw or steamed veggies as you can.
☐ For dinner, eat a palm-sized portion of protein with steamed or stir-fried vegetables.
☐ At 8 P.M.: Hot lemon water. Brush teeth. Do NOT eat again until morning.

Exercise:
☐ Walk briskly for forty-five minutes.

DAY SEVENTY-SEVEN	TODAY'S DATE

Scripture to memorize:

Praise the Lord, O my soul;
all my inmost being, praise his holy name.
Praise the Lord, O my soul,
and forget not all his benefits.

PSALM 103:1–2

Passage to read:

When the woman saw that the fruit of the tree was good for food and pleasing to the eye, and also desirable for gaining wisdom, she took some and ate it. She also gave some to her husband, who was with her, and he ate it. Then the eyes of both of them were opened, and they realized they were naked; so they sewed fig leaves together and made coverings for themselves.

GENESIS 3:6–7

Guided prayer:

Dear Lord, today's passage is a humbling reminder. We are all capable of blowing it when faced with tempting food. Eve saw food that looked good and she wanted to eat it, even though she knew it was against God's command. Throughout the course of this renewal, you have shown me those foods that cause me to stumble. Yet I confess I continue to reach for them, rather than reaching for you. Forgive me. Holy Spirit, strengthen me as I turn to you for wisdom regarding my daily food choices. Amen.

A prayer from your heart:

_____

_____

_____

_____

Affirmation to recite:

I exercise wisdom concerning my eating habits, because I know food can be a stumbling block to me.

BASED ON GENESIS 3:1–7

Action to take:

Prayerfully consider which food remains a stumbling block to you. Undertake another ten-day limited fast, abstaining from that food entirely. Food you will abstain from: _____

Dates of fast: From _____ until _____. Mark your calendar.

Attitude adjustment:

If I were honest with myself, had I been standing at that tree, my mouth and my hands would be covered with fruit.

SARA GROVES

I think it's interesting how the very first fall of mankind involved a woman being tempted by food that looked too good to pass up. I don't know about you, but I am certainly in no position to judge Eve! I *love* tempting treats: doughnuts, cookies, cakes, etc. I'm always tempted to indulge my taste buds, even though I know these foods will lead me into sin (by making me irritable within thirty minutes, then depressed when I can't fit my clothes anymore). I also find it fascinating that Adam and Eve both needed new outfits after demonstrating their inability to resist food temptations. Wow! Things haven't changed much after all these centuries, have they?

Use wisdom when dealing with food issues. In addition to overeating, many people stumble into bulimia, anorexia, and other eating disorders. Ask the Holy Spirit to continue leading you into a balanced approach to your eating habits.

Diet:
☐ Free day—eat whatever you like.

Exercise:
☐ Rest.

Week 12

Scripture to memorize:

Praise the Lord, O my soul;
all my inmost being, praise his holy name.
Praise the Lord, O my soul,
and forget not all his benefits.

PSALM 103:1–2

Passage to read:

For you created my inmost being; you knit me together in my mother's womb. I praise you because I am fearfully and wonderfully made; your works are wonderful, I know that full well. My frame was not hidden from you when I was made in the secret place. When I was woven together in the depths of the earth, your eyes saw my unformed body. All the days ordained for me were written in your book before one of them came to be.

PSALM 139:13–16

Guided prayer:

Dear Lord, thank you for creating me. Thank you for my mother, who carried me in her womb and toiled to bring me into this world. I praise you because I am fearfully and wonderfully made. Everything you made is wonderful. And I am wonderful, exactly the way I am, because you hand-made me. I am one of a kind. Lord, you knit me together and designed me to have a specific body type. Help me to find peace with the fact that certain parts of my body don't live up to our culture's ideal. Nevertheless, I am thankful for every properly functioning part of my body. Help me to focus on getting fit so I can serve you more effectively. All the days ordained for me were written in your book before one of them came to be. Help me, Lord, to make the most of each one! Amen.

A prayer from your heart:

_____

_____

_____

_____

Affirmation to recite:
I am fearfully and wonderfully made.

BASED ON PSALM 139:13–16

Action to take:
Consider canceling your subscription to any magazine that leaves you feeling inadequate.

Attitude adjustment:
Before two hours of hair and makeup, even I don't look like
Cindy Crawford!

CINDY CRAWFORD

I hope you've been following the diet and exercise portion of the renewal. You should have noticed a difference when you stand on the bathroom scale. Your clothes should also be fitting better. The improved health of your spirit and soul should be reflected in your mirror as the peace within smoothes the lines on your face. However, don't expect to be transformed into a supermodel. It's important for you to maintain realistic goals based on a realistic body image.

About a year or so ago, I noticed how discontent I felt every time I glanced through a fitness magazine. It gradually dawned on me: I am never again going to look like the teenage models it featured. And you know what? That's okay! I am fearfully and wonderfully made, exactly as I am. I don't have to drive myself to exhaustion trying to be someone I'm not. God wants me to take care of my body so I can serve him with more energy, not so I can look like a fitness model.

So guess what I did? I cancelled my subscriptions to fitness magazines. In reality, each month they all rehash the same basic information. If your stomach is flabby, there are a handful of abdominal exercises everyone recommends. The same thing goes for your buns, thighs, and upper arms. The rest of the magazine is designed to make you discontent with your appearance so you'll feel compelled to purchase the products and renewals being promoted by the advertisers. In fact, many women's magazines serve a similar purpose. If the magazines you routinely read leave you feeling inadequate or discontent . . . stop reading them!

Diet:

- [ ] Drink 8 oz. water mixed with 1 Tbs. ACV and 1 t. local honey.
- [ ] Take multivitamin, Ester-C, EFAs.
- [ ] Drink sixty-four ounces of water throughout the day.
- [ ] Eat two eggs sometime today.
- [ ] Eat an apple or half a grapefruit midmorning.
- [ ] Have a salad with your lunch.
- [ ] Eat as many raw or steamed veggies as you can.
- [ ] Eat a small serving of fruit or lean protein midafternoon.
- [ ] For dinner, eat a palm-sized portion of protein with steamed or stir-fried vegetables.
- [ ] At 8 P.M.: Hot lemon water. Brush teeth. Do NOT eat again until morning.

Exercise:

- [ ] Bounce for ten minutes.
- [ ] Walk briskly for thirty minutes.

Scripture to memorize:

Praise the Lord, O my soul;
all my inmost being, praise his holy name.
Praise the Lord, O my soul,
and forget not all his benefits.

PSALM 103:1–2

Passage to read:

The man without the Spirit does not accept the things that come from the Spirit of God, for they are foolishness to him, and he cannot understand them, because they are spiritually discerned. The spiritual man makes judgments about all things, but he himself is not subject to any man's judgment:

"For who has known the mind of the Lord that he may instruct him?"
But we have the mind of Christ.

1 CORINTHIANS 2:14–16

Guided prayer:

Dear Lord, I thank you for the gift of your Holy Spirit. Apart from the Spirit's work in my life, I would understand nothing! I would be as lost as anyone else on the planet, unable to discern spiritual truth from error. I thank you for giving me the ability to make proper judgments concerning all things (not all people, but all things!) and for the knowledge that no person has the right to judge me. If they want to, that's fine. But I need not concern myself with what anyone else thinks of my choices. Lord, I thank you for giving me the mind of Christ. Help me to grow in my understanding of what it means to have the mind of Christ, as I transform my thinking patterns by a determined act of my will. Help me to align myself with your Word, so your truth can set my emotions free. Amen.

A prayer from your heart:

_____

_____

_____

_____

Affirmation to recite:

When I call to God He answers me. He tells me things I wouldn't know otherwise.

BASED ON JEREMIAH 33:3

Action to take:

Today, think about what you are thinking about! Jot down things you hear yourself saying that are clearly in opposition to the truth of God's Word. (William Backus, author of *Learning to Tell Myself the Truth*, labels these "misbeliefs.")[1] For example, "I'll never change" and "This is hopeless" are classic examples of misbeliefs. The truth is, people change all the time and no situation is hopeless. After you've listed examples of your internal monologue (what you say to yourself all day), you may have some fresh insight into why you feel the way you do. Our thoughts profoundly affect our emotions. The next step is to go back and write out the truth to counteract each misbelief.

---

[1] William Backus, *Learning to Tell Myself the Truth* (Minneapolis, MN: Bethany House Publishers, 1994).

Misbelief (what you say to yourself)	Truth (what God's Word says)
_____	_____
_____	_____
_____	_____
_____	_____
_____	_____

Attitude adjustment:

Your internal monologue is the never-silent stream of words or images running through your head night and day, the automatic thoughts that habitually pop into your head unbidden, generated automatically from your beliefs. . . . All too often we make ourselves miserable and keep ourselves miserable by listening to a nonstop stream of inner nonsense [and self-defeating self-criticism]. . . . We can know scriptural truth, yet still allow ourselves to be [negatively] influenced by untrue self-talk. . . . The cause of our emotional ups and downs comes from within us— not what happens to us, but what we tell ourselves as we interpret what's happening to us. . . . What we tell ourselves determines the quality of our lives.

WILLIAM BACKUS[2]

Few books have had greater impact on my life than William Backus's *Telling Yourself the Truth,* which was given to me by a church counselor. I had struggled with depression my whole life, even as a small child. That book was probably the first step on my journey to recovery, as I realized that I couldn't possibly *feel* better until I started *thinking* better thoughts. The book you now hold in your hands contains the holistic approach—spirit, soul, and body—which God used to deliver me from depression. But as they say, every journey begins with a single step. Reading Backus's book was that step for me. If, after completing today's assignment, you realize your thought life is a major stumbling block, I would urge you to obtain a copy of *Telling Yourself the Truth.*[3]

---

[2]Ibid., 42–43, 59, 61.
[3]Bethany House Publishers. Available at your local bookstore.

Diet:

- [ ] Drink 8 oz. water mixed with 1 Tbs. ACV and 1 t. local honey.
- [ ] Take multivitamin, Ester-C, EFAs.
- [ ] Drink sixty-four ounces of water throughout the day.
- [ ] Eat two eggs sometime today.
- [ ] Eat an apple or half a grapefruit midmorning.
- [ ] Have a salad with your lunch.
- [ ] Eat a small serving of fruit or lean protein midafternoon.
- [ ] Eat as many raw or steamed veggies as you can.
- [ ] For dinner, eat a palm-sized portion of protein with steamed or stir-fried vegetables.
- [ ] At 8 P.M.: Hot lemon water. Brush teeth. Do NOT eat again until morning.

Exercise:

- [ ] Bounce for ten minutes.
- [ ] Walk briskly for thirty minutes.
- [ ] Optional: strength training.

DAY EIGHTY	TODAY'S DATE

Scripture to memorize:

Praise the Lord, O my soul;
all my inmost being, praise his holy name.
Praise the Lord, O my soul,
and forget not all his benefits.

PSALM 103:1–2

Passage to read:

Then Jesus said to his disciples, "If anyone would come after me, he must deny himself and take up his cross and follow me. For whoever wants to save his life will lose it, but whoever loses his life for me will find it. What good will it be for a man if he gains the whole world, yet forfeits his soul? Or what can a man give in exchange for his soul?"

MATTHEW 16:24–26

Guided prayer:

Dear Lord, your kingdom is upside down from this world's perspective. I've been told all my life, "Look out for number one," but your command is "Look up to me and I'll take care of you." The world tells me, "Don't deny yourself anything," but you ask me to deny myself. The world created crucifixion as the most shameful form of death, but you tell me it is the pathway to life. The world tells me to "find myself," but you say if I want to save my life, I have to lose it. My mind says, "That's crazy," but there's a place deep within my spirit that recognizes the truth.

Every time I try to pursue my own agenda, I end up frantic and frustrated. Even when I manage to succeed, the emptiness haunts me. Lord, I don't want to gain all this world has to offer if it means sacrificing my soul—my peace of mind. Lord, I don't want the road to riches. I want the path to peace. Please lead me there, step by step. Amen.

A prayer from your heart:

_____

_____

_____

_____

Affirmation to recite:

I realize nothing good comes from worrying, so I refuse to worry. My responsibility is to make it through today with a grateful heart and let God handle tomorrow.

BASED ON MATTHEW 6:34

Action to take:

You know the old expression: "Something's got to give." Although that slogan isn't directly taken from the Bible, it is certainly based in scriptural truth. Note below some of the things in the world's economy that people try to "gain" and what they have to "give up" to get it. I've given you one example to get you started.

Gain	Give up
Financial success	*Time with family*

Now evaluate yourself. What have you been giving up in pursuit of worldly gain?

Attitude adjustment:

> *He is no fool who gives what he cannot keep*
> *to gain what he cannot lose.*

JIM ELLIOT, MISSIONARY MARTYR

Is it possible you've been giving up what matters in a mad dash to gain things that don't? Re-examine the list you wrote above and pray about the priorities shaping your life. Is it possible God is calling you to make some radical lifestyle changes to become the woman you want to be? Maybe he wants you to use some of your newfound energy to serve him in ways you never dreamed possible—in places you never dreamed you'd visit!

Over the last several years I have been sending copies of my *Ten-Week Journey* books to missionaries in Papua New Guinea. I felt this was the least I could do for women who are laying down their lives in such a difficult place to bring God's Word to people who otherwise wouldn't be able to read it in their native language. I recalled reading the book *Peace Child* shortly after becoming a Christian and being amazed by the courage of Don Richardson and others who first brought the Gospel to that country. The thought of journeying there never even entered my mind until several months ago. Much to my astonishment and delight, I have now been invited by Wycliffe Bible Translators to lead a retreat for 120 female missionaries from around the world. I know a lot of sacrifice will be necessary to make this journey possible, but I believe the gains will far outweigh the difficulties.

Be open to the possibilities for ministry in your own life. God may have quite a surprise in store for you.

Diet:

- [ ] Drink 8 oz. water mixed with 1 Tbs. ACV and 1 t. local honey.
- [ ] Take multivitamin, Ester-C, EFAs.
- [ ] Drink sixty-four ounces of water throughout the day.
- [ ] Eat two eggs sometime today.
- [ ] Eat an apple or half a grapefruit midmorning.
- [ ] Have a salad with your lunch.
- [ ] Eat as many raw or steamed veggies as you can.

- [ ] Eat a small serving of fruit or lean protein midafternoon.
- [ ] For dinner, eat a palm-sized portion of protein with steamed or stir-fried vegetables.
- [ ] At 8 P.M.: Hot lemon water. Brush teeth. Do NOT eat again until morning.

Exercise:

- [ ] Walk briskly for thirty minutes.

DAY EIGHTY-ONE   TODAY'S DATE

Scripture to memorize:

*Beloved, I pray that you may prosper in every way and [that your body]
may keep well, even as [I know] your soul keeps well and prospers.*

3 JOHN 2 AMP

Passage to read:

*The Lord is the everlasting God,
the Creator of the ends of the earth.
He will not grow tired or weary,
and his understanding no one can fathom.
He gives strength to the weary
and increases the power of the weak.
Even youths grow tired and weary,
and young men stumble and fall;
but those who hope in the Lord
will renew their strength.
They will soar on wings like eagles;
they will run and not grow weary,
they will walk and not be faint.*

ISAIAH 40:28–31

Guided Prayer

Dear Lord, I praise you, the everlasting God. I marvel at all you have created. I thank you because you never grow tired or weary. When I have nothing left to give, you have not even begun to tap into your infinite supply of wisdom and strength. Lord, you have promised to give me strength and increase my power if I place my hope in you. Lord, I place my hope in you right now. I believe, with all my heart, that you have good plans for my future. I want to soar like the eagle, who does what you created him to do with effortless grace. That's what I want my life to look like: effortless grace. I don't want to strive anymore. I don't want to wear myself out in vain pursuits. I want to be the woman you've called me to be, nothing more, nothing less. May it be so! Amen.

A prayer from your heart:

_____

_____

_____

_____

Affirmation to recite:

God gives me power and increases my strength. I run and am not weary. I walk and do not faint.

BASED ON ISAIAH 40:28–31

Action to take:

Spend an extra thirty minutes in prayer today, expressing your hope and trust in God. What are some things you are hoping for?

Attitude adjustment:

Lessons will be repeated until learned.

CHERIE CARTER-SCOTT

Every morning when you wake up, you have two basic choices. One is to refuse to get out of bed. The other is to get up and face the world. Ideally, on most days, you will choose to get out of bed. Then you have a new set of choices to make. You can grumble your way through the day, mumbling about how "nothing ever changes." Or you can keep hope alive. You can say to yourself, "No matter how yesterday turned out, I am hoping for better things today." God wants you to live hopefully, expecting the best. Yes, there will be disappointments in life, but God will get you through those. In fact, even the most disappointing turn of events may hold important life lessons fundamental to your Christian maturity. If you find yourself facing the same disappointment over and over again, you should stop and ask God to show you what he's trying to teach you. Maybe you can't move forward to *Victory 201* until you've mastered *Dealing with Disappointment 101*. Learn the lesson so you can move on.

Diet:
☐ Free day—eat whatever you can.

Exercise:
☐ Bounce for ten minutes.
☐ Walk briskly for thirty minutes.
☐ Optional: strength training.

DAY EIGHTY-TWO	TODAY'S DATE

Scripture to memorize:
Beloved, I pray that you may prosper in every way and [that your body] may keep well, even as [I know] your soul keeps well and prospers.

3 JOHN 2 AMP

268

Passage to read:

For the word of God is living and active. Sharper than any double-edged sword, it penetrates even to dividing soul and spirit, joints and marrow; it judges the thoughts and attitudes of the heart. Nothing in all creation is hidden from God's sight. Everything is uncovered and laid bare before the eyes of him to whom we must give account.

HEBREWS 4:12–13

Guided prayer:

Dear Lord, thank you for giving me your Word, the Bible—which reveals my Basic Instructions Before Leaving Earth. Without it, I would have no clue how to live the kind of life that brings true joy and fulfillment. My natural tendency is to think of myself and have a selfish attitude. But your Word says if I want to live an abundant life, I need to focus my thoughts on you and maintain a God-centered attitude of gratitude. Lord, I acknowledge my desire to live according to what I think, what I want, and what I feel, rather than according to your Word. I've come to you, many times, with my own agenda and called it a prayer list. Help me distinguish between my desires and your will—so often they are at cross-purposes. I invite you to show me, through your Word, any thoughts and attitudes I must change in order to become the woman I want to be. Renew my heart, O God! Amen.

A prayer from your heart:

_____

_____

_____

_____

Affirmation to recite:

Greater is he who is in me than he who is in the world. Me plus God is always a majority.

BASED ON 1 JOHN 4:4

Action to take:

Plan what you will do for the health of your spirit, soul, and body when you complete your ninety-day journey. Just a little more than a week left!

For your spirit: _____

For your soul: _____

For your body: _____

Attitude adjustment:

*Since habits become power, make them work with you
and not against you.*

E. STANLEY JONES

If you have been faithfully following the ninety-day plan, by now you have developed some new, more positive daily habits, including:

- ✠ Memorizing and meditating upon Scripture
- ✠ Reading a passage from the Bible
- ✠ Praying Scripture-based prayers
- ✠ Writing out your prayers
- ✠ Reciting positive affirmations, designed to transform you by the renewing of your mind
- ✠ Exerting the strength of your own will to take productive action, applying what you are learning to the real world

- ✠ Adjusting your beliefs and attitudes to line them up with the Word of God
- ✠ Exercising daily
- ✠ Praying while you walk
- ✠ Healthier eating habits
- ✠ Occasional days set aside for prayer and fasting

If you hold on to these habits, they will continue to benefit you for years to come. All humans are creatures of habit. The only question is: are they good habits or bad habits? Your habits can either work for you or against you—and they will accomplish their purpose every day, without your conscious awareness. Decide, right now, to cultivate positive habits.

Diet:

- ☐ Drink 8 oz. water mixed with 1 Tbs. ACV and 1 t. local honey.
- ☐ Take multivitamin, Ester-C, EFAs.
- ☐ Drink sixty-four ounces of water throughout the day.
- ☐ Eat two eggs sometime today.
- ☐ Eat an apple or half a grapefruit midmorning.
- ☐ Have a salad with your lunch.
- ☐ Eat as many raw or steamed veggies as you can.
- ☐ Eat a small serving of fruit or lean protein midafternoon.
- ☐ For dinner, eat a palm-sized portion of protein with steamed or stir-fried vegetables.
- ☐ At 8 P.M.: Hot lemon water. Brush teeth. Do NOT eat again until morning.

Exercise:

- ☐ Walk briskly for forty-five minutes.

DAY EIGHTY-THREE	TODAY'S DATE

Scripture to memorize:

*Beloved, I pray that you may prosper in every way and [that your body]
may keep well, even as [I know] your soul keeps well and prospers.*

3 JOHN 2 AMP

Passage to read:

*My son, pay attention to what I say;
listen closely to my words.
Do not let them out of your sight,
keep them within your heart;
for they are life to those who find them
and health to a man's whole body.
Above all else, guard your heart,
for it is the wellspring of life.
Put away perversity from your mouth;
keep corrupt talk far from your lips.
Let your eyes look straight ahead,
fix your gaze directly before you.
Make level paths for your feet
and take only ways that are firm.
Do not swerve to the right or the left;
keep your foot from evil.*

PROVERBS 4:20–27

Guided prayer:

*Dear Lord, I come before you today, paying careful attention to your Word.
I have committed myself to storing your Word in my heart. I know Scripture
memorization requires setting aside time and focused energy, but it will pay rich
dividends. You have said your words will bring life to me and health to my body.*

Lord, I want to experience the abundant life Jesus promised. I know we live in a fallen world—this isn't heaven yet. But I want to experience all the health and wholeness you desire for me, even while I'm in this earthly body.

I play a vital role in maintaining my own health by caring for my spirit, soul, and body—not just my body. I realize the pathway to holiness is also the pathway to my optimal health. So I am fixing my eyes straight ahead and making level paths for my feet. I am determined to walk the road to righteousness, not swerving to the right or the left. Lord, help me fulfill my vows and keep my feet from evil. Amen.

A prayer from your heart:

_____

_____

_____

_____

Affirmation to recite:

I promote health in my body by fixing my mind on God and keeping my feet firmly set on the road to holiness.

BASED ON PROVERBS 4:20–27

Action to take:

Jot down the names of as many sick people as you can think of and commit to pray for them at least once per week.

_____ _____ _____ _____

_____ _____ _____ _____

_____ _____ _____ _____

Attitude adjustment:

Research indicates 80 percent of church prayer requests are related to physical ailments.

SHERI ROSE SHEPHERD

Think about your own experience of listening to prayer requests at Sunday school or your weekly women's Bible class. Or maybe you're on the church prayer chain. Doesn't the statistic—80 percent of requests are related to physical problems—ring true? Christians should be the healthiest people on earth! The Bible says meditating upon God's Word can make you healthier. There is an increasing body of medical science to support the truth of the Bible, not that the Bible needs any support. There is a tremendous connection between the mind and the body. You can have a healthier body just by filling your mind with thoughts of God's loving care. That's a prescription we can all live with, one with zero potential for adverse side effects.

Diet:

☐ Drink 8 oz. water mixed with 1 Tbs. ACV and 1 t. local honey.
☐ Take multivitamin, Ester-C, EFAs.
☐ Drink sixty-four ounces of water throughout the day.
☐ Eat two eggs sometime today.
☐ Eat an apple or half a grapefruit midmorning.
☐ Have a salad with your lunch.
☐ Eat as many raw or steamed veggies as you can.
☐ Eat a small serving of fruit or lean protein midafternoon.
☐ For dinner, eat a palm-sized portion of protein with steamed or stir-fried vegetables.
☐ Prepare to fast tomorrow.
☐ At 8 P.M.: Hot lemon water. Brush teeth. Do NOT eat again until morning.

Exercise:

☐ Bounce for ten minutes.
☐ Walk briskly for thirty minutes.
☐ Optional: strength training.

DAY EIGHTY-FOUR	TODAY'S DATE

Scripture to memorize:

Beloved, I pray that you may prosper in every way and [that your body] may keep well, even as [I know] your soul keeps well and prospers.

3 JOHN 2 AMP

Passage to read:

This is what the Lord says—your Redeemer, the Holy One of Israel: "I am the Lord your God, who teaches you what is best for you, who directs you in the way you should go."

ISAIAH 48:17

Guided prayer:

Dear Lord, thank you for redeeming me. Thank you for sending Jesus to pay the price for my sins so that I might enjoy eternity in heaven. I praise you, O Lord, because you are holy and blameless. Thank you for being my personal trainer and teacher. I have total God-confidence knowing you always desire the best for me. I ask you now to direct me in the way I should go. Amen.

A prayer from your heart:

_____

_____

_____

_____

Affirmation to recite:

I am more than a conqueror through Christ who loves me. I am a winner.

BASED ON ROMANS 8:37

Action to take:

At the beginning of your ninety-day renewal, you completed a self-evaluation like the one below. Now reevaluate your progress as we near the end of the journey. For each category, indicate how fully you are experiencing God's best, from 1 (meaning not at all, because you are in flat-out disobedience in this area and your life reflects it) to 10 (meaning you are walking in obedience in this area and enjoying tremendous blessings as a result).

Spiritual

Consistent quiet time   1 – – – – 5 – – – – 10

Prayerful (practice the presence of God)   1 – – – – 5 – – – – 10

Increasing in knowledge of the Scriptures   1 – – – – 5 – – – – 10

Routinely memorize and meditate on Scripture   1 – – – – 5 – – – – 10

Mental

Maintain a positive attitude   1 – – – – 5 – – – – 10

Read uplifting material   1 – – – – 5 – – – – 10

Regulate TV viewing   1 – – – – 5 – – – – 10

Learn something new on a regular basis   1 – – – – 5 – – – – 10

Emotional

Moods are stable, rather than up and down   1 – – – – 5 – – – – 10

Able to express and receive love   1 – – – – 5 – – – – 10

Listen carefully when others speak   1 – – – – 5 – – – – 10

Physical

Overall health is good   1 – – – – 5 – – – – 10

Weight is appropriate   1 – – – – 5 – – – – 10

Eating habits are well-balanced   1 – – – – 5 – – – – 10

Personal appearance is appealing   1 – – – – – 5 – – – – – 10

Relational

(evaluate the quality of each that is applicable)

Spouse   1 – – – – – 5 – – – – – 10

Children   1 – – – – – 5 – – – – – 10

Extended family   1 – – – – – 5 – – – – – 10

Church family   1 – – – – – 5 – – – – – 10

Neighbors   1 – – – – – 5 – – – – – 10

Friends   1 – – – – – 5 – – – – – 10

Co-workers   1 – – – – – 5 – – – – – 10

Strangers   1 – – – – – 5 – – – – – 10

Practical

Home is in good order   1 – – – – – 5 – – – – – 10

Car is in good order   1 – – – – – 5 – – – – – 10

Bills are paid on time   1 – – – – – 5 – – – – – 10

Obligations fulfilled on time (no procrastination)   1 – – – – – 5 – – – – – 10

Diet:

☐ Fast, drinking only lemon water.

Exercise:

☐ Do only light stretching exercises. Do not overexert yourself while fasting.

Week 13

Scripture to memorize:

Beloved, I pray that you may prosper in every way and [that your body] may keep well, even as [I know] your soul keeps well and prospers.

3 JOHN 2 AMP

Passage to read:

"I am the true vine, and my Father is the gardener. He cuts off every branch in me that bears no fruit, while every branch that does bear fruit he prunes so that it will be even more fruitful. You are already clean because of the word I have spoken to you. Remain in me, and I will remain in you. No branch can bear fruit by itself; it must remain in the vine. Neither can you bear fruit unless you remain in me.

"I am the vine; you are the branches. If a man remains in me and I in him, he will bear much fruit; apart from me you can do nothing. If anyone does not remain in me, he is like a branch that is thrown away and withers; such branches are picked up, thrown into the fire and burned. If you remain in me and my words remain in you, ask whatever you wish, and it will be given you. This is to my Father's glory, that you bear much fruit, showing yourselves to be my disciples."

JOHN 15:1–8

Guided prayer:

Dear Lord, I know you desire for my soul to prosper. You desire for me to enjoy good health and vitality. Forgive me for indulging harmful emotions that rob me of stamina and lower my body's natural defenses. Forgive me for neglecting my body, then praying for health. How foolish! Lord, I want to remain in you. I do not want to be cut off, so I invite you to cut off those parts of me that drag me down and hinder my effectiveness for your kingdom. Apart from you, I can do nothing. But if I remain in you, spending time with you throughout each day, I will bear much fruit. God, it is the earnest desire of my heart to live a fruitful Christian life. I desire to be a blessing to everyone I meet and to leave this world a better place when I return to you. Father, please establish the work of my hands. Make me fruitful. Amen.

A prayer from your heart:

_____

_____

_____

_____

Affirmation to recite:

Apart from God, I can do nothing. Therefore, I stay connected to him throughout the day by practicing the presence of God.

BASED ON JOHN 15:1–8

Action to take:

For this, your final week, you will be setting specific goals and strategies in each of the five self-evaluation categories. Today, begin with the most important area: Spiritual.

What are some practical steps you can take to ensure you maintain a consistent quiet time? List at least three ideas:

1. _____

2. _____

3. _____

What are some practical ways you can incorporate more prayer into your life? List three ideas:

1. _____
2. _____
3. _____

How can you remind yourself to practice the presence of God?

1. _____
2. _____
3. _____

How will you increase your knowledge of Scripture?

1. _____
2. _____
3. _____

How will you incorporate Scripture memorization and meditation into your daily routine?

1. _____
2. _____
3. _____

Attitude adjustment:

> *He who fails to pray does not cheat God. He cheats himself.*

GEORGE FAILING

For the sake of your spiritual health, you must convince yourself once and for all that God prescribes spiritual disciplines for your sake. He does not need you to perform for him. You cannot add anything to God's holiness by practicing holy habits. Instead, God has revealed these principles in his Word so that we can live a more abundant life. When you fail to pray, you are only cheating your-self out of a blessing. You can never save time by skipping time with God. You have nothing to lose and everything to gain by waking up earlier. Don't make your decision each morning when the alarm rings. Make your decision, right now, once for all time. Then never think about it or mentally debate it again. Just do it!

Diet:

- [ ] Drink 8 oz. water mixed with 1 Tbs. ACV and 1 t. local honey.
- [ ] Take multivitamin, Ester-C, EFAs.
- [ ] Drink sixty-four ounces of water throughout the day.
- [ ] Eat two eggs sometime today.
- [ ] Eat an apple or half a grapefruit midmorning.
- [ ] Have a salad with your lunch.
- [ ] Eat as many raw or steamed veggies as you can.
- [ ] Eat a small serving of fruit or lean protein midafternoon.
- [ ] For dinner, eat a palm-sized portion of protein with steamed or stir-fried vegetables.
- [ ] At 8 P.M.: Hot lemon water. Brush teeth. Do NOT eat again until morning.

Exercise:

- [ ] Bounce for ten-plus minutes.
- [ ] Walk briskly for thirty minutes.
- [ ] Optional: strength training.

Scripture to memorize:

Therefore, prepare your minds for action; be self-controlled; set your hope fully on the grace to be given you when Jesus Christ is revealed. As obedient children, do not conform to the evil desires you had when you lived in ignorance. But just as he who called you is holy, so be holy in all you do; for it is written: "Be holy, because I am holy."

1 PETER 1:13–16

Passage to read:

For if you live according to the sinful nature, you will die; but if by the Spirit you put to death the misdeeds of the body, you will live, because those who are led by the Spirit of God are sons of God.

ROMANS 8:13–14

Guided prayer:

Dear Lord, thank you for revealing truth concerning life and death principles. Every decision I make each day is a vote for life or death. Not in terms of my eternal destiny, which was settled at the cross, but in terms of the quality of my life experience here on earth. Lord, today I want to choose life. Therefore, I am actively putting to death the misdeeds of the body, like overeating and over-indulgence. I want to have enough physical energy to follow the leading of the Holy Spirit. I want to be ready for anything! Amen.

A prayer from your heart:

_____

_____

_____

_____

Affirmation to recite:

   I have compassion on people—especially people who tend to annoy me—because I realize we are all jars of clay.

BASED ON 2 CORINTHIANS 4:7

Action to take:

   Today we turn our attention to the physical:
What are three practical steps you can take to improve your overall health?

1. _____

2. _____

3. _____

Are you currently at your ideal weight?

_____ Yes   _____ No

If not, what steps can you take to return to your ideal weight? And if so, how can you maintain your weight?

1. _____

2. _____

3. _____

What components of the diet do you plan to continue incorporating into your daily routine?

1. _____

2. _____

3. _____

What other strategies do you have for eating a well-balanced, healthy diet?

1. _____

2. _____

3. _____

Do you think your personal appearance reflects well on your Father, the King of kings?

_____ Yes _____ No

What daily steps do you need to take to look your best?

1. _____

2. _____

3. _____

What are some one-time measures you can take to improve your appearance?

1. _____

2. _____

3. _____

Attitude adjustment:

Don't Diet—Live-it!

SLOGAN FROM WWW.EDIETS.COM

The word "diet" has become misconstrued in our culture. It is now understood to mean "a temporary fix for a long-term problem." When you think about it that way, you realize how unworkable the concept really is. No weekend or weeklong or even twelve-week diet can permanently take weight off your body. Yet at any given moment, an estimated 80 to 115 million Americans are on a diet of some kind. Would you believe dieting is a $10-billion industry in the United States? More than 90 percent of dieters end up feeling like failures, because the moment they go off the diet, the weight begins to creep back on. It is inevitable.

You have to make a permanent lifestyle change. Discover a new way of living and eating. Don't diet. Live-it!

Diet:

- [ ] Drink 8 oz. water mixed with 1 Tbs. ACV and 1 t. local honey.
- [ ] Take multivitamin, Ester-C, EFAs.
- [ ] Drink sixty-four ounces of water throughout the day.
- [ ] Eat two eggs sometime today.
- [ ] Eat an apple or half a grapefruit midmorning.
- [ ] Have a salad with your lunch.
- [ ] Eat as many raw or steamed veggies as you can.
- [ ] Eat a small serving of fruit or lean protein midafternoon.
- [ ] For dinner, eat a palm-sized portion of protein with steamed or stir-fried vegetables.
- [ ] At 8 P.M.: Hot lemon water. Brush teeth. Do NOT eat again until morning.

Exercise:

- [ ] Walk briskly for forty-five minutes.

Scripture to memorize:

Therefore, prepare your minds for action; be self-controlled; set your hope fully on the grace to be given you when Jesus Christ is revealed. As obedient children, do not conform to the evil desires you had when you lived in ignorance. But just as he who called you is holy, so be holy in all you do; for it is written: "Be holy, because I am holy."

1 PETER 1:13–16

Passage to read:

Therefore I tell you, do not worry about your life, what you will eat or drink; or about your body, what you will wear. Is not life more important than food, and the body more important than clothes? Look at the birds of the air; they do not sow or reap or store away in barns, and yet your heavenly Father feeds them. Are you not much more valuable than they? Who of you by worrying can add a single hour to his life?

And why do you worry about clothes? See how the lilies of the field grow. They do not labor or spin. Yet I tell you that not even Solomon in all his splendor was dressed like one of these. If that is how God clothes the grass of the field, which is here today and tomorrow is thrown into the fire, will he not much more clothe you, O you of little faith? So do not worry, saying, "What shall we eat?" or "What shall we drink?" or "What shall we wear?" For the pagans run after all these things, and your heavenly Father knows that you need them. But seek first his kingdom and his righteousness, and all these things will be given to you as well. Therefore do not worry about tomorrow, for tomorrow will worry about itself. Each day has enough trouble of its own.

MATTHEW 6:25–34

Guided prayer:

Dear Lord, you have commanded me not to worry. Therefore, whenever I choose to worry, I am also choosing to disobey you. Lord, I trust in your loving care. I know you will meet all of my needs. You clothe me and feed me. You keep a roof over my head. That is so much more than many people in this world have. I am thankful. Lord, I know I cannot make a single positive change by worrying. I can only do harm to my physical and emotional well-being, not to mention damaging my vital relationships.

Lord, I commit myself to seeking first your kingdom and your righteousness. I know you will take care of everything else in my life, as I fix my eyes on you. I am determined to stop worrying about tomorrow and will instead do my best to live a life that honors you today. Amen.

A prayer from your heart:

_____

_____

_____

_____

Affirmation to recite:

I choose not to be a critical or judgmental person because I know people will treat me the way I treat others. The less critical I am, the less critical people will be of me.

BASED ON MATTHEW 7:1

Action to take:

Now let's turn to your mental and emotional well-being:

What are three ways you can continue maintaining a positive attitude?

1. _____

2. _____

3. _____

List three uplifting books you plan to read in the near future. Perhaps set deadlines for their completion.

1. _____
2. _____
3. _____

Indicate how much time you are willing to devote to television viewing each week:

_____ hours

How will you regulate your viewing to insure you do not go beyond the time you have allotted?

_____

_____

What subject would you like to become an expert on?

_____

List three resources (books, audiotapes, seminar, college class, Sunday school class, etc.) you can avail yourself of to increase your knowledge.

1. _____
2. _____
3. _____

List three practical steps you plan to take to keep your moods stable.

1. _____
2. _____
3. _____

Attitude adjustment:

> *Yesterday is history*
> *Tomorrow is a mystery*
> *Today is a gift*
> *That's why we call it the present.*

UNKNOWN

Few things are sadder than a woman whose highest aspiration is to become what she used to be. You see them all the time: women chasing after the lost glory of their youth, women who don't believe the best is yet to come. Wisdom comes with wrinkles. It's a package deal. Would you really trade the lessons you've learned for thin thighs? The woman you want to be cannot be found in your past. Nor will she suddenly turn up on your doorstep tomorrow just because you sit around dreaming she will. No, the woman you want to be can only be created in the present moment, as you cooperate with God and he transforms you from the inside out.

Diet:

- [ ] Drink 8 oz. water mixed with 1 Tbs. ACV and 1 t. local honey.
- [ ] Take multivitamin, Ester-C, EFAs.
- [ ] Drink sixty-four ounces of water throughout the day.
- [ ] Eat two eggs sometime today.
- [ ] Eat an apple or half a grapefruit midmorning.
- [ ] Have a salad with your lunch.
- [ ] Eat as many raw or steamed veggies as you can.
- [ ] Eat a small serving of fruit or lean protein midafternoon.
- [ ] For dinner, eat a palm-sized portion of protein with steamed or stir-fried vegetables.
- [ ] At 8 P.M.: Hot lemon water. Brush teeth. Do NOT eat again until morning.

Exercise:

- [ ] Rest.

Scripture to memorize:

Therefore, prepare your minds for action; be self-controlled; set your hope fully on the grace to be given you when Jesus Christ is revealed. As obedient children, do not conform to the evil desires you had when you lived in ignorance. But just as he who called you is holy, so be holy in all you do; for it is written: "Be holy, because I am holy."

1 PETER 1:13–16

Passage to read:

Therefore confess your sins to each other and pray for each other so that you may be healed. The prayer of a righteous man is powerful and effective.

JAMES 5:16

Guided prayer:

Dear Lord, please bring one person into my life with whom I can be completely open. Someone I can confess my sins to so that we might pray for one another and experience healing. I know my prayers will be powerful and effective as I walk with my conscience cleansed of sin. Amen.

A prayer from your heart:

_____

_____

_____

_____

Affirmation to recite:

I choose to spend time with people who are wise, so I will become wise.

BASED ON PROVERBS 13:20

Action to take:

Today, evaluate your relationships:

List three practical steps you can take, right away, to improve your relationship with your spouse or, if not married, the person you are closest to:

1. _____

2. _____

3. _____

List three practical steps you can take, right away, to improve your relationships with your own children or other children God has placed in your life. (If you aren't in a close relationship with any children, perhaps you should be. There is no shortage of children in need of a godly influence.)

1. _____

2. _____

3. _____

List three practical steps you can take to improve your relationships with your extended family:

1. _____
2. _____
3. _____

List three practical steps you can take to improve your relationships with your church family:

1. _____
2. _____
3. _____

List three practical steps you can take to improve your relationships with your neighbors:

1. _____
2. _____
3. _____

List three practical steps you can take to improve your relationships with your co-workers (if applicable):

1. _____
2. _____
3. _____

List three practical steps you can take to improve your casual interaction with strangers (waitresses, check-out clerks, etc.):

1. _____

2. _____

3. _____

Attitude adjustment:

When you pray for anyone you tend to modify your personal attitude toward him. You thereby lift the relationship to a higher level.

NORMAN VINCENT PEALE

One of the most practical steps you can take to improve any relationship is simply to begin praying for the other person. It is almost impossible to remain angry, bitter, or indifferent toward someone when you are actively praying for his or her welfare. It is difficult to treat someone cruelly while asking God to bring about the best in his or her life. And it is much easier to forgive an offense as you pray for someone and begin to see that person broken at the foot of the cross—or in need of a Savior.

Begin praying for everyone you meet. Even total strangers! One way to move people from your list of acquaintances to your list of friends is to inquire how you can pray for them. Then pray for them each day, asking for updates on a routine basis. Soon you will know this person's nearest concerns and they will know you truly care. How much more important is it to pray for our own family! Some of us live such hectic lives, we hardly know our nearest relatives. But ask how you can pray for each one. Listen attentively, with a pen and prayer notebook in your hand. This will surely get their attention and, ultimately, win their affection.

Diet:

- ☐ Drink 8 oz. water mixed with 1 Tbs. ACV and 1 t. local honey.
- ☐ Take multivitamin, Ester-C, EFAs.
- ☐ Drink sixty-four ounces of water throughout the day.
- ☐ Eat two eggs sometime today.
- ☐ Eat an apple or half a grapefruit midmorning.
- ☐ Have a salad with your lunch.
- ☐ Eat as many raw or steamed veggies as you can.

☐ Eat a small serving of fruit or lean protein midafternoon.
☐ For dinner, eat a palm-sized portion of protein with steamed or stir-fried vegetables.
☐ At 8 P.M.: Hot lemon water. Brush teeth. Do NOT eat again until morning.

Exercise:
☐ Bounce for ten-plus minutes.
☐ Walk briskly for thirty minutes.

DAY EIGHTY-NINE	TODAY'S DATE

Scripture to memorize:
> *Therefore, prepare your minds for action; be self-controlled; set your hope fully on the grace to be given you when Jesus Christ is revealed. As obedient children, do not conform to the evil desires you had when you lived in ignorance. But just as he who called you is holy, so be holy in all you do; for it is written: "Be holy, because I am holy."*

1 PETER 1:13–16

Passage to read:
*Though the fig tree does not bud
and there are no grapes on the vines,
though the olive crop fails
and the fields produce no food,
though there are no sheep in the pen
and no cattle in the stalls,
yet I will rejoice in the Lord,
I will be joyful in God my Savior.
The Sovereign Lord is my strength;
he makes my feet like the feet of a deer,
he enables me to go on the heights.*

HABAKKUK 3:17–19

Guided prayer:

Dear Lord, I am ready to prepare my mind for action! I am ready to live a self-controlled life. I have set my hope fully on you and all the wonderful things you have in store for me, both in this life and throughout eternity. I want to be an obedient child, not one who surrenders to the sinful impulses seeking to rule my body, mind, will, and emotions. I want to be holy, just as you are holy. Lord, I know life won't always turn out exactly the way I might want. Sometimes "the crops fail"—disappointments inevitably come. But even at those times, I know you will be my strength. You will enable me to be surefooted and not lose my step. God, I am counting on you to bring to completion the good work you have started in me. I know you will be faithful to do it. Amen.

A prayer from your heart:

_____

_____

_____

_____

Affirmation to recite:

Joy is not a result of what happens to me; it is a result of how I respond to what happens to me. I choose to be joyful.

BASED ON 1 THESSALONIANS 5:16

Action to take:

Although we haven't addressed the following practical matters directly, I am certain that as the health of your spirit, soul, and body has improved, you have seen improvements in the way you attend to the everyday details of life. Please evaluate how you can continue to improve in the following areas:

List three practical ways you can keep your home in good order:

1. _____
2. _____
3. _____

List three practical ways you can keep your car in good order:

1. _____
2. _____
3. _____

Are your bills paid on time?

_____ Yes _____ No

If not, what specific changes do you need to make?

1. _____
2. _____
3. _____

Do you fulfill your obligations on time or do you tend to procrastinate? If you are inclined to procrastination, list some practical ways you can overcome it (don't put off answering this question!):

1. _____
2. _____
3. _____

Attitude adjustment:

I had planned to write something about the importance of overcoming procrastination, but I decided to put it off.

DONNA PARTOW

One of the most powerful little booklets ever written is *The Tyranny of the Urgent,* by Charles Hummel (InterVarsity Press). Even though I first read it nearly two decades ago, his words still resonate in my mind: "Our unfinished tasks *haunt quiet moments.*" Oh, how true that is! Our energy is often drained, not by work we do, but by work we've left undone. I experienced this firsthand when I moved into my current house several months ago. I had only two days to house hunt. This one was in the right neighborhood at the right price, so I bought it after a quick walk-through. I didn't stop to examine every nook and cranny; instead, I just took in the house's "big picture," which appeared suitable. When we moved in, I immediately realized the house was absolutely filthy. Not only did the prior owners leave behind surface dirt—unwiped counters and cabinets, grungy toilets and showers, etc.—the house was deep-down dirty—the kind of dirt that comes from many years of neglect.

Ever since move-in day, almost every quiet moment has been haunted by the filth. Almost from the minute I open my eyes in the morning, I'm exhausted by the mere thought of the work I know needs to be done. I'm just now admitting to myself what part of me has known all along: rolling up my sleeves will ultimately prove less draining than looking at the unfinished task. When I finish this book, I'm going to start by cleaning one of the fourteen filthy ceiling fans!

What unfinished tasks are haunting you right now? Resolve to roll up your sleeves and get to work. A task begun is half done. And I bet you'll feel energized by the momentum . . . so much so that you'll move on to the next task. And the next. At least that's what I'm hoping is going to happen. That's the kind of woman I want to be.

Diet:

- [ ] Drink 8 oz. water mixed with 1 Tbs. ACV and 1 t. local honey.
- [ ] Take multivitamin, Ester-C, EFAs.
- [ ] Drink sixty-four ounces of water throughout the day.
- [ ] Eat two eggs sometime today.
- [ ] Eat an apple or half a grapefruit midmorning.
- [ ] Have a salad with your lunch.
- [ ] Eat as many raw or steamed veggies as you can.
- [ ] Eat a small serving of fruit or lean protein midafternoon.

☐ For dinner, eat a palm-sized portion of protein with steamed or stir-fried vegetables.

☐ At 8 P.M.: Hot lemon water. Brush teeth. Do NOT eat again until morning.

Exercise:

☐ Bounce for ten-plus minutes.

☐ Walk briskly for thirty minutes.

☐ Optional: strength training.

DAY NINETY	TODAY'S DATE

Scripture to memorize:

Therefore, prepare your minds for action; be self-controlled; set your hope fully on the grace to be given you when Jesus Christ is revealed. As obedient children, do not conform to the evil desires you had when you lived in ignorance. But just as he who called you is holy, so be holy in all you do; for it is written: "Be holy, because I am holy."

1 PETER 1:13–16

Passage to read:

My heart is steadfast, O God;
I will sing and make music with all my soul.
Awake, harp and lyre!
I will awaken the dawn.
I will praise you, O Lord, among the nations;
I will sing of you among the peoples.
For great is your love, higher than the heavens;
your faithfulness reaches to the skies.
Be exalted, O God, above the heavens,
and let your glory be over all the earth.

PSALM 108:1–5

Guided prayer:

Dear Lord, we made it! Thank you for giving me the strength to travel this ninety-day journey. I want to sing and make music with all of my heart, mind, and soul. Lord, I praise you for giving me a fresh start on my life. The woman I want to be is becoming a reality. Thank you for your great love and faithfulness. Thank you for never giving up on me, even when I'm tempted to give up on myself. Lord, I want to glorify your name through my life. I want the whole world to know what a wonderful God you are, just by taking note of the radical changes you have made in my life. I want to be a walking testimony to your life-changing power. Today, bring someone across my path that I can tell of your marvelous deeds on my behalf! Amen.

A prayer from your heart:

_____

_____

_____

_____

Affirmation to recite:

The One who began a good work in me will see it through to completion. Therefore, I don't feel stressed-out or disappointed when I see my weaknesses and failures. I stay focused on God and trust the process. I believe I am well on my way to enjoying maximum health in my spirit, soul, and body.

BASED ON PHILIPPIANS 1:6

Action to take:

Reread the lists you made on Day 2. Revise them if appropriate.

Call a friend and tell her what you have accomplished! Go out and celebrate. You deserve it.

Attitude adjustment:

True abundance comes not from amassing [more], but from appreciating what you already have.

CHERIE CARTER-SCOTT

If you have made it this far, I am truly proud of you. By now, you will have noticed some dramatic changes in your spirit, soul, and body. Many of your friends will have noticed the outward changes, but be sure to tell them what has taken place in your spirit and soul, as well.

Now may God himself, the God of peace, sanctify you through and through. May your whole self—spirit, soul, and body—be kept blameless until the coming of our Lord Jesus Christ. The one who called you is faithful. And he will do it. Amen.

Diet:

☐ Fast or feast for your final day. Your choice!!!

Exercise:

☐ Your choice!

Becoming the Woman I Want to Be
Leader's Guide

A Note to Leaders

Thank you for choosing *Becoming the Woman I Want to Be* to encourage and help the women entrusted to your care. I pray it will enrich your lives as you undertake this ninety-day program together with the Lord's help. While I wrote the book for individual use, it's easily adapted to a small-group setting.

Use your time together to encourage women in their journey both spiritually and physically. I have made suggestions—not a lesson plan—for each week's meeting. If you sense the Spirit's leading, adapt the content for your group by choosing a different day's Scripture passage or activity/discussion topic. While this isn't a formal Bible study, you may want to have a short discussion of the Scripture passage and talk about how it applies to life. The weekly meeting will be more meaningful if the women have already completed the material you are discussing.

Praying together is also important at every meeting. Some weeks you may use one of the guided prayers; other times women may share their written prayers. In addition, a time of praying for one another is valuable.

Finally, I encourage you to spur the women on in Scripture memory each week. It is a powerful way to renew the mind.

Read through all the weekly suggestions now, making note where advance planning or equipment is needed.

At your first meeting, be sure to emphasize that although this is an individual journey, because you are taking it together you can help one another along. Women should not compare their goals or their progress so as to feel inferior or superior but rather rejoice together in how far each one has come. Ask the women to commit to one another that they will respect one another's privacy—

that everything shared in the meetings must stay there. Emphasize this as strongly as you know how! If any person's trust is violated, then everyone's trust will be violated and the effectiveness of your group will be greatly diminished. Meanwhile, please visit my Web site for more information and on-going support as your group works through the ninety-day journey.

I would love to hear from you when your group has completed its ninety-day journey. You may e-mail your comments to *donnapartow@cox.net*. It is my earnest prayer that this program will bring each person closer to becoming the woman *she* wants to be.

His Vessel,
Donna Partow

Discussion Leader's Guide

WEEK 1

- Read the Day 3 Scripture passage and pray the guided prayer together.
- Ask the women to share a couple of their Have/Do/Become list items from Day 2. Talk together about practical ways they can incorporate the renewal plan in their schedules. Encourage them to find an exercise partner and a prayer partner for their journey.
- Provide a tempting array of fresh veggies (from the approved list) to munch during the meeting.
- Take a "before" picture of each individual and provide her with a print of the picture.

WEEK 2

- Read the Day 11 Scripture passage and pray the guided prayer together or pray in pairs.
- Invite a personal trainer or other qualified person to share the benefits of lifelong weight training for women. To encourage women just getting started with weight training, bring in a variety of weights and exercise videos and try them out (see Day 11).
- Discuss the importance of sealing one's lips and sharing the good things God is doing (Day 12). Take turns affirming each person in the group. To ensure that everyone is treated the same way, focus attention on each individual in turn, asking the rest of the group to make three positive statements about her.

WEEK 3

- Read the Day 16 Scripture passage and pray the guided prayer together or ask a few individuals to read their written prayers.
- Sing together (or read the words aloud) "I Surrender All."

All to Jesus I surrender,
All to Him I freely give;
I will ever love and trust Him,
In His presence daily live.

All to Jesus I surrender,
Make me, Savior, wholly Thine;
Let me feel the Holy Spirit—
Truly know that Thou art mine.

All to Jesus I surrender,
Humbly at His feet I bow;
Worldly pleasures all forsaken,
Take me, Jesus, take me now.

All to Jesus I surrender,
Lord, I give myself to Thee;
Fill me with Thy love and power,
Let Thy blessings fall on me.

Chorus:
I surrender all,
I surrender all,
All to Thee, my blessed Savior,
I surrender all.[1]

- This might be a good time to discuss fasting, especially if it is a new discipline for some in your group. Encourage those who fast regularly or occasionally to talk about how it helps them spiritually. Plan strategies for fasting while caring for a hungry family, going about daily work, or other obstacles that may be encountered.
- Ask each woman to bring copies of a *healthy* salad recipe for a recipe exchange next week.

WEEK 4

- Read the Day 24 Scripture passage and pray the guided prayer together.
- Hang large easel paper around the room and have women write as many blessings as they can on the sheets within a few minutes. Discuss how blessed they are and encourage individuals to share special blessings.
- Using the book *Operation World,* missionary publications, or newspapers/magazines, pray together for the persecuted church worldwide.
- Exchange recipes and ask for volunteers to talk about the benefits they're seeing as they follow the diet and exercise guidelines.

[1]Judson W. Van de Venter. Public domain.

WEEK 5

- Read the Day 30 Scripture passage and pray the guided prayer together or pray in pairs.
- If anyone in the group has taken a silent retreat, ask her (in advance) to share her experience. Let those who practiced keeping quiet (Day 30, Attitude Adjustment) talk about the benefits—or frustrations—of the day.
- Provide information about local retreat centers that can be used for silent retreats.
- Celebrate being one-third of the way through the ninety days. Rejoice with those who are seeing benefits and support those who might be discouraged. Enjoy healthy fruit smoothies or protein shakes together.

WEEK 6

- Read the Day 38 Scripture passage and pray the guided prayer together or ask a few people to read their written prayers.
- This is a good time to review the Scripture passages that the group has memorized over the past six weeks. Share together how these verses have blessed the group.
- Watch the movie *Chariots of Fire* (or a portion of it) together. Ask the group this question: How does the concept of athletic training relate to the Christian life?

WEEK 7

- Read the Day 43 Scripture passage and pray the guided prayer together.
- Invite a spiritually vibrant woman (or more than one) over age seventy-five to the group. What is the secret of her blessed life? Ask her to share her faith journey. Then discuss what the group members want to be like when they're eighty.
- Ask for volunteers to give progress reports at the halfway point of the ninety-day journey. Address the spirit, soul, and body. Spend an extended time in prayer either in small groups or pairs, praying for specific needs.

WEEK 8

- Read the Day 52 Scripture passage and pray the guided prayer together.
- Talk about the choices women make every day and how knowing Colossians

3:2–4 can help in making the best choices. How do the choices they make impact their families, co-workers, and friends?
- Enjoy an exercise-related outing together. Go ice-skating, roller-skating, biking, swimming, or hiking, for example. Or bring an easy-to-follow workout video to the group if an outing isn't possible.

WEEK 9

- Read the Day 60 Scripture passage and pray the guided prayer together or pray in pairs.
- Together compile a list of good things in your lives. Encourage women to share the stories behind the good things they mention.
- Ask: Which of the Affirmations has helped you the most? What impact are they having in your faith journey?
- Provide a variety of craft supplies for women to make a poster or wall hangings of the Affirmation that is most meaningful to her.

WEEK 10

- Read the Day 68 Scripture passage and pray the guided prayer together.
- Discuss the attributes of God that the women listed (Action to take, Day 60).
- Sing together "Thou Art Worthy"[2] or another hymn or worship song that focuses on God's attributes. Spend time in prayer praising God for his attributes.
- Invite a creative cook to share healthy creative ways to prepare or season vegetables and salads. Provide recipes and/or samples to taste.

WEEK 11

- Read the Day 71 Scripture passage and pray the guided prayer together or ask for volunteers to read the prayers from their heart.
- Ask someone to read the story behind the hymn " 'Tis So Sweet to Trust in Jesus" (Attitude Adjustment, Day 71) and then sing together or read aloud verses one and four.

'Tis so sweet to trust in Jesus,
Just to take Him at His word,
Just to rest upon His promise,
Just to know, "Thus saith the Lord."

I'm so glad I learned to trust Thee,
Precious Jesus, Savior, Friend;
And I know that Thou art with me,
Wilt be with me to the end.

---

[2]Pauline Michael Mills, "Thou Art Worthy" (Tarzana, CA: Fred Bock Music Company, 1991).

Chorus:
Jesus, Jesus, how I trust Him!
How I've proved Him o'er and o'er!
Jesus, Jesus, precious Jesus!
O for grace to trust Him more![3]

- In advance, ask women to bring tapes or CDs with music that inspires and encourages them. Let several play a short selection and tell how God has spoken to them through it.
- If someone in your group plays a guitar or flute or other instrument, ask her to prepare and play several minutes of quiet music while the rest of the women meditate and pray silently. Or use a recording of instrumental music.

WEEK 12

- Read the Day 82 Scripture passage and pray the guided prayer together.
- Review the habits developed during the past three months (Attitude Adjustment, Day 82). Discuss which of the habits various group members plan to continue—and why—when the ninety-day program is completed.
- Plan to send each woman in the group an encouraging note or e-mail in about a month. Note what specific habits she said she wanted to continue.
- Review the Scripture passages that the group has memorized. Share together how these verses have blessed the group.
- Together, plan your celebration for next week. How will you commemorate becoming the women you want to be? See below for a few ideas.

WEEK 13

- Read the Day 90 Scripture passage and pray the guided prayer together. Then open the prayer time for individuals to add their specific prayer from the heart.
- Celebrate together. You could
    - ★ enjoy a healthy meal or activity together.
    - ★ give verbal or fun homemade awards to each group member for goals met or progress made.
    - ★ share testimonies of what God has done in lives.

---

[3]Louisa M. R. Stead, "'Tis So Sweet to Trust in Jesus," Public domain.

★ take individual "after" pictures and give each woman a print, plus a picture of the group.
★ do a service project for others (your women's ministry leader or pastor may have suggestions).

Affirmations

You can transform your life by filling your mind with the Word of God. The following Scripture-based affirmations are positive statements describing, not necessarily who you are right now, but the woman you *want* to be and the woman you *can become* through the power of the Holy Spirit. Read these **aloud** daily:

- ✠ I forget those things that are behind me, including all of my personal short-comings in the area of spiritual disciplines, diet, and exercise. I am pressing toward what lies ahead: a bright future filled with health in my spirit, soul, and body.—Based on Philippians 3:13
- ✠ I have the power to change my life, because the spirit of the Lord rests upon me. I can learn a new way of living because I have a spirit of wisdom and understanding.—Based on Isaiah 11:2
- ✠ I am cooperating with God as he transforms me day by day. I am pressing on toward the prize God has in store for me.—Based on Philippians 3:14
- ✠ I rest securely in God's loving care. I know he has an awesome plan for my future. Plans to prosper me and not to harm me.—Based on Jeremiah 29:11
- ✠ Goodness and love follow me wherever I go. I am richly blessed!—Based on Psalm 23
- ✠ I meditate on God's Word day and night. I love to memorize Scripture!—Based on Psalm 119:97
- ✠ I am blessed because I look to God's Word for advice and direction. As I live by the principles of God's Word, I will be blessed and bear fruit.—Based on Psalm 1
- ✠ I actively strive for health in my spirit, soul, and body. I seek healing whenever needed so that my spirit, soul, and body may be kept blameless.—Based on 1 Thessalonians 5:23–24
- ✠ I've made it my goal to be steadfast, unmovable, always abounding in the

work of the Lord.—Based on 1 Corinthians 15:58

✠ I diligently guard my body, because it is the only living sacrifice I have to offer God. But I am even more diligent in guarding my heart because I know out of it flow the issues of life.—Based on Proverbs 4:23

✠ I don't overeat because I know food can never satisfy me. My soul is satisfied with the things of God.—Based on Psalm 84:1–2

✠ Any hardships I face in this world are nothing compared to the glory that will be revealed in me.—Based on Romans 8:18

✠ I am persuaded that nothing can separate me from the love of God.—Based on Romans 8:38–39

✠ I know nothing is impossible with God. He is able to transform my life from the inside out.—Based on Luke 1:37

✠ I don't let negative people in my life drag me down; instead, I strive to be a positive, loving influence on everyone I meet.—Based on 1 John 5:4

✠ I am a slave to righteousness. I am no longer free to live however I please.—Based on Romans 6:19–23

✠ I know God is able to do exceedingly abundantly above all that I could possibly ask or imagine.—Based on Ephesians 3:20

✠ My body belongs to God—he bought and paid for it. I have no right to treat God's temple like a trash can, filling it with junk food and abusing it through neglect. Instead, I have an obligation to take care of myself.—Based on Romans 12:1–2

✠ I lay up for myself treasures in heaven. I do not store treasure here on earth. I realize that where my treasure is, there my heart will also be.—Based on Matthew 6:19–21

✠ I am confident that God will reward me as I diligently seek him. I don't know what form the reward will take, but I know it will be awesome.—Based on Hebrews 11:6

✠ I remain calm no matter what happens. I keep a clear head in all situations because I trust God to provide for my every need.—Based on Isaiah 26:3

✠ I am one of God's treasured possessions. He handpicked me to be his own.—Based on Deuteronomy 26:16–19

✠ I take dominion over my body; I don't allow my body to have dominion over me.—Based on Matthew 5:29–30

✠ I am a blessing to God when I choose to be grateful and hopeful, no matter how difficult my circumstances.—Based on Luke 1:46–52

✠ I remember all God's benefits: He forgives me, heals me, and surrounds me with loving-kindness. He has rescued me from an eternity in hell and has blessed me in this life as well.—Based on Psalm 103:1–5

✠ My faith makes me whole in spirit, soul, and body. Jesus offers me the same healing he offered others when he walked the earth.—Based on Mark 5:34

✠ My life is a life of contribution. I am making a positive difference in this world and for eternity.—Based on 1 Peter 2:11–12

✠ When my emotions go haywire, I turn to God's Word and it revives my soul.—Based on Psalm 19:7–8

✠ I firmly believe God desires for me to prosper and enjoy good health.—Based on 3 John 2

✠ I trust in God and he shows me the way I should go.—Based on Psalm 143:8

✠ God has called me to serve others. I fulfill that call enthusiastically in the power of the Holy Spirit.—Based on Isaiah 61:1–3

✠ As a follower of God, I am automatically in a position of leadership in this world. I take that responsibility seriously and always seek to set a good example.—Based on 1 Kings 2:2–3

✠ I walk in love and humility. I am patient and kind in every situation.—Based on 1 Corinthians 13

✠ I spend more time praying than grumbling, therefore I have less to grumble about.—Based on Philippians 2:14

✠ I don't have to rely on cosmetics to make me beautiful. I look to the Lord, so my face is radiant. He makes me beautiful from the inside out.—Based on Psalm 34:1–5

✠ I build myself up through wisdom. Through increasing knowledge, I fill my life with blessings and every good thing.—Based on Proverbs 24:3–4

✠ Nothing I have to do today is more important than spending time in prayer. My day goes more smoothly when I begin it on my knees.—Based on Mark 1:35–37

✠ I reject negative thinking patterns, focusing instead on the positive promises of God. When negative thoughts come, I stop them in their tracks and take them captive.—Based on 2 Corinthians 10:5

✠ I keep my mind at peace by focusing on God's goodness, rather than striving after my fair share.—Based on Isaiah 26:3

✠ When someone asks me how I am, I say, "I am richly blessed," because that is always true—no matter what else is happening in my life.—Based on Proverbs 28:20

✠ I protect my body by keeping my mind at peace. The more confidence I have in God's loving care for me, the more my mind will remain at peace.—Based on Isaiah 26:3

✛ I am in strict training as a disciple of Christ and I work hard. But I don't drive myself to exhaustion trying to prove I'm worth something. I know I am worthwhile because I am a child of God.—Based on 1 John 3:1

✛ I don't get worked up when things don't turn out the way I had hoped. I simply adjust to circumstances as they unfold, trusting that God has a better plan in mind.—Based on Jeremiah 29:11

✛ I am not shaken by tough times, because I am confident God will bring something good out of every circumstance, even if I don't understand the how, when, or why.—Based on Romans 8:28

✛ I desire and work toward peace within and around me. I cultivate harmony in all my relationships by being gracious, no matter how difficult the circumstances.—Based on Psalm 34:11–14

✛ I fill my mind with loving, positive thoughts concerning my family rather than mentally rehearsing their faults.—Based on Philippians 4:8

✛ I live my life in a spirit of prayer, practicing the presence of God at all times and in all my affairs.—Based on Ephesians 6:10–18

✛ I am not easily provoked. Instead, I give other people the benefit of the doubt, knowing others are probably doing the best they can.—Based on 1 Corinthians 13

✛ I trust in the Lord with all my heart, rather than trying to figure things out for myself. I know he has everything figured out already.—Based on Proverbs 3:5-6

✛ I enjoy meditating on God's Word. It's such a blessing to have God's Word in my mouth—to be able to speak a word in due season to those who are weary or discouraged.—Based on Psalm 1:2

✛ I realize self-control is a marvelous fruit of the Holy Spirit, so I actively seek to cultivate it in my life. My life is so much better when I practice self-control, rather than living by impulse.—Based on Galatians 5:22–23

✛ I believe God's Word rather than what I might believe by looking at my circumstances. Circumstances can deceive me, but God's Word never will.—Based on Proverbs 4:20–22

✛ I love giving because I know that in the same measure I give, it will be given back to me—good measure, pressed down, shaken together, and running over.—Based on Luke 6:38

✛ The more I fill my mind with "whatever is true, noble, excellent, and praiseworthy," the less room there will be in my mind for negative thoughts. Therefore I choose to think about such things.—Based on Philippians 4:8–9

✛ I am controlled by the Spirit, not by my taste buds.—Based on Romans 8:6

- I am richly blessed. I am not missing out on anything. I enjoy every spiritual blessing!—Based on Ephesians 1:3
- Tough times will either make me bitter or better. I choose to learn my life lessons, rather than resenting or resisting them, so I will become a better person.—Based on Hebrews 12:15
- Even before I was born, God had a specific assignment in mind for my life. My greatest fulfillment comes as I fulfill God's plans and purposes.—Based on Jeremiah 1:5
- My vindication comes from God, so I don't waste time trying to prove I'm right.—Based on Isaiah 54:17
- My life is full of good things. All I have to do is open my eyes to see how fortunate I really am.—Based on Matthew 6:20
- I desire to be blessed with long life so that I can be a blessing to others.—Based on Joshua 14:6–14
- The eyes of my understanding are enlightened. I understand how powerful God is in my life—more powerful than any obstacles I face.—Based on Ephesians 1:18–19
- I choose to feed my spirit.—Based on Galatians 5:16–18
- I choose to be joyful and gracious, no matter how difficult the circumstance.—Based on Philippians 4:4–7
- I have committed the rest of my life to serving God with all my heart and with all my soul.—Based on Joshua 22:5
- I have made a conscious decision to eliminate complaining from my life—for my sake and for the sake of everyone around me. I do everything—especially the simple, everyday tasks of life—without complaint.—Based on Philippians 2:14–15
- God shows me the way to go. All I have to do is listen and he will tell me which path to take.—Based on Proverbs 3:5–8
- My sinful response to the sin of others has far more destructive power than anything others can do to me. Therefore, I respond to everyone in a loving fashion no matter how they treat me.—Based on Proverbs 17:22
- I choose to forgive everyone, just as God has forgiven me. Hanging on to unforgiveness cannot benefit me in any way.—Based on Colossians 3:13
- I don't waste my time looking for the "speck" in other people's eyes. Instead, I focus on removing the plank from my own eye—realizing the "plank" is my own critical spirit.—Based on Matthew 7:1–5
- I let the peace of Christ rule in my heart by choosing to be thankful for what

I do have, rather than complaining about what I don't have.—Based on Colossians 3:15–16

✠ When I choose to be thankful, I am obeying and honoring God. He, in turn, will bless my obedience.—Based on Colossians 3:15

✠ I eat to live. I don't live to eat.—Based on Proverbs 23:2

✠ I reap what I sow. Therefore, I choose to sow wisely.—Based on Galatians 6:7–9

✠ I enjoy life and peace, because I keep my mind fixed on the things of God. When my life lacks peace, I refocus my mind on him and watch my peace be restored.—Based on Isaiah 26:3

✠ I try to live every day, every moment, enthusiastically. I give thanks for every opportunity and encounter, even the challenges, because they help me grow.—Based on Psalm 103:1–2

✠ I exercise wisdom concerning my eating habits, because I know food can be a stumbling block to me.—Based on Genesis 3:1–7

✠ I am fearfully and wonderfully made.—Based on Psalm 139:13–16

✠ When I call to God He answers me. He tells me things I wouldn't know otherwise.—Based on Jeremiah 33:3

✠ I realize nothing good comes from worrying, so I refuse to worry. My responsibility is to make it through today with a grateful heart and let God handle tomorrow.—Based on Matthew 6:34

✠ God gives me power and increases my strength. I run and am not weary. I walk and do not faint.—Based on Isaiah 40:28–31

✠ Greater is he who is in me than he who is in the world. Me plus God is always a majority.—Based on 1 John 4:4

✠ I promote health in my body by fixing my mind on God and keeping my feet firmly set on the road to holiness.—Based on Proverbs 4:20–27

✠ I am more than a conqueror through Christ who loves me. I am a winner.—Based on Romans 8:37

✠ Apart from God, I can do nothing. Therefore, I stay connected to him throughout the day by practicing the presence of God.—Based on John 15:1–8

✠ I have compassion on people—especially people who tend to annoy me—because I realize we are all jars of clay.—Based on 2 Corinthians 4:7

✠ I choose not to be a critical or judgmental person because I know people will treat me the way I treat others. The less critical I am, the less critical people will be of me.—Based on Matthew 7:1

✣ I choose to spend time with people who are wise, so I will become wise.—Based on Proverbs 13:20

✣ Joy is not a result of what happens to me; it is a result of how I respond to what happens to me. I choose to be joyful.—Based on 1 Thessalonians 5:16

✣ The One who began a good work in me will see it through to completion. Therefore, I don't feel stressed-out or disappointed when I see my weaknesses and failures. I stay focused on God and trust the process. I believe I am well on my way to enjoying maximum health in my spirit, soul, and body.—Based on Philippians 1:6

2 Timothy 1:7

For God did not give us a spirit of timidity, but a spirit of power, of love and of self-discipline.

Becoming the Woman I Want to Be, Donna Partow

Psalm 51:10–12

Create in me a pure heart, O God, and renew a steadfast spirit within me. Do not cast me from your presence or take your Holy Spirit from me. Restore to me the joy of your salvation and grant me a willing spirit, to sustain me.

Becoming the Woman I Want to Be, Donna Partow

---

1 Thessalonians 5:23–24

May God himself, the God of peace, sanctify you through and through. May your whole spirit, soul and body be kept blameless at the coming of our Lord Jesus Christ. The one who calls you is faithful and he will do it.

Becoming the Woman I Want to Be, Donna Partow

Psalm 31:7–8

I will be glad and rejoice in your love, for you saw my affliction and knew the anguish of my soul. You have not handed me over to the enemy but have set my feet in a spacious place.

Becoming the Woman I Want to Be, Donna Partow

Psalm 143:8

Let the morning bring me word of your unfailing love, for I have put my trust in you. Show me the way I should go, for to you I lift up my soul.

Becoming the Woman I Want to Be, Donna Partow

Psalm 62:1–2

My soul finds rest in God alone; my salvation comes from him. He alone is my rock and my salvation; he is my fortress, I will never be shaken.

Becoming the Woman I Want to Be, Donna Partow

---

1 Corinthians 9:24–25

Do you not know that in a race all the runners run, but only one gets the prize? Run in such a way as to get the prize. Everyone who competes in the games goes into strict training. They do it to get a crown that will not last; but we do it to get a crown that will last forever.

Becoming the Woman I Want to Be, Donna Partow

---

1 Corinthians 6:19–20

Do you not know that your body is a temple of the Holy Spirit, who is in you, whom you have received from God? You are not your own; you were bought at a price. Therefore honor God with your body.

Becoming the Woman I Want to Be, Donna Partow

---

2 Corinthians 7:1

Since we have these promises, dear friends, let us purify ourselves from everything that contaminates body and spirit, perfecting holiness out of reverence for God.

Becoming the Woman I Want to Be, Donna Partow

Psalm 103:1–2

Praise the Lord, O my soul; all my inmost being, praise his holy name. Praise the Lord, O my soul, and forget not all his benefits.

Becoming the Woman I Want to Be, Donna Partow

1 Corinthians 3:16–17

Don't you know that you yourselves are God's temple and that God's Spirit lives in you? If anyone destroys God's temple, God will destroy him; for God's temple is sacred, and you are that temple.

Becoming the Woman I Want to Be, Donna Partow

1 Corinthians 9:26–27

Therefore I do not run like a man running aimlessly; I do not fight like a man beating the air. No, I beat my body and make it my slave so that after I have preached to others, I myself will not be disqualified for the prize.

Becoming the Woman I Want to Be, Donna Partow

3 John 2 AMP

Beloved, I pray that you may prosper in every way and [that your body] may keep well, even as [I know] your soul keeps well and prospers.

Becoming the Woman I Want to Be, Donna Partow

Proverbs 17:22

A cheerful heart is good medicine, but a crushed spirit dries up the bones.

Becoming the Woman I Want to Be, Donna Partow

Colossians 3:2–4

Set your minds on things above, not on earthly things. For you died, and your life is now hidden with Christ in God. When Christ, who is your life, appears, then you also will appear with him in glory.

Becoming the Woman I Want to Be, Donna Partow

1 Peter 1:13–16

Therefore, prepare your minds for action; be self-controlled; set your hope fully on the grace to be given you when Jesus Christ is revealed. As obedient children, do not conform to the evil desires you had when you lived in ignorance. But just as he who called you is holy, so be holy in all you do; for it is written: "Be holy, because I am holy."

Becoming the Woman I Want to Be, Donna Partow

Psalm 34:15

The eyes of the Lord are on the righteous and his ears are attentive to their cry.

Becoming the Woman I Want to Be, Donna Partow

Psalm 34:4–5

I sought the Lord, and he answered me; he delivered me from all my fears. Those who look to him are radiant; their faces are never covered with shame.

Becoming the Woman I Want to Be, Donna Partow

OVERCOME THE STING OF LIFE'S DISAPPOINTMENTS

Not long ago it all seemed possible. You'd have a great marriage, great kids, lifelong friendships, and fulfillment to all your dreams. But now you look around and say, this isn't what I signed up for. What's going on here?

Get ready to discover a new approach to life that promises hope and healing. As Donna says, "If God can breathe new life into my weary heart and soul...there's hope for everyone!"

This Isn't the Life I Signed Up For

BIBLE STUDIES TO REVIVE YOU!

Donna Partow's EXTRACTING THE PRECIOUS Bible study guides help you discover for yourself what God's Word teaches. Each title helps you apply God's truth to your daily life.

Mine Deep Wisdom
   From Paul's Letter to Corinth

A Glimpse of God's Faithfulness
   With Isaiah

Extracting the Precious From 2 Corinthians
Extracting the Precious From Isaiah